CARL WILLIAM MAXWELL

Civilization: The Great Cities of the Ancient World

Contents

III Levant

IV Anatolia

V Greece

VI Italy

VII Iran

VIII   South Asia

IX   East Asia

X   Central America

Preface

In the quiet whispers of ancient ruins, beneath the layers of time, lies the story of humanity's most profound achievements—the rise and fall of cities that once stood as the beating hearts of civilization. These cities, with their towering walls, sacred temples, bustling markets, and intricate networks of streets, were not just the physical embodiments of human ingenuity; they were the crucibles where culture, power, and knowledge were forged. They were the places where myths were born, where empires were built, and where the pulse of the ancient world was felt in every stone, every artifact, every whispered legend.

"Civilization: The Great Cities of the Ancient World" invites you on a journey through time and space, to the very foundations of human history. From the sacred waters of Eridu, the birthplace of civilization, to the majestic spires of Teotihuacan, the City of the Gods, this book delves into the stories of cities that once shaped the destiny of our world. Each city, whether it's the moonlit majesty of Ur, the radiant heart of Thebes, or the vibrant crossroads of Damascus, is a testament to the resilience, creativity, and ambition of the people who lived, loved, and dreamed within their walls.

As we explore these ancient metropolises—stretching from the fertile plains of Mesopotamia to the sun-drenched shores of the Mediterranean, from the lush jungles of Central America to the serene valleys of East Asia—we are reminded that these cities were not just places; they were the epicenters of human experience. They were where the great questions of existence were pondered, where art and architecture reached new heights, and where the echoes of the past still resonate in the present.

In the ruins of Pompeii, frozen in time by the fury of Vesuvius, we see the fragility of life; in the labyrinthine streets of Knossos, the myth of the Minotaur comes to life; and in the towering ziggurats of Babylon, we glimpse the aspirations of a people reaching for the heavens. Each city in this book is a chapter in the grand narrative of human civilization, a story of ambition, innovation, and the indomitable spirit of mankind.

This book is not just an exploration of ancient cities; it is a journey into the heart of what it means to be human. It is a celebration of our shared heritage, a reflection on the forces that shaped our world, and a tribute to the cities that, though long fallen, continue to inspire awe and wonder.

Welcome to the great cities of the ancient world. Welcome to the echoes of civilization.

C.W.M.

I

Mesopotamia

Eridu: The Birthplace of Civilization and the Sacred Waters

The Primordial Oasis

In the cradle of the world where the Tigris and Euphrates rivers converge, there lies a city that whispers the secrets of humanity's earliest days: Eridu. Often hailed as the oldest city in the world, Eridu is a place where myth and history intertwine, forming the bedrock of Sumerian civilization. This ancient metropolis, enveloped by the fertile marshlands of southern Mesopotamia, is not just a city but a symbol of the dawn of human ingenuity and spiritual awakening.

Enki's Sacred Abode

Eridu was the divine city of Enki, the god of wisdom, water, and creation. His temple, E-abzu (House of the Abzu), stood as the spiritual heart of the city, a sanctuary built over a sacred spring that was believed to be the source of all fresh water. The Abzu, a subterranean aquifer, was a mystical domain where the waters of life originated, and Enki, as its keeper, was revered as the bringer of fertility and knowledge.

The temple complex of E-abzu was a marvel of early architecture. Its ziggurat, a stepped platform ascending to the heavens, symbolized the connection between the earthly and the divine. Priests performed rituals and offerings here to honor Enki, seeking his wisdom and blessings. The temple was not just a place of worship but a center of learning, where scribes and scholars gathered to study the mysteries of the cosmos and the natural world.

The Cradle of Kingship

Eridu holds a revered place in Sumerian mythology as the first city where kingship descended from heaven. According to the Sumerian King List, it was in Eridu that the gods first bestowed the gift of kingship upon humanity, establishing the foundation of organized society and governance. The legendary figure Alulim is cited as the first king of Eridu, ruling for an astonishing 28,800 years, a testament to the city's ancient and mythical origins.

This divine kingship set the precedent for the future rulers of Sumer, who saw their authority as sanctioned by the gods. The concept of kingship, as practiced in Eridu, emphasized the ruler's role as a shepherd of the people, a protector, and a mediator between the gods and humanity. The city's governance and religious practices laid the groundwork for the development of other great Sumerian cities, such as Uruk, Ur, and Nippur.

A Center of Agriculture and Innovation

Eridu's location at the edge of the Mesopotamian marshes provided abundant natural resources, which were harnessed by its inhabitants to create a thriving agricultural society. The city's farmers developed advanced irrigation techniques, digging canals and constructing levees to control the flow of water from the Euphrates, transforming the arid landscape into fertile fields.

These innovations allowed Eridu to produce surplus crops, supporting a growing population and enabling trade with neighboring regions. The city's economy was diversified, with craftsmen producing pottery, tools, and textiles, which were traded for resources not found locally. This trade network extended across Mesopotamia and beyond, making Eridu a hub of commerce and cultural exchange.

The Legacy of Eridu

Eridu's significance transcends its physical remnants. As the earliest known city, it represents the birth of urban civilization, a place where humanity first organized itself into a structured society with governance, religion, and economy. The city's myths and legends influenced the cultural and religious narratives of Mesopotamia, shaping the identity of the Sumerians and their successors.

The decline of Eridu began around 2000 BCE, as shifting political and environmental conditions led to the rise of other city-states. However, its legacy endured through the stories and traditions passed down through generations. The ruins of Eridu, excavated in the 20th century, have revealed layers of history, from the earliest mudbrick structures to the grand temple complexes, offering invaluable insights into the dawn of civilization.

Key Events

1. **c. 5400 BCE** - Founding of Eridu: Considered one of the oldest cities in Mesopotamia.
2. **c. 5000 BCE** - Construction of the Temple of Enki: Early religious center dedicated to the water god Enki.
3. **c. 3800 BCE** - Urban Expansion: Growth of Eridu into a significant urban center.
4. **c. 2900 BCE** - Decline: Gradual decline as other cities like Ur and Uruk rose in prominence.

Ur: The City of Moonlight and Majesty

A Jewel in the Mesopotamian Crown

Picture an ancient city shimmering under the silver glow of the moon, its ziggurat rising majestically above the landscape like a staircase to the heavens. This is Ur, a city that once stood as one of the greatest urban centers of the ancient world. Nestled on the banks of the Euphrates River in modern-day southern Iraq, Ur was not just a city but a beacon of Sumerian culture, innovation, and spirituality.

The Moon God's Sanctuary

Ur's identity is deeply intertwined with its patron deity, Nanna (or Sin), the god of the moon. The Great Ziggurat of Ur, a massive terraced structure, was the heart of the city and served as Nanna's earthly abode. This towering monument, built by King Ur-Nammu around 2100 BCE, was a place where priests and worshippers gathered to honor the moon god, performing rituals that harmonized the celestial and terrestrial realms. The ziggurat's design, with its grand staircases and imposing presence, symbolized the connection between humanity and the divine.

Urban Splendor and Sophistication

Walking through Ur's ancient streets, one would encounter a city meticulously planned and constructed. The residential quarters were a maze of narrow lanes flanked by mudbrick houses, each home reflecting the social status and wealth of its inhabitants. Wealthy families lived in spacious two-story houses with central courtyards, while artisans and laborers resided in more modest dwellings.

Ur was a city of contrasts, where the grandeur of royal palaces and temples stood alongside bustling markets and workshops. The city's layout showcased advanced urban planning, with well-defined residential, commercial, and religious districts. Public spaces and granaries ensured that the city's inhabitants had access to essential goods and services, fostering a vibrant and self-sustaining community.

Economic Powerhouse

Ur's prosperity was fueled by its strategic location and access to trade routes. The city's economy was a complex web of agriculture, trade, and craft production. Fertile lands surrounding Ur yielded abundant crops of barley, dates, and other staples, which supported a thriving agricultural base. The city's artisans produced fine textiles, pottery, and metalwork, goods that were highly valued in trade.

Ur was a nexus of commerce, connecting the resources of Mesopotamia with distant regions. Merchants from Ur traded with cities across the ancient Near East, from the Indus Valley to Anatolia, bringing in exotic goods such as lapis lazuli, ivory, and precious metals. The wealth generated from trade and agriculture funded grand architectural projects and supported a high standard of living for its citizens.

Cultural and Intellectual Hub

Ur was not only an economic and religious center but also a hub of cultural and intellectual activity. The city was home to schools where scribes learned the art of cuneiform writing, a skill essential for administering the city's complex bureaucracy. The scribes of Ur documented everything from commercial transactions to religious hymns and epic poetry, contributing to the rich literary heritage of Mesopotamia.

One of Ur's most significant contributions to world literature is the "Epic of Gilgamesh," a story that has echoed through the ages with its themes of heroism, friendship, and the quest for immortality. The city's intellectual pursuits extended to astronomy, mathematics, and law, with the famous Code of Ur-Nammu being one of the earliest known legal codes.

Life and Afterlife

The people of Ur placed great importance on the afterlife, as evidenced by the Royal Cemetery of Ur. This necropolis, dating back to the Early Dynastic period, reveals a society that honored its dead with elaborate burials and grave goods. The tombs of Ur's royalty were filled with treasures, including jewelry, musical instruments, and intricately crafted artifacts, reflecting the city's wealth and the belief in an opulent afterlife.

The famous "Standard of Ur," a decorative box depicting scenes of war and peace, was discovered in these royal graves. This artifact, with its vivid imagery and intricate craftsmanship, offers a glimpse into the life and values of Ur's elite.

Decline and Legacy

Like many ancient cities, Ur's fortunes waxed and waned with the tides
of history. The city reached its zenith during the Third Dynasty of Ur
(circa 2100-2000 BCE), a period marked by architectural and cultural
achievements. However, shifting political and environmental conditions
led to its decline. The city was eventually abandoned, its glory fading into
the sands of time.

Yet, the legacy of Ur endures. Archaeological excavations in the early 20th
century by Sir Leonard Woolley brought to light the splendor of this ancient
metropolis, capturing the world's imagination. The artifacts and ruins
of Ur continue to tell the story of a civilization that achieved remarkable
advancements in architecture, governance, and culture.

Key Events

1. **c. 3800 BCE** - Founding of Ur: Emergence as a significant settlement.
2. **c. 2600 BCE** - Early Dynastic Period: Ur becomes a powerful city-state.
3. **c. 2100 BCE** - Third Dynasty of Ur: Flourishes under rulers like Ur-
   Nammu, who built the Great Ziggurat.
4. **c. 2000 BCE** - Decline: Decline and eventual fall to the Elamites and
   later the Amorites.

Nippur: The Sacred Heart of Sumer

A Divine Crossroads

In the fertile plains of ancient Mesopotamia, where the Tigris and Euphrates rivers carve their paths, lies a city unlike any other: Nippur. Revered as the spiritual epicenter of Sumerian civilization, Nippur was not just a city but a divine crossroads, a place where the earthly and celestial realms intertwined. It was here that the god Enlil, the lord of the winds and king of the gods, made his presence felt, imbuing Nippur with an aura of sacredness that echoed through the ages.

The Temple of Enlil: Ekur

At the heart of Nippur stood the majestic Ekur, the temple of Enlil. This grand sanctuary, whose name means "House of the Mountain," was the focal point of religious life in the city. The temple complex, with its towering ziggurat and sprawling courtyards, was a marvel of ancient architecture and devotion. Priests and pilgrims alike gathered here to offer their prayers, sacrifices, and rituals, seeking Enlil's favor and guidance.

The Ekur was more than just a place of worship; it was a symbol of divine authority and cosmic order. Enlil, as the chief deity of the Sumerian pantheon, held sway over the destinies of gods and men. Nippur, as his chosen city, was considered the spiritual axis of the world, where the decrees of fate were issued and the balance of the cosmos maintained.

A Hub of Knowledge and Culture

Nippur was not merely a religious center but also a hub of intellectual and cultural activity. The city's scribes were renowned for their scholarship, and Nippur housed one of the most significant libraries of the ancient world. Clay tablets inscribed with cuneiform writing recorded a vast array of knowledge, from administrative records and legal codes to hymns, myths, and astronomical observations.

The "Nippur Tablets" are a treasure trove of Sumerian literature and science. Among them are some of the earliest known versions of the "Epic of Gilgamesh," a testament to Nippur's role in preserving and transmitting the cultural heritage of Mesopotamia. The city's scholars were adept in various disciplines, including mathematics, medicine, and divination, making Nippur a beacon of enlightenment in the ancient world.

The Urban Tapestry

Nippur's urban landscape was a tapestry of bustling activity and communal life. The city's layout reflected its dual role as a religious and administrative center. The sacred precincts of the Ekur temple complex were surrounded by residential neighborhoods, markets, and workshops. The people of Nippur lived in mudbrick houses, engaged in daily routines that included farming, trading, and crafting.

The Euphrates River, flowing nearby, provided water for irrigation, enabling the cultivation of crops that sustained the city's population. Nippur's strategic location along trade routes facilitated the exchange of goods and ideas with neighboring regions. Merchants brought exotic commodities from distant lands, enriching the city's markets and fostering a cosmopolitan atmosphere.

Political Significance

Despite its lack of political ambition, Nippur held immense influence over the Sumerian city-states. Its religious significance meant that kings and rulers sought Enlil's blessing to legitimize their reigns. Control over Nippur was often a strategic goal for aspiring dynasts, who understood that the city's spiritual authority could enhance their political power.

Nippur's role as a neutral ground for diplomacy and religious observance made it a center for alliances and treaties. Leaders from various city-states convened in Nippur to resolve disputes and forge agreements, recognizing the city's unique position as the keeper of divine justice.

Decline and Rediscovery

Nippur's prominence endured for millennia, but like all great cities, it eventually faced decline. Environmental changes, shifting trade routes, and the rise of new powers contributed to its gradual fading into obscurity. By the time of the Babylonian and Assyrian empires, Nippur had lost much of its former glory, remembered more as a site of ancient reverence than a living city.

The rediscovery of Nippur in the 19th century by archaeologists brought to light the city's enduring legacy. Excavations revealed the remnants of the Ekur temple, residential quarters, and libraries, offering a glimpse into the spiritual and cultural heart of ancient Sumer. The artifacts and inscriptions uncovered at Nippur continue to illuminate our understanding of early urban civilization and the profound connection between humanity and the divine.

Key Events

1. **c. 5000 BCE** - Early Settlement: One of the earliest sites of civilization in Mesopotamia.
2. **c. 3200 BCE** - Religious Importance: Becomes a major religious center

dedicated to the god Enlil.

3. **c. 2200 BCE** - Akkadian Empire: Nippur continues to be a key religious and cultural site under Sargon of Akkad.

4. **c. 2100 BCE** - Third Dynasty of Ur: Nippur flourishes again under the control of Ur.

5. **c. 1750 BCE** - Decline: Begins to lose prominence but remains an important religious site.

Kish: The Cradle of Kings

A Kingdom Born of Clay

In the heart of ancient Mesopotamia, where the fertile lands of the Tigris and Euphrates rivers nurtured early human settlements, rose the city of Kish. A city born from the very clay that defined its landscape, Kish is often considered one of the earliest cradles of human civilization. This was a city where kingship itself was said to have descended from the heavens, marking the dawn of organized society and governance.

The First Kingship

Kish holds a unique place in the Sumerian King List, a record of rulers that chronicles the divine origins of kingship. According to this ancient text, after the great flood, it was Kish where the gods reestablished kingship on earth. Etana, the first recorded king of Kish, is depicted in myth as the one who ascended to the heavens on the back of an eagle, seeking the plant of birth to secure an heir and thus, the future of his people.

This mythological ascent symbolizes Kish's role as a bridge between the divine and the earthly realms, a place where the authority of kings was seen as a sacred trust bestowed by the gods. The kings of Kish were not just rulers but divine intermediaries, their authority rooted in celestial mandate.

A Nexus of Power and Innovation

Kish's strategic location made it a nexus of power and innovation in the ancient world. Situated near modern-day Tell al-Uhaymir in Iraq, the city commanded key trade routes that connected it to other major centers of Mesopotamia. This prime location facilitated the flow of goods, ideas, and technologies, making Kish a bustling hub of commerce and cultural exchange.

The city's architecture reflects its early advancements. Excavations have revealed impressive structures, including palaces, temples, and fortifications built from the abundant clay and mudbrick. The Temple of Zababa, the warrior god, stood as a testament to Kish's martial prowess and its devotion to deities of war and protection. The city's layout, with its organized streets and public spaces, speaks to an advanced understanding of urban planning and community life.

Economy and Daily Life

Kish's economy was diverse and dynamic, supported by agriculture, trade, and craftsmanship. The fertile lands surrounding the city yielded abundant crops, including barley, wheat, and dates, which sustained its population and created surplus for trade. Kish's artisans were skilled in pottery, metallurgy, and textile production, creating goods that were highly valued both locally and in distant markets.

The city's markets were vibrant places where merchants from across Mesopotamia and beyond converged to buy and sell wares. Goods such as lapis lazuli from Afghanistan, timber from the Zagros Mountains, and copper from Oman found their way to Kish, enriching the city's material culture and connecting it to a broader network of trade.

Daily life in Kish was a tapestry of activities. Its residents lived in modest mudbrick houses, engaged in farming, trade, and religious observances. The city's administrative records, written in early cuneiform script, provide a glimpse into the lives of its inhabitants, documenting everything from legal disputes and commercial transactions to religious rituals and royal decrees.

The Heart of Sumerian Civilization

Kish was more than just a political and economic center; it was the beating heart of Sumerian civilization. The city's scholars and scribes played a crucial role in the development of writing, governance, and law. The Code of Ur-Nammu, one of the earliest known legal codes, owes much to the administrative and legal innovations that originated in cities like Kish.

Religious life in Kish was rich and complex. The city's pantheon included gods such as Zababa and Inanna, to whom grand temples were dedicated. These temples were not only places of worship but also centers of economic and social life, where offerings were made, festivals celebrated, and community decisions enacted.

Legacy and Rediscovery

Kish's prominence waned over time, as the shifting sands of history favored other cities and empires. Yet, its legacy endured, remembered as the place where kingship first touched the earth. Archaeological excavations in the early 20th century unveiled the layers of Kish's past, revealing the remnants of its grandeur and the echoes of its ancient splendor.

Artifacts uncovered at Kish, from intricate jewelry and pottery to monumental inscriptions, provide a window into the life of a city that once stood at the forefront of human progress. These discoveries continue to inform our understanding of the early stages of urban development, governance, and culture.

Key Events

1. **c. 3100 BCE** – Early Dynastic Period: Kish becomes a major political and military center.
2. **c. 2900 BCE** – First Dynasty of Kish: Prominent early rulers include Enmebaragesi.
3. **c. 2300 BCE** – Sargon of Akkad: Sargon conquers Kish and uses it as a base for his empire.
4. **c. 1800 BCE** – Decline: Declines in political significance but remains an important city.

Uruk: The City of Legends

The Dawn of Urban Civilization

In the vast and fertile plains of ancient Mesopotamia, along the winding banks of the Euphrates River, rose a city that would forever change the course of human history: Uruk. Known as the birthplace of writing, the cradle of kings, and the setting for epic tales, Uruk was more than a city—it was the epicenter of the dawn of civilization, where myths were born, and legends walked among men.

The Epic of Gilgamesh

No story of Uruk is complete without the tale of its most famous king, Gilgamesh. Immortalized in the "Epic of Gilgamesh," one of humanity's earliest and greatest literary works, Gilgamesh's exploits captured the imaginations of ancient and modern audiences alike. The epic recounts his heroic deeds, his friendship with Enkidu, and his quest for immortality, reflecting the universal themes of human ambition, companionship, and the desire to conquer death.

Gilgamesh's legacy is etched into the very fabric of Uruk, with its towering walls and grandiose temples said to be the work of his reign. As you walk through the ruins of Uruk, you can almost hear the echoes of his footsteps and the whispers of his epic adventures, reminding us of the timeless nature of human aspiration.

The City of Temples

Uruk was renowned for its monumental architecture and religious significance. The city was divided into two main districts: Eanna and Anu, each dedicated to a major deity. The Eanna district, dedicated to Inanna (or Ishtar), the goddess of love, beauty, and war, was a marvel of ancient engineering. The complex included the famed White Temple, a shining beacon atop a ziggurat, symbolizing the city's spiritual and political power.

In the Anu district, the sky god Anu was worshipped. The massive ziggurat here was another architectural feat, serving as a bridge between the heavens and the earth. These temples were not only places of worship but also centers of economic and administrative activities, underscoring the intertwining of religion and governance in Sumerian society.

The Birth of Writing

Uruk's most profound contribution to humanity is the invention of writing. It was here that the earliest form of writing, cuneiform, emerged. Initially developed for record-keeping and administrative purposes, cuneiform soon became a tool for capturing literature, laws, and scientific knowledge. The tablets uncovered in Uruk's ruins reveal a sophisticated society that valued knowledge, communication, and the power of the written word.

The invention of writing in Uruk marked the beginning of recorded history, allowing us to glimpse into the lives, thoughts, and achievements of ancient peoples. This breakthrough laid the foundation for the rich literary traditions of Mesopotamia and influenced countless civilizations to come.

Economic and Cultural Hub

Uruk was a bustling metropolis that thrived on agriculture, trade, and craftsmanship. The city's location provided fertile land for farming, supporting a large and growing population. Uruk's markets were teeming with activity, where traders exchanged goods such as grains, textiles, pottery, and precious metals. The city's artisans were skilled in various crafts, creating intricate jewelry, fine pottery, and impressive statuary.

The economic prosperity of Uruk was complemented by its vibrant cultural life. The city was a melting pot of ideas and traditions, attracting scholars, artists, and merchants from across Mesopotamia and beyond. Festivals dedicated to Inanna and other deities were grand events that showcased Uruk's religious devotion and cultural richness.

The Walls of Uruk

One of the most iconic features of Uruk was its massive walls, which encircled the city and stood as a testament to its strength and ingenuity. According to legend, these walls were built by King Gilgamesh himself.

Made of mudbrick, the walls stretched over six miles and protected the city from invasions while symbolizing its might and resilience.

The walls of Uruk not only served a defensive purpose but also delineated the sacred space of the city, separating the divine order within from the chaos outside. They were a physical manifestation of the city's identity and pride, celebrated in literature and history as one of Uruk's greatest achievements.

Decline and Rediscovery

Uruk's prominence lasted for millennia, but like all great cities, it eventually declined. Environmental changes, shifting trade routes, and the rise of new powers contributed to its gradual fading into obscurity. By the time of the Babylonian and Persian empires, Uruk had lost much of its former glory, its temples and palaces abandoned to the sands of time.

The rediscovery of Uruk in the 19th century by archaeologists brought to light the grandeur of this ancient city. Excavations revealed the remnants of its temples, walls, and tablets, offering a window into a world that laid the foundations of civilization. The artifacts and inscriptions uncovered at Uruk continue to inform our understanding of early urban life and the profound legacy of Sumerian culture.

Key Events

1. **c. 4500 BCE** - Founding of Uruk: Becomes a major urban center in the Ubaid period.
2. **c. 3400 BCE** - Urban Revolution: Growth into one of the world's first major cities during the Uruk period.
3. **c. 2900 BCE** - Gilgamesh: Reigns as one of the most famous kings of Uruk.
4. **c. 2100 BCE** - Decline: Begins to decline but remains a cultural and religious center.

Mari: The Oasis of Diplomacy

A Desert Jewel

Amidst the arid expanse of the Syrian desert, along the banks of the Euphrates River, lies a city that once glittered like a jewel: Mari. This ancient metropolis, with its lush gardens and bustling streets, was a beacon of diplomacy, innovation, and cultural richness. Known for its strategic location and impressive palatial complex, Mari served as a crucial link between the civilizations of Mesopotamia, the Levant, and beyond.

The Palace of Zimri-Lim

At the heart of Mari stood one of the most magnificent structures of the ancient world: the Palace of Zimri-Lim. This sprawling complex, covering over six hectares, was not only the residence of the king but also a center of administration, culture, and diplomacy. The palace boasted more than 260 rooms, including audience halls, administrative offices, storerooms, and private apartments.

The walls of the palace were adorned with vibrant frescoes depicting scenes of divine rituals, royal processions, and everyday life. These artworks, preserved by the dry desert climate, offer a vivid glimpse into the opulence and sophistication of Mari's royal court. The throne room, with its grandeur and ceremonial importance, was where King Zimri-Lim received envoys and dignitaries from across the ancient world, forging alliances and securing Mari's place on the international stage.

A Hub of Diplomacy

Mari was renowned for its diplomatic prowess. The city's strategic position along the Euphrates made it a vital crossroads for trade and communication between Mesopotamia, the Levant, and Anatolia. As a result, Mari became a melting pot of cultures and a center for diplomatic activity. The archives of Mari, discovered in the palace, contain thousands of clay tablets that document diplomatic correspondences, treaties, and administrative records.

These tablets reveal a city deeply engaged in the politics of the region, where diplomacy was an art form and alliances were carefully cultivated. Mari's kings corresponded with rulers from distant lands, negotiating trade agreements, military alliances, and marriage treaties. The city's influence extended far beyond its walls, shaping the political landscape of the ancient Near East.

Architectural Marvels

Mari's urban landscape was a testament to its architectural innovation and planning. The city's streets were laid out in a grid pattern, flanked by mudbrick houses, temples, and public buildings. The use of sophisticated irrigation systems enabled the cultivation of gardens and orchards, transforming the desert city into a verdant oasis.

The Temple of Ishtar, dedicated to the goddess of love and war, was one of Mari's prominent religious structures. This temple, with its intricate carvings and ceremonial significance, played a central role in the city's spiritual life. The Great Temple of Dagan, another key religious site, underscored Mari's devotion to its deities and its role as a religious center.

Innovation and Culture

Mari was a center of innovation, particularly in the fields of art, admin-istration, and engineering. The city's artisans were skilled in producing intricate jewelry, pottery, and statuary, which were highly prized in trade. Mari's scribes developed an advanced system of cuneiform writing, used for recording everything from commercial transactions to epic poetry.

The city's cultural life was vibrant, with festivals, music, and religious ceremonies playing an integral role in the daily lives of its inhabitants. The archives of Mari contain hymns, prayers, and literary texts that reflect a rich tradition of storytelling and religious devotion. The fusion of various cultural influences created a unique and dynamic society that thrived on diversity and exchange.

Decline and Rediscovery

Mari's prosperity was eventually overshadowed by the rise of powerful neighbors. The city faced multiple conquests, the most devastating being its destruction by Hammurabi of Babylon around 1760 BCE. Despite this, Mari's legacy endured, its ruins silently guarding the secrets of its past.

The rediscovery of Mari in the 20th century by French archaeologist André Parrot brought the city back to light. Excavations revealed the grandeur of the palace, the sophistication of its urban planning, and the richness of its cultural life. The treasures unearthed from Mari's ruins provide invaluable insights into the history and achievements of this ancient city.

Key Events

1. **c. 2900 BCE** - Founding of Mari: Emergence as a significant settle-ment in the Euphrates River valley.
2. **c. 2600-2300 BCE** - Early Dynastic Period: Mari becomes a major trade and political center.
3. **c. 1800-1750 BCE** - Zimri-Lim's Reign: Mari reaches its peak as a

diplomatic and cultural hub.

4. **c. 1759 BCE** - Sack by Hammurabi: Mari is conquered and destroyed by Babylonian king Hammurabi.

5. **c. 1300 BCE** - Decline: Continued decline and eventual abandonment.

Babylon: The Enchanted City of Wonders and Wisdom

A Vision of Splendor

Envision a city that rises like a phoenix from the plains of Mesopotamia, its towering ziggurats piercing the heavens and its hanging gardens cascading with lush greenery. This is Babylon, a city that has captured the imagination of poets, historians, and adventurers for millennia. Situated along the Euphrates River, Babylon was more than a city; it was a legend come to life, a symbol of human ingenuity and divine grandeur.

The Hanging Gardens: A Lost Wonder

One of the most enchanting tales of Babylon is that of the Hanging Gardens, one of the Seven Wonders of the Ancient World. According to legend, these gardens were constructed by King Nebuchadnezzar II for his homesick wife, Amytis of Media, who longed for the verdant mountains of her homeland. The gardens were said to be an astonishing feat of engineering, with terraces of exotic plants and flowers, irrigated by an ingenious system that brought water from the Euphrates up to the highest levels.

While the exact existence and location of the Hanging Gardens remain shrouded in mystery, their story embodies the essence of Babylon: a city where the impossible became possible, and where the boundaries of human creativity were constantly pushed.

The Tower of Babel: A Gateway to Heaven

The Tower of Babel, another emblematic structure of Babylon, speaks to the city's ambition and its place in biblical lore. Described as a towering ziggurat, this structure was intended to reach the heavens, a testament to the Babylonians' desire to connect with the divine. Although the tower's construction was halted, its legend underscores Babylon's role as a bridge between earth and the cosmos.

The actual ziggurat of Babylon, Etemenanki, dedicated to the god Marduk, stood as a monumental expression of the city's religious devotion and architectural prowess. Its name, meaning "House of the Foundation of Heaven and Earth," captures the spirit of a city that saw itself as the center of the universe.

The Ishtar Gate: A Portal of Majesty

As you approach Babylon, you would be greeted by the awe-inspiring Ishtar Gate, a dazzling entrance adorned with glazed bricks in vibrant blues, depicting lions, dragons, and bulls. This grand gateway was dedicated to Ishtar, the goddess of love and war, and served as a symbol of Babylon's wealth and artistic excellence. Passing through the Ishtar Gate, one would enter the Processional Way, a grand boulevard lined with statues and reliefs, leading to the heart of the city.

A Center of Learning and Law

Babylon was not only a city of architectural marvels but also a center of learning and law. The city's scholars made significant contributions to astronomy, mathematics, and literature. The Babylonian astronomers meticulously mapped the stars and planets, laying the groundwork for future astronomical studies. Their mathematical innovations, including the use of a base-60 system, influenced the development of modern timekeeping and geometry.

One of Babylon's most enduring legacies is the Code of Hammurabi, one of the oldest and most comprehensive legal codes in history. Inscribed on a towering stone stele, this code established laws governing everything from trade and property to family and criminal justice. "An eye for an eye" became a foundational principle of justice, reflecting the Babylonians' commitment to order and fairness.

The Splendor of Nebuchadnezzar's Reign

The zenith of Babylon's glory came during the reign of Nebuchadnezzar II (605–562 BCE). Under his rule, Babylon became the largest and most magnificent city of its time. Nebuchadnezzar embarked on extensive building projects, including the reconstruction of the city's walls and temples, the creation of the Hanging Gardens, and the enhancement of the Ishtar Gate. His reign marked a period of unparalleled prosperity and cultural flourishing.

A Cultural Melting Pot

Babylon was a cosmopolitan hub where diverse cultures, languages, and traditions converged. Merchants, artisans, and scholars from across the ancient world flocked to the city, bringing with them goods, ideas, and innovations. This cultural melting pot enriched Babylonian society, making it a vibrant center of exchange and creativity.

Festivals and religious ceremonies played a central role in Babylonian life. The New Year festival, Akitu, was a grand celebration involving processions, rituals, and the reaffirmation of the king's divine mandate. The city's temples and shrines, dedicated to gods such as Marduk, Ishtar, and Nabu, were focal points of worship and community life.

Decline and Legacy

Babylon's fortunes waned with the rise of new empires. The city fell to the Persians under Cyrus the Great in 539 BCE, marking the end of Babylonian independence. However, Babylon's influence endured through the ages. Alexander the Great envisioned Babylon as the capital of his vast empire and died there in 323 BCE, further cementing the city's legendary status.

The rediscovery of Babylon in the 19th century by archaeologists, including Robert Koldewey, unveiled the splendor of its ruins. Excavations revealed the grandeur of the Ishtar Gate, the foundations of the ziggurat, and the remnants of the city's walls and palaces. These discoveries continue to inspire awe and provide insights into the life of one of history's greatest cities.

Key Events

1. **c. 2300 BCE** - First mention of Babylon: Appears in records as a small town.
2. **c. 1894 BCE** - Amorite Dynasty: Founded by Sumu-abum, marking the rise of Babylon as a significant city.
3. **c. 1792-1750 BCE** - Reign of Hammurabi: Babylon becomes a major empire, famous for the Code of Hammurabi.
4. **c. 1595 BCE** - Hittite Sack: Babylon is sacked by the Hittites but later recovers.
5. **c. 626-539 BCE** - Neo-Babylonian Empire: Flourishes under Nebuchadnezzar II, who builds the Hanging Gardens and the Ishtar Gate.
6. **539 BCE** - Fall to Persia: Conquered by Cyrus the Great of Persia.

Larsa: The Radiant Sun of Sumer

A City Awakened by the Dawn

As the first light of dawn breaks over the plains of southern Mesopotamia, it illuminates a city that once shone brightly in the annals of history: Larsa. Nestled near the banks of the Euphrates River, Larsa was more than just a city; it was a beacon of light, prosperity, and divine favor. This ancient metropolis, dedicated to the sun god Utu (Shamash), was a center of innovation, culture, and religious devotion, where the radiance of the sun god's blessings touched every aspect of life.

The Temple of Utu: Sanctuary of the Sun

At the heart of Larsa stood the magnificent E-Babbar, the White Temple, dedicated to Utu, the sun god and arbiter of justice. This sacred sanctuary was a place where the people of Larsa gathered to worship, seek justice, and celebrate the divine light that governed their lives. The temple, with its gleaming white walls and towering ziggurat, symbolized purity, enlightenment, and the unbroken connection between the heavens and the earth.

Priests performed daily rituals and offerings to honor Utu, ensuring the sun's benevolent light continued to bless the city with warmth and prosperity. The temple was not only a religious center but also a judicial one, where legal matters were resolved under the watchful eyes of the sun god, reflecting Larsa's commitment to justice and order.

A Hub of Innovation and Prosperity

Larsa's economy was a testament to its innovative spirit and strategic location. The city's proximity to the Euphrates provided fertile lands for agriculture, enabling the cultivation of barley, dates, and flax. Sophisticated irrigation systems, including canals and dikes, maximized agricultural output, supporting a thriving population and fostering trade.

The artisans of Larsa were renowned for their craftsmanship. Pottery, textiles, and metalwork produced in the city were highly prized, both locally and in distant markets. Larsa's merchants engaged in extensive trade networks, exchanging goods with cities across Mesopotamia and beyond, bringing wealth and diversity to the city's markets.

A City of Architectural Marvels

Larsa's urban landscape was characterized by its impressive architecture and urban planning. The city's buildings, constructed from sun-dried mudbrick, showcased the ingenuity of its builders. Residential quarters, administrative buildings, and temples were arranged in an orderly manner, reflecting a well-organized society.

One of the most remarkable features of Larsa was its extensive library of cuneiform tablets. These tablets, inscribed with records of commercial transactions, legal codes, hymns, and literary texts, offer a window into the intellectual life of the city. Larsa's scribes were adept in the use of cuneiform, preserving the city's knowledge and traditions for future generations.

The Reign of King Rim-Sin I

The zenith of Larsa's power came during the reign of King Rim-Sin I (1822–1763 BCE). Under his rule, Larsa expanded its influence across southern Mesopotamia, engaging in both military campaigns and diplomatic endeavors. Rim-Sin's reign was marked by significant architectural projects, including the enhancement of the E-Babbar temple and the construction of public works that improved the city's infrastructure.

Rim-Sin's long reign brought stability and prosperity to Larsa, making it a dominant power in the region. His legacy is remembered not only for his military and administrative achievements but also for his contributions to the cultural and religious life of the city.

Cultural Flourishing

Larsa was a city of cultural richness, where religion, art, and scholarship flourished. The city's festivals and religious ceremonies were grand events that brought the community together in celebration and reverence. Music, dance, and feasting were integral parts of these festivities, reflecting the joyous spirit of Larsa's inhabitants.

The city's dedication to the sun god Utu permeated its culture. Hymns and prayers composed in his honor celebrated his role as the bringer of light and justice. These literary works, along with administrative and legal texts, were meticulously recorded by the city's scribes, ensuring the preservation of Larsa's cultural heritage.

Decline and Legacy

Larsa's fortunes began to wane with the rise of rival powers, particularly Babylon under the rule of Hammurabi. In 1763 BCE, Hammurabi conquered Larsa, incorporating it into his burgeoning empire. Despite this conquest, the legacy of Larsa endured, remembered as a city of innovation, justice, and cultural achievement.

The rediscovery of Larsa in modern times has shed light on its significant contributions to Mesopotamian civilization. Archaeological excavations have uncovered the remains of its temples, palaces, and residential areas, revealing the grandeur of its past. The cuneiform tablets found at Larsa continue to provide invaluable insights into the city's history, economy, and culture.

Key Events

1. **c. 2700 BCE** - Founding: Early settlement in Sumer.
2. **c. 2000 BCE** - Rise of Larsa: Emerges as an important city-state in Sumer.
3. **c. 1900-1800 BCE** - Period of Independence: Flourishes under the reign of rulers like Gungunum and Rim-Sin I.
4. **c. 1763 BCE** - Conquest by Hammurabi: Larsa is conquered by Babylon and incorporated into its empire.
5. **c. 1500 BCE** - Decline: Gradual decline in importance and influence.

Harran: The Crossroads of Time and Stars

A City Steeped in Starlight

Imagine a city where the desert sands whisper ancient secrets and the night sky is a map of celestial wonder. This is Harran, a city that thrived as a beacon of knowledge, commerce, and spirituality in ancient Mesopotamia. Nestled in what is now southeastern Turkey, Harran's history is woven with threads of mythology, astronomy, and trade, making it a unique and enduring center of human endeavor.

The Moon God's Sanctuary

At the heart of Harran stood the grand Temple of Sin, dedicated to the moon god. Sin, also known as Nanna, was revered as the god of wisdom, time, and the celestial bodies. The temple, an architectural marvel, was the focal point of religious life in Harran. Pilgrims from far and wide would journey to this sacred site, drawn by the city's reputation as a place where the divine met the mortal.

The temple complex, with its imposing ziggurat and lush courtyards, was a hub of activity where priests conducted rituals and offered sacrifices to honor the moon god. The nightly rituals, performed under the vast canopy of stars, imbued the city with a sense of cosmic connection, linking the heavens and earth in a harmonious dance.

A Nexus of Knowledge

Harran was more than a religious center; it was a seat of learning and intellectual pursuit. The city's scholars were renowned for their expertise in astronomy and mathematics. They meticulously observed the movements of the stars and planets, recording their findings on clay tablets that have survived the millennia. These ancient astronomers developed sophisticated methods for tracking celestial events, contributing to our understanding of the cosmos.

The House of Wisdom in Harran was a renowned institution where scholars studied the mysteries of the universe. This early academy attracted intellectuals from across the ancient world, fostering an environment of inquiry and discovery. The knowledge produced in Harran influenced subsequent civilizations, leaving a legacy that endured long after the city's decline.

The Silk Road's Embrace

Strategically located at the crossroads of major trade routes, Harran was a vital link between the East and West. The city's markets bustled with activity as merchants traded goods from distant lands. Silk from China, spices from India, precious metals from Anatolia, and textiles from Persia all flowed through Harran, enriching its economy and cultural fabric.

The caravanserais of Harran were havens for weary travelers and traders, offering respite and opportunity for cultural exchange. These inns were not only places of rest but also hubs of information, where news and ideas were exchanged as freely as goods. The vibrant marketplace was a testament to Harran's role as a melting pot of cultures, languages, and traditions.

A City of Resilience and Adaptation

Harran's strategic importance made it a coveted prize for empires throughout history. The city saw the rise and fall of many great powers, from the Akkadians and Assyrians to the Babylonians and Persians. Each empire left its mark on Harran, enriching its cultural tapestry and architectural heritage.

One of Harran's most remarkable features was its ability to adapt and thrive despite the tumultuous changes. The city's inhabitants were resilient, rebuilding and fortifying their city in the face of invasions and natural disasters. This spirit of perseverance ensured Harran's continuity as a center of civilization for thousands of years.

Legacy of the Ancients

The decline of Harran began with the changing tides of history and the shifting of trade routes. By the time of the Roman and Byzantine periods, Harran had diminished in political and economic significance but retained its cultural and religious importance. The city remained a bastion of learning and spirituality, with its traditions continuing to influence the surrounding regions.

In the 20th century, archaeological excavations brought to light the hidden treasures of Harran. The ruins of the Temple of Sin, the remains of ancient observatories, and the remnants of bustling markets revealed a city that had once been a jewel of ancient Mesopotamia. These discoveries have provided invaluable insights into the life and achievements of Harran's inhabitants.

Key Events

1. **c. 2000 BCE** - Early Settlement: Harran is established as a key trading and religious center.
2. **c. 1800 BCE** - Growth as a Trade Hub: Becomes a significant center

for commerce and astronomy.

3. **c. 1200 BCE** - Assyrian Influence: Harran falls under the influence of the Assyrian Empire.

4. **c. 610 BCE** - Neo-Assyrian Period: Harran remains important, serving as a religious center for the moon god Sin.

5. **c. 610 BCE** - Fall to Babylonians: Conquered by the Neo-Babylonian Empire.

6. **c. 300 BCE** - Hellenistic Period: Harran continues to be a center of learning and trade under the Greeks.

Ashur: The Sacred Citadel of the Gods

The Cradle of Empire and Devotion

Perched on a rocky promontory overlooking the swift currents of the Tigris River, surrounded by arid plains and rolling hills, lies Ashur, the ancient city that gave birth to one of history's most formidable empires. More than just a city, Ashur was the sacred heart of the Assyrian civilization, a place where gods and kings intertwined their destinies. Founded around 2500 BCE, Ashur became the spiritual and political nucleus of the Assyrian Empire, its temples and palaces serving as symbols of divine favor and imperial power. With its towering ziggurats, sacred precincts, and military might, Ashur remains a testament to the enduring legacy of a civilization that once dominated the ancient Near East.

The Temple of Ashur: The Divine Throne

At the center of Ashur stood the Temple of Ashur, dedicated to the city's patron god after whom the city was named. This temple was not just a place of worship; it was the spiritual and political heart of the Assyrian Empire. The god Ashur was seen as the divine king who granted victory in battle and prosperity to the land, and his temple was the axis mundi—the point where heaven and earth met.

The temple's architecture was imposing, with its high walls and grand entranceways leading to inner sanctums where the god's presence was believed to dwell. Rituals performed within the temple were of paramount importance, ensuring the favor of Ashur for the king and the empire. These ceremonies included offerings, prayers, and processions, all designed to maintain the cosmic order and the empire's dominance. The Temple of Ashur was more than just a religious structure; it was a symbol of the divine mandate that justified Assyrian rule and expansion.

The Ziggurat: A Stairway to the Heavens

Rising alongside the temple was the great ziggurat of Ashur, a towering stepped pyramid that reached towards the sky. The ziggurat was a monumental structure, built from mud-brick and designed as a stairway to the heavens, allowing priests and kings to ascend to the realm of the gods. Each tier of the ziggurat symbolized a different level of the universe, from the earthly plane to the celestial spheres.

At the summit of the ziggurat, a shrine housed the statue of the god Ashur, where the most sacred rituals were conducted. The ziggurat was not only a religious center but also a powerful symbol of the Assyrian king's connection to the divine. By ascending the ziggurat, the king demonstrated his role as the intermediary between the gods and his people, reinforcing his authority and the sacred nature of his rule. The ziggurat of Ashur stood as a testament to the Assyrians' architectural prowess and their profound spiritual beliefs.

The Royal Palace: A Fortress of Power

The royal palace of Ashur was a vast complex that served as the residence of the Assyrian kings and the administrative center of the empire. Built on a raised platform within the city's fortified walls, the palace was both a symbol of the king's authority and a fortress designed to protect the ruler and his court. The palace was adorned with intricate reliefs, depicting scenes of warfare, hunting, and divine favor, celebrating the king's achievements and his close relationship with the gods.

The throne room, the heart of the palace, was where the king held court, received foreign dignitaries, and made decisions that shaped the fate of the empire. The palace's courtyards and gardens provided spaces for relaxation and reflection, while its storerooms and archives contained the wealth and knowledge of the empire. The royal palace of Ashur was more than just a residence; it was the nerve center of Assyrian power, where the king's word was law and the empire's future was forged.

The City Walls: Guardians of the Empire

The city of Ashur was surrounded by massive walls, constructed from mud-brick and stone, which protected it from invaders and symbolized the might of the Assyrian Empire. These walls, reinforced with towers and gates, were a testament to the city's strategic importance and its role as the empire's spiritual and administrative capital. The walls of Ashur were not just physical barriers; they were a symbol of the strength and resilience of the Assyrian people, who defended their city against numerous threats over the centuries.

The gates of Ashur, adorned with carvings of protective deities and symbols of power, controlled access to the city and served as entry points for both merchants and warriors. The walls and gates of Ashur were more than just defensive structures; they were a statement of the city's invincibility and the divine protection afforded by its patron god. The walls of Ashur guarded not only the city but also the heart of an empire that once ruled vast territories from the Persian Gulf to the Mediterranean.

The Archives: The Wisdom of the Ages

Within the city of Ashur, in the shadow of its great temples and palaces, lay the archives—repositories of knowledge and records that chronicled the history, laws, and achievements of the Assyrian Empire. These archives, housed in the palace and temple complexes, contained clay tablets inscribed with cuneiform script, the world's earliest form of writing. The records included royal decrees, treaties, religious texts, and chronicles of military campaigns, preserving the memory of the empire for future generations.

The archives of Ashur were a testament to the Assyrians' commitment to documentation and governance, ensuring that the wisdom and decisions of the past were not lost to time. These records also served as tools of statecraft, enabling the king to enforce laws, collect taxes, and maintain control over the vast territories of the empire. The archives of Ashur were more than just collections of documents; they were the written legacy of a civilization that valued knowledge and its power to shape the world.

The Rise and Fall of an Empire

Ashur's rise as the heart of the Assyrian Empire was marked by centuries of expansion, conquest, and cultural achievement. The city's influence reached its zenith during the reigns of powerful kings such as Tiglath-Pileser I and Ashurbanipal, who extended Assyrian control over much of the Near East. However, the empire's relentless ambition and the harshness of its rule eventually led to internal strife and external enemies.

By the end of the 7th century BCE, Ashur faced destruction at the hands of the Medes and Babylonians, who saw the fall of the city as a symbolic end to Assyrian dominance. The city's great temples and palaces were reduced to ruins, and its once-powerful empire crumbled. Yet, the memory of Ashur lived on, preserved in the annals of history and the ruins that still stand today.

Key Events

1. **c. 2500 BCE** – Early Settlement: Ashur is established as a small settlement along the Tigris River, becoming a key religious center for the worship of the god Ashur.
2. **c. 2000-1800 BCE** – Old Assyrian Period: Ashur becomes the capital of the Old Assyrian Kingdom, a hub for trade and commerce, particularly with Anatolia.
3. **c. 1350-1200 BCE** – Middle Assyrian Empire: Ashur rises to prominence as the capital of the Assyrian Empire, with the construction of grand temples and palaces.
4. **c. 900-600 BCE** – Neo-Assyrian Empire: Ashur continues to be a major religious and cultural center, although the political capital shifts to other cities like Nineveh and Nimrud.
5. **c. 614 BCE** – Destruction by the Medes and Babylonians: Ashur is sacked and destroyed during the fall of the Assyrian Empire.

6. **c. 1st century CE** – Brief Resurgence: Ashur is partially rebuilt under the Parthians but never regains its former glory.

Nineveh: The Majestic Guardian of Assyria

The Lion Among Cities

In the heart of ancient Mesopotamia, where the Tigris River courses through fertile plains, lay Nineveh, a city of unparalleled grandeur and might. Nineveh was not just a city; it was the roaring lion of Assyria, the embodiment of its power and splendor. This ancient metropolis, with its soaring walls, magnificent palaces, and bustling streets, stood as a testament to human ambition and divine favor.

The Walls of Nineveh: Defenders of the Realm

Nineveh was famed for its colossal walls, which stretched for over seven miles, encircling the city like the protective embrace of a mighty lion. These walls, some of the most formidable of the ancient world, were both a defensive masterpiece and a symbol of Assyrian strength. Adorned with massive gates and intricately carved reliefs depicting scenes of war and triumph, the walls told the story of Assyria's dominance.

The Nergal Gate, one of the grand entrances to Nineveh, was a marvel of engineering and artistry. Flanked by towering statues of lamassu—mythical creatures with the body of a bull, wings of an eagle, and the head of a human—this gate was both a protective barrier and a statement of the city's invincibility and grandeur.

The Palaces of Kings

Nineveh's palaces were the heart of its splendor, serving as both the residences and administrative centers of Assyria's greatest kings. The most renowned of these was the Palace of Sennacherib, also known as the

"Palace Without Rival." This sprawling complex boasted over 80 rooms, decorated with exquisite bas-reliefs and adorned with lush gardens and elaborate water features.

King Sennacherib's palace was a testament to his ambition and vision. The walls were lined with reliefs depicting his military campaigns, his victories, and the grandeur of his reign. The famous "Garden Room" contained intricate carvings of lush landscapes and exotic animals, creating a paradise within the palace walls. This opulence was not merely for show; it was a display of the king's power, his divine right to rule, and the prosperity of his empire.

The Library of Ashurbanipal: A Treasure of Knowledge

Nineveh was not only a center of political and military might but also a beacon of learning and culture. The city's intellectual heart was the Library of Ashurbanipal, one of the most significant collections of knowledge in the ancient world. King Ashurbanipal, a ruler as devoted to wisdom as he was to conquest, amassed a vast collection of cuneiform tablets on subjects ranging from literature and religion to science and law.

The library contained the Epic of Gilgamesh, one of humanity's oldest and most profound literary works, along with thousands of other texts that chronicled the knowledge and achievements of Mesopotamian civilization. This treasure trove of information was meticulously cataloged and preserved, reflecting Ashurbanipal's commitment to education and cultural heritage. The library served as a foundation for future generations, preserving the wisdom of the ancients and inspiring scholars for millennia.

A City of Temples and Gods

Religion played a central role in the life of Nineveh. The city's skyline was dominated by towering temples dedicated to the gods of the Assyrian pantheon. The most significant of these was the Temple of Ishtar, the goddess of love, war, and fertility. This grand temple was a place of worship and pilgrimage, where priests conducted elaborate rituals and offerings to honor the goddess and seek her favor.

The ziggurat of Nineveh, a massive terraced structure, stood as a bridge between heaven and earth, a place where the divine and mortal realms intersected. The city's religious festivals were grand events, drawing people from across the empire to partake in celebrations, processions, and ceremonies that reinforced the bond between the people and their gods.

The Heartbeat of an Empire

Nineveh was a bustling metropolis, a hub of commerce, culture, and daily life. Its markets were alive with the sounds and smells of merchants selling goods from across the known world—spices from India, gold from Egypt, textiles from Phoenicia. The city's streets were filled with artisans, traders, and citizens going about their daily routines, contributing to the vibrant tapestry of urban life.

The city's infrastructure reflected advanced urban planning, with well-paved roads, efficient water supply systems, and grand public buildings. Nineveh was a city that thrived on innovation and enterprise, where the pulse of the empire could be felt in every corner.

Decline and Rediscovery

The glory of Nineveh was not eternal. The city fell to a coalition of Babylonians, Medes, and Scythians in 612 BCE, marking the end of Assyrian supremacy. Nineveh's fall was swift and brutal, its grand structures reduced to ruins and its treasures scattered.

Yet, the memory of Nineveh endured. Archaeological excavations in the 19th century, led by pioneers such as Austen Henry Layard, brought the city's wonders back to light. The rediscovery of Nineveh's palaces, temples, and libraries unveiled the grandeur of a civilization that had once been the heartbeat of the ancient world. The artifacts and inscriptions found within its ruins continue to provide invaluable insights into Assyrian culture, governance, and daily life.

Key Events

1. **c. 3000 BCE** - Early Settlement: Nineveh is established as a small settlement.
2. **c. 1800 BCE** - Assyrian Growth: Nineveh grows in importance under the Assyrian Empire.
3. **c. 705-681 BCE** - Reign of Sennacherib: Nineveh becomes the capital of the Assyrian Empire, undergoing massive architectural and cultural development.
4. **c. 668-627 BCE** - Reign of Ashurbanipal: Nineveh reaches its peak, known for the great library of Ashurbanipal.
5. **612 BCE** - Fall of Nineveh: Conquered by a coalition of Babylonians, Medes, and others, marking the end of the Assyrian Empire.

Nimrud: The Glorious Citadel of Assyrian Power

The Jewel of the Tigris

In the cradle of ancient Mesopotamia, where the Tigris River winds its way through the heartland of the Assyrian Empire, stood Nimrud, a city of unparalleled splendor and might. Known in antiquity as Kalhu, Nimrud was not just a city; it was a citadel of power, a symbol of Assyrian dominance, and a beacon of architectural and artistic achievement.

The Royal Citadel: A Fortress of Majesty

Nimrud's most striking feature was its royal citadel, a fortified complex that dominated the city's skyline. This citadel was home to the grand palaces of Assyrian kings, whose reigns marked the zenith of the empire's glory. The most magnificent of these was the Northwest Palace, constructed by Ashurnasirpal II (883-859 BCE). This palace was an architectural marvel, boasting over 200 rooms adorned with intricate reliefs and luxurious decorations.

The palace's grand halls were lined with bas-reliefs depicting scenes of royal hunts, battles, and religious ceremonies. These artworks, meticulously carved into alabaster panels, showcased the king's prowess, divine favor, and the empire's might. The palace was not just a residence; it was a statement of power, designed to awe and intimidate visitors with its scale and opulence.

The Winged Bulls: Guardians of the Gateways

One of Nimrud's most iconic symbols was the lamassu, colossal winged bulls with human heads that stood guard at the entrances to the city and its royal palaces. These imposing statues, standing over three meters tall, were both protective deities and expressions of the king's authority. They conveyed a message of strength and invincibility, ensuring that all who entered Nimrud understood they were in the presence of greatness.

The lamassu's detailed craftsmanship, with their intricate wings, muscular bodies, and serene faces, reflected the high level of artistry and skill possessed by Assyrian sculptors. These guardians of the gateways were more than mere statues; they were embodiments of the city's divine protection and royal power.

A Center of Art and Culture

Nimrud was a hub of artistic and cultural innovation. The city's craftsmen were renowned for their expertise in various arts, from sculpture and metalwork to ivory carving and jewelry. The artifacts unearthed from Nimrud's ruins, such as the famed Nimrud Ivories, reveal a society that valued beauty, luxury, and craftsmanship.

The city's libraries and scribal schools were centers of learning where scholars studied and copied texts on diverse subjects, including astronomy, medicine, and literature. The intellectual life of Nimrud was vibrant, with the city's scribes preserving and advancing the knowledge inherited from earlier Mesopotamian civilizations.

The Temples of Nimrud: Houses of the Gods

Religion was integral to life in Nimrud, and the city's temples were grand edifices dedicated to the gods of the Assyrian pantheon. The Temple of Ninurta, the god of war and agriculture, was one of Nimrud's most significant religious sites. This temple, with its imposing ziggurat and sacred precincts, was a place of worship and pilgrimage, where priests conducted rituals to invoke the favor of the gods.

The temples of Nimrud were not only spiritual centers but also economic and administrative hubs. They played a crucial role in the city's daily life, managing vast estates and resources, and serving as centers of redistribution and social welfare.

The Empire's Stronghold

Nimrud's strategic location and formidable defenses made it a vital military stronghold. The city's fortifications included massive walls and towers that protected against invasions and ensured the security of the Assyrian heartland. The city's garrison was well-equipped and trained, ready to defend the empire's interests and expand its territories through conquest.

Under kings like Shalmaneser III and Tiglath-Pileser III, Nimrud became a launching point for military campaigns that extended Assyrian control over vast regions. The city's strategic importance and military might were reflected in its grand architecture and the presence of elite soldiers and commanders.

Decline and Rediscovery

The decline of Nimrud began with the fall of the Assyrian Empire in the late 7th century BCE. The city was sacked by a coalition of Babylonians, Medes, and Scythians, leading to its abandonment and eventual decay. For centuries, Nimrud lay buried beneath the sands of time, its grandeur forgotten.

The rediscovery of Nimrud in the 19th century by archaeologists such as Austen Henry Layard brought to light the city's hidden treasures. Excavations revealed the remnants of its palaces, temples, and artworks, providing a glimpse into the splendor of ancient Assyria. The artifacts and inscriptions unearthed from Nimrud continue to illuminate our understanding of Assyrian culture, politics, and art.

Key Events

1. **c. 1250 BCE** - Early Foundation: Nimrud (ancient Kalhu) is established as an important city.
2. **c. 884-859 BCE** - Reign of Ashurnasirpal II: Becomes the capital of Assyria, known for grand palaces and temples.
3. **c. 745-727 BCE** - Reign of Tiglath-Pileser III: Nimrud remains a major administrative and military center.
4. **c. 705-681 BCE** - Sennacherib: Moves the capital to Nineveh, but Nimrud remains significant.
5. **c. 612 BCE** - Fall of Nimrud: Sacked along with other Assyrian cities during the fall of the Assyrian Empire.

II

Africa

Giza: The Eternal City of Stone and Stars

A City Carved from Eternity

Beneath the scorching sun of the Egyptian desert, where the sands stretch endlessly towards the horizon, rises a city that defies time itself: Giza. Unlike any other, Giza is a city of monumental grandeur, where the ambitions of pharaohs and the mysteries of the cosmos intertwine. Known primarily for its awe-inspiring pyramids and the enigmatic Sphinx, Giza stands as a testament to the ancient Egyptians' pursuit of immortality and their profound connection to the heavens.

The Pyramids: Mountains of the Pharaohs

Giza's skyline is dominated by the three great pyramids, each a colossal mountain of stone built for eternity. The Great Pyramid of Khufu, the largest and most famous, stands as a marvel of ancient engineering. Originally rising to a height of 146 meters, this pyramid was the tallest man-made structure in the world for over 3,800 years. Its precise alignment with the cardinal points and the stars reflects the Egyptians' astronomical knowledge and their belief in the afterlife.

Next to Khufu's pyramid are the slightly smaller pyramids of Khafre and Menkaure. Khafre's pyramid, often mistaken for the Great Pyramid due to its prominent position and still intact limestone casing at the apex, is part of a larger complex that includes the Great Sphinx. Menkaure's pyramid, though smaller, is no less impressive, with its intricate mortuary temple and statues that once adorned its surroundings.

These pyramids were more than just tombs; they were gateways to the afterlife, designed to ensure the pharaohs' eternal journey among the stars.

The construction of these monumental structures required a vast workforce and meticulous planning, showcasing the organizational prowess and technological capabilities of ancient Egypt.

The Great Sphinx: Guardian of Secrets

Lying in silent vigil at the foot of Khafre's pyramid is the Great Sphinx, a colossal statue with the body of a lion and the head of a pharaoh, believed to represent Khafre himself. The Sphinx, carved from a single limestone outcrop, measures 73 meters in length and 20 meters in height, making it one of the largest monolithic statues in the world.

The Great Sphinx, with its serene and enigmatic expression, has been a symbol of mystery and power for millennia. Its purpose remains a subject of debate among scholars, but it is widely believed to serve as a guardian of the Giza Plateau, protecting the pharaohs' eternal resting places and watching over the sacred land.

A City of the Living and the Dead

Giza was not only a necropolis but also a thriving city of the living, where priests, workers, and craftsmen resided. The workers' village, discovered near the pyramids, reveals a well-organized settlement with bakeries, breweries, and workshops. This community was responsible for the daily operations of the pyramid complexes, from constructing the monuments to performing the rituals that sustained the pharaohs' spirits.

The priests of Giza played a crucial role in the religious life of the city. They conducted elaborate ceremonies and offerings to honor the gods and the deceased pharaohs, ensuring the smooth passage of the souls to the afterlife. The temples and shrines scattered across Giza were centers of worship and pilgrimage, drawing devotees from across the land.

The Celestial Connection

Giza's monuments were designed with a deep understanding of the cosmos. The pyramids' alignment with the Orion constellation and the positioning of the Sphinx to face the rising sun during the equinoxes reflect the Egyptians' astronomical prowess. This celestial connection was integral to their belief system, linking the pharaohs' eternal journey with the cycles of the stars and the sun.

The Pyramid Texts, inscribed on the walls of the pyramids, contain spells and hymns that guide the pharaohs through the afterlife, emphasizing the importance of the celestial realm in their spiritual journey. These texts are among the oldest religious writings in the world, providing invaluable insights into ancient Egyptian cosmology and theology.

Legacy and Rediscovery

The grandeur of Giza endured through the ages, even as the sands of time buried its secrets. The ancient Greeks and Romans marveled at the pyramids, considering them among the Seven Wonders of the Ancient World. In the modern era, explorers and archaeologists, such as Giovanni Battista Belzoni and Howard Carter, unveiled the mysteries of Giza, bringing its wonders to global attention.

Today, Giza remains a symbol of ancient Egypt's architectural brilliance and spiritual depth. The pyramids and the Sphinx attract millions of visitors from around the world, inspiring awe and admiration. The ongoing archaeological work continues to uncover new facets of this ancient city, deepening our understanding of its history and significance.

Key Events

1. **c. 2600-2500 BCE** - Construction of Pyramids: Great Pyramids of Giza, including the Pyramid of Khufu, are built.
2. **c. 2500 BCE** - Construction of the Great Sphinx: Monumental statue

constructed during the reign of Pharaoh Khafre.

3. **c. 2100-2000 BCE** - Old Kingdom Decline: Decline in Giza's prominence as the political center shifts.

4. **c. 1550-1070 BCE** - New Kingdom Period: Giza remains an important religious and burial site.

5. **c. 500 BCE - 30 BCE** - Greco-Roman Period: Continued use of Giza as a necropolis.

Memphis: The Living Heart of Ancient Egypt

The Pulse of the Nile

Where the life-giving waters of the Nile River split into the delta, forming a lush and fertile landscape, lay the ancient city of Memphis. Known as the "White Walls" for its brilliant limestone constructions, Memphis was the living heart of Egypt for over 3,000 years. This grand metropolis served as the political, cultural, and spiritual center of one of history's greatest civilizations.

The Throne of the Pharaohs

Founded around 3100 BCE by the legendary King Menes, who unified Upper and Lower Egypt, Memphis was more than a city; it was the cradle of Egyptian power. Here, amidst the palaces and administrative buildings, the pharaohs ruled with divine authority, their decrees shaping the destiny of the Nile Valley. The Great Temple of Ptah, the city's patron deity and god of craftsmen and architects, was a hub of religious and political activity. This temple complex, one of the largest and most important in ancient Egypt, was where the pharaohs sought the blessings of the gods and consulted with priests on matters of state and spirituality.

The Colossus of Ramses

One of the city's most iconic symbols was the colossal statue of Ramses II, which stood sentinel at the entrance to the temple of Ptah. This massive sculpture, over 10 meters tall, depicted the pharaoh in a pose of eternal strength and serenity. Carved from red granite, the statue reflected the artistry and engineering prowess of the ancient Egyptians, who could create such monumental works with the simplest of tools. The Colossus of Ramses served as a reminder of the pharaoh's divine status and the enduring legacy of his reign.

A Center of Commerce and Culture

Memphis was a bustling hub of commerce, attracting traders, artisans, and laborers from across Egypt and beyond. The city's strategic location at the apex of the Nile Delta made it a natural center for trade, where goods from Africa, the Mediterranean, and Asia were exchanged. Markets teemed with activity as merchants sold everything from grain and papyrus to gold and incense.

The city's workshops were renowned for their craftsmanship. Artisans in Memphis produced exquisite jewelry, pottery, and statues, their skills honed over generations. The city's proximity to the limestone quarries of Tura ensured a steady supply of high-quality stone for building and sculpture, contributing to Memphis's architectural grandeur.

The Necropolis of Saqqara

Just outside the city lay the vast necropolis of Saqqara, a testament to Memphis's enduring significance. Saqqara was home to the Step Pyramid of Djoser, the earliest colossal stone building in Egypt, designed by the legendary architect Imhotep. This pyramid, with its innovative stepped design, marked the beginning of the pyramid age and set the stage for the construction of the great pyramids at Giza.

Saqqara's tombs and mortuary temples, decorated with intricate carvings and vibrant frescoes, chronicled the lives and achievements of Egypt's elite. The necropolis was a place of reverence and remembrance, where the deceased were honored and their spirits guided to the afterlife. The complex rituals and offerings performed here reflected the Egyptians' deep belief in the afterlife and the importance of maintaining the cosmic order.

The Cult of Apis

One of the unique religious practices of Memphis was the worship of the Apis bull, considered a living incarnation of the god Ptah. The Apis bull, identified by specific markings, was housed in the temple and worshipped during its lifetime. Upon its death, the bull was mummified and buried in the Serapeum, a vast underground catacomb in Saqqara. The cult of Apis played a central role in the religious life of Memphis, symbolizing fertility, strength, and the divine connection between the gods and the pharaoh.

Decline and Legacy

The fortunes of Memphis waxed and waned with the shifting tides of history. As new capitals like Thebes and Alexandria rose to prominence, Memphis gradually declined, though it remained a significant cultural and religious center. The city's decline was accelerated by the changing course of the Nile and the rise of new political powers.

Despite its decline, the legacy of Memphis endured. The city's ruins, including the remains of the Great Temple of Ptah and the Colossus of Ramses, have provided invaluable insights into the life and achievements of ancient Egypt. Archaeological excavations have uncovered a wealth of artifacts, from statues and stelae to pottery and tools, shedding light on the daily life, religious practices, and artistic achievements of this great city.

Key Events

1. **c. 3100 BCE** - Founding of Memphis: Established by Pharaoh Menes (or Narmer) as the capital of united Egypt.
2. **c. 2686-2181 BCE** - Old Kingdom Period: Memphis flourishes as the administrative and religious capital.
3. **c. 1991-1802 BCE** - Middle Kingdom: Memphis remains an important cultural and religious center.

4. **c. 1550-1070 BCE** - New Kingdom: Memphis serves as a major city, with large temples and monuments.

5. **c. 332 BCE** - Alexander the Great: Memphis becomes the administrative center under Alexander's rule.

6. **c. 30 BCE-641 CE** - Roman and Byzantine Periods: Continues to be a significant city until the rise of Fustat (Cairo).

Thebes: The Splendor of the Nile

The City of Eternal Dawn

Imagine a city where the first rays of the sun illuminate grand temples and majestic statues, a city where the gods themselves seemed to have laid their blessings. This is Thebes, the city of eternal dawn, nestled on the banks of the Nile River. Known as Waset to the ancient Egyptians and later as Thebes by the Greeks, this city was the heart of Egyptian civilization during the height of its power and glory.

The Temples of Karnak and Luxor: Pillars of Divinity

Thebes was renowned for its monumental temples, the most impressive of which were the Temple of Karnak and the Temple of Luxor. Karnak, a vast complex of chapels, pylons, and obelisks, was dedicated to the god Amun-Ra, the king of the gods. Walking through its grand Hypostyle Hall, with its forest of colossal columns etched with hieroglyphs, one could feel the divine presence that permeated the air.

Luxor Temple, connected to Karnak by the Avenue of Sphinxes, was equally magnificent. Built by Amenhotep III and expanded by Ramses II, this temple was a center of religious and political power. Its imposing statues, grand courtyards, and sanctuaries reflected the city's wealth and the pharaohs' devotion to the gods. The annual Opet Festival, where statues of the gods were paraded from Karnak to Luxor, underscored the city's role as a spiritual nexus.

The Valley of the Kings: The Eternal Resting Place

Across the river, hidden in the shadow of the cliffs, lies the Valley of the Kings, the eternal resting place of Egypt's greatest pharaohs. This necropolis, with its tombs carved deep into the rock, was designed to protect the royal mummies and their treasures from tomb robbers. The tomb of Tutankhamun, discovered nearly intact in 1922, remains one of the most significant archaeological finds, offering a glimpse into the opulence of the New Kingdom.

The tombs of Seti I, Ramses II, and other illustrious rulers are adorned with intricate wall paintings and hieroglyphs that narrate their journey through the afterlife. These tombs reflect the Egyptians' profound belief in immortality and the meticulous preparations made to ensure the pharaohs' safe passage to the next world.

The Colossi of Memnon: Guardians of the West

Standing sentinel on the western bank of the Nile are the Colossi of Memnon, two towering statues of Amenhotep III. These colossal figures, each over 18 meters high, once guarded the entrance to the pharaoh's mortuary temple. Although the temple itself has long since disappeared, the statues remain, their faces weathered by time yet still exuding an aura of majesty.

The Colossi of Memnon were famed in antiquity for the phenomenon known as the "Vocal Memnon." At dawn, the northern statue emitted a musical sound, believed by the Greeks to be the voice of the hero Memnon calling to his mother Eos, the goddess of dawn. This mysterious occurrence added to the allure and mystique of Thebes.

A Center of Learning and Culture

Thebes was not only a religious and political center but also a hub of learning and culture. The city's scribes and scholars worked in the temples and palaces, recording historical events, religious texts, and literary works on papyrus scrolls. The Library of Thebes, though not as famous as Alexandria's, was a repository of knowledge that contributed to the intellectual life of ancient Egypt.

The arts flourished in Thebes, with craftsmen creating exquisite jewelry, pottery, and statuary. The city's artisans were renowned for their skill, producing works that adorned the temples and tombs. The vibrant frescoes and reliefs that decorate the tombs in the Valley of the Kings and the temples of Karnak and Luxor are testament to their mastery.

The Legacy of Thebes

Thebes reached its zenith during the New Kingdom, particularly under the rule of pharaohs like Thutmose III, Hatshepsut, and Ramses II. These rulers expanded the city's influence, embarking on ambitious building projects and military campaigns that extended Egypt's borders. However, the city's fortunes declined with the rise of the Assyrians and later the Persians, and by the time of Alexander the Great, Thebes had lost much of its former glory.

Despite its decline, the legacy of Thebes endured. The city's ruins, explored and documented by archaeologists, have provided invaluable insights into ancient Egyptian civilization. The grandeur of its temples, the artistry of its tombs, and the historical records inscribed on its walls continue to captivate and inspire.

Key Events

1. **c. 3200 BCE** - Early Settlement: Thebes established as a small settlement.
2. **c. 2055-1650 BCE** - Middle Kingdom: Becomes the religious capital and site of great temples like Karnak and Luxor.
3. **c. 1550-1070 BCE** - New Kingdom: Flourishes as the political, religious, and cultural heart of Egypt.
4. **c. 1350 BCE** - Akhenaten's Reign: Brief decline during the religious revolution of Akhenaten.
5. **c. 1070-664 BCE** - Third Intermediate Period: Thebes remains an important religious center.
6. **c. 30 BCE-641 CE** - Roman and Byzantine Periods: Thebes continues to be revered, though its political importance wanes.

Athribis: The Hidden Gem of the Nile Delta

A City of Blossoms and Mysteries

In the lush, fertile expanse of the Nile Delta, where the river branches into a labyrinth of waterways and green fields, lies a city steeped in myth and mystery: Athribis. Known to the ancient Egyptians as Hut-Heryib and to the Greeks as Athribis, this city was a thriving center of culture, religion, and innovation. Often overshadowed by its more famous neighbors, Athribis remains a hidden gem, offering glimpses into the intricate tapestry of ancient Egyptian civilization.

The Temple of Min and Repyt: Sanctuary of Fertility

Athribis was renowned for its grand temple complex dedicated to Min, the god of fertility and harvest, and his consort, Repyt. This temple, one of the largest in the Delta, was the heart of the city's religious life. The towering pylons, adorned with intricate carvings and hieroglyphs, welcomed worshippers and pilgrims who came to seek blessings for bountiful harvests and prosperous lives.

Inside the temple, priests conducted elaborate rituals and ceremonies to honor Min and Repyt, ensuring the fertility of the land and the prosperity of the people. The sanctity of the temple extended to its sacred gardens, where exotic plants and flowers bloomed, symbolizing the fertility and abundance that the gods bestowed upon Athribis.

The Nile Festival: A Celebration of Life

Athribis was famous for its vibrant Nile Festival, an annual celebration marking the inundation of the Nile River. This festival was a joyous occasion, filled with music, dance, and feasting, as the rising waters rejuvenated the land and brought life to the fields. The festival began with a grand procession from the temple, with priests carrying statues of Min and Repyt to the riverbanks, where offerings and prayers were made to ensure a generous flood.

The streets of Athribis came alive with the sounds of drums and flutes, and the air was filled with the scent of incense and blooming flowers. People from across the Delta and beyond flocked to the city to partake in the festivities, reinforcing the bonds of community and the shared reverence for the life-giving Nile.

A Hub of Innovation and Craftsmanship

Athribis was a center of innovation and craftsmanship, known for its skilled artisans who produced exquisite jewelry, pottery, and textiles. The city's workshops buzzed with activity, as craftsmen created goods that were highly prized in both local and distant markets. The intricate designs and superior quality of Athribis's products reflected the city's artistic heritage and its role as a hub of trade and commerce.

The city's proximity to the Nile provided easy access to transportation and trade routes, enabling the flow of goods and ideas. Merchants from Athribis engaged in extensive trade networks, exchanging their finely crafted wares for exotic materials and luxuries from across the ancient world. This vibrant trade enriched the city's economy and cultural life, making Athribis a dynamic and prosperous community.

The Enigmatic Necropolis

Just outside the city lay the enigmatic necropolis of Athribis, a testament to the city's spiritual and cultural significance. This sprawling burial ground was the final resting place for the city's elite, with tombs and mastabas that reflected the wealth and status of their occupants. The tombs were adorned with elaborate carvings and paintings, depicting scenes of daily life, religious rituals, and the journey to the afterlife.

The necropolis was also home to the mysterious "House of Life," a library and scriptorium where priests and scribes copied sacred texts and conducted astronomical observations. This institution was a center of learning and preservation, ensuring the continuity of knowledge and tradition through the generations.

The Legacy of Athribis

Athribis thrived during various periods of ancient Egyptian history, particularly during the Ptolemaic and Roman eras. The city's strategic location and its cultural and economic vitality ensured its prominence over the centuries. However, as the political and economic landscape of Egypt shifted, Athribis gradually declined, its temples and workshops falling into ruin.

Despite its decline, the legacy of Athribis endures. Archaeological excavations have uncovered the remnants of its temples, tombs, and workshops, shedding light on the city's rich history and cultural achievements. The artifacts and inscriptions discovered in Athribis provide invaluable insights into the daily lives, beliefs, and artistic endeavors of its inhabitants.

Key Events

1. **c. 3000 BCE** - Early Settlement: Athribis established as a local administrative center in the Nile Delta.
2. **c. 1550-1070 BCE** - New Kingdom: Flourishes with temples dedicated to gods like Amun and Horus.

3. **c. 664-332 BCE** - Late Period: Continues to thrive as a religious and administrative center.
4. **c. 332-30 BCE** - Ptolemaic Period: Significant development under the Greek rulers of Egypt.
5. **c. 30 BCE-641 CE** - Roman and Byzantine Periods: Remains an important local center until the early Islamic period.

Heliopolis: The City of the Sun's Ascendancy

The Dawn of the Divine

In the sun-drenched expanse of the Egyptian desert, where the Nile River gives life to the surrounding lands, there once stood a city that embodied the very essence of light and creation: Heliopolis. Known to the ancient Egyptians as Iunu or On, Heliopolis was more than a city; it was a celestial beacon, a place where the divine sun god Ra was worshipped and the mysteries of the cosmos were unraveled. This ancient metropolis, bathed in the golden glow of the rising sun, was a center of religious, intellectual, and cultural enlightenment.

The Temple of the Sun: Ra's Sacred Abode

At the heart of Heliopolis was the Great Temple of Ra, the god of the sun and creation. This temple, one of the largest and most significant in ancient Egypt, was the focal point of worship and pilgrimage. The temple complex, with its grand pylons and vast courtyards, was designed to honor Ra and to capture the sun's rays, symbolizing the power and energy of the divine.

The temple's architecture was aligned with the cardinal points, emphasizing the importance of solar movements in Egyptian cosmology. Each morning, as the sun rose, its first light would strike the temple's central obelisk, a towering stone monument that represented a ray of the sun frozen in time. This obelisk was not just a marker of religious devotion but also an astronomical instrument, used by priests to track the solar calendar and mark important seasonal events.

The House of Life: A Beacon of Knowledge

Heliopolis was a renowned center of learning and intellectual pursuit, home to the prestigious "House of Life." This institution functioned as a combination of library, school, and scriptorium, where priests and scholars studied a wide array of subjects, from theology and astronomy to medicine and philosophy. The House of Life was a repository of knowledge, housing sacred texts and scientific treatises that were meticulously copied and preserved by scribes.

The city's scholars were instrumental in the development of the Egyptian calendar, which was based on the solar year. Their observations of the sun and stars, recorded in astronomical texts, contributed significantly to the understanding of celestial phenomena. The intellectual legacy of Heliopolis influenced not only Egyptian science and religion but also Greek and Roman thought, as scholars from these cultures later studied the works of Heliopolitan priests.

The Ennead: Gods of Creation

Heliopolis was the birthplace of the Ennead, a group of nine deities who played a central role in Egyptian cosmology. This pantheon included Atum, Shu, Tefnut, Geb, Nut, Osiris, Isis, Set, and Nephthys. According to Heliopolitan mythology, Atum, the creator god, emerged from the primordial waters of Nun and gave birth to the other gods through his own efforts.

The priests of Heliopolis developed complex theological doctrines based on the interactions and stories of the Ennead, explaining the creation of the world and the functioning of the cosmos. These myths were central to Egyptian religion and were depicted in temple reliefs, hymns, and religious texts. The Ennead's narratives provided a framework for understanding the natural and divine order, reinforcing the city's status as a spiritual and intellectual epicenter.

A City of Light and Life

Heliopolis was more than a religious and intellectual center; it was a vibrant urban hub. The city's markets bustled with activity, offering goods from across Egypt and beyond. Merchants traded papyrus, linen, jewelry, and exotic spices, contributing to Heliopolis's prosperity. The fertile lands surrounding the city supported agriculture, ensuring a steady supply of food and resources.

The people of Heliopolis lived in harmony with the cycles of the sun, their daily lives intertwined with religious rituals and agricultural practices. Festivals dedicated to Ra and the Ennead were grand celebrations, featuring processions, music, and feasting. These events reinforced the community's connection to the divine and celebrated the city's role as a source of light and life.

The Obelisks: Pillars of the Sun

Heliopolis was famed for its obelisks, which were symbols of solar worship and markers of the city's sacred landscape. These towering monoliths, carved from single blocks of red granite, were erected in pairs at the entrances of temples and along ceremonial routes. The obelisks were inscribed with hieroglyphs that praised Ra and commemorated the deeds of pharaohs.

One of the most famous obelisks from Heliopolis was transported to Rome by Emperor Augustus and now stands in the Piazza del Popolo. These obelisks, scattered across the world, continue to serve as enduring symbols of Heliopolis's legacy and the far-reaching influence of its culture and religion.

Legacy and Rediscovery

The glory of Heliopolis faded with the rise of new political centers and the changing religious landscape of Egypt. However, the city's influence endured through the ages. Greek and Roman scholars, such as Herodotus and Strabo, wrote about the wonders of Heliopolis, preserving its memory in their histories.

Archaeological excavations in the 19th and 20th centuries brought to light the ruins of Heliopolis, revealing the remnants of its temples, obelisks, and inscriptions. These discoveries have provided valuable insights into the city's religious practices, architectural achievements, and intellectual contributions.

Key Events

1. **c. 3000 BCE** - Early Settlement: Heliopolis is established as a major religious center dedicated to the sun god Ra.
2. **c. 2613-2181 BCE** - Old Kingdom: Heliopolis becomes one of the most important religious cities in Egypt, with its priesthood wielding

significant influence.

3. **c. 2055-1650 BCE** – Middle Kingdom: Continues to flourish as a center of learning and religious thought.

4. **c. 1353-1336 BCE** – Amarna Period: Brief decline in religious significance as Akhenaten focuses on Aten.

5. **c. 664-332 BCE** – Late Period: Revival as a major center for the worship of Ra.

6. **c. 30 BCE-641 CE** – Roman and Byzantine Periods: Heliopolis remains an important religious site but gradually declines.

Elephantine: The Isle of Boundaries and Beginnings

The Island at the Edge of the World

In the southern reaches of ancient Egypt, where the mighty Nile flows past rocky cataracts and into the sands of Nubia, lies Elephantine, an island that served as both a boundary and a beginning. Known to the ancient Egyptians as Abu, Elephantine was more than just a city; it was a gateway to the unknown, a place where the familiar world of Egypt met the mysteries of Africa. This ancient city, perched on the first cataract of the Nile, was a hub of trade, culture, and spiritual significance.

The Island of Khnum: Guardian of the Inundation

Elephantine was sacred to Khnum, the ram-headed god of the Nile's inundation and the creator of human beings. The Temple of Khnum, a focal point of worship, stood proudly on the island, where priests conducted rituals to honor the god who controlled the life-giving waters of the Nile. According to mythology, Khnum fashioned humans on his potter's wheel from the clay of the Nile, breathing life into their forms.

The temple complex was an architectural marvel, with its grand courtyards, towering columns, and intricately carved reliefs. Pilgrims and worshippers flocked to Elephantine to offer prayers and sacrifices to Khnum, seeking his favor for a plentiful inundation and bountiful harvests. The island was also home to the Nilometer, a vital instrument that measured the river's flood levels, enabling the prediction of agricultural cycles and ensuring the prosperity of the land.

A Center of Trade and Exchange

Elephantine's strategic location made it a crucial center for trade and exchange. Positioned at the southern border of Egypt, the island was a bustling gateway between Egypt and Nubia, facilitating the flow of goods, ideas, and cultures. Traders from distant lands brought gold, ivory, incense, ebony, and exotic animals, enriching the markets of Elephantine and connecting it to the broader world.

The island's harbors were filled with boats laden with treasures, and its markets buzzed with activity. Merchants, craftsmen, and traders from diverse backgrounds mingled in Elephantine, creating a cosmopolitan atmosphere that reflected the island's importance as a commercial hub. The fusion of Egyptian and Nubian cultures on the island fostered a unique blend of art, language, and traditions, making Elephantine a melting pot of ancient civilizations.

The Island of Boundaries

Elephantine's significance extended beyond trade; it was also a place of boundaries and defense. As the southernmost settlement of ancient Egypt, the island marked the frontier of the Egyptian world. Fortresses and military outposts were established on the island to protect against incursions from Nubia and other southern lands. These fortifications, constructed from sturdy granite, symbolized Egypt's determination to defend its borders and control the vital trade routes along the Nile.

The island's position at the first cataract of the Nile, where the river's flow was interrupted by granite boulders and rapids, made it a natural boundary. The challenging terrain served as a deterrent to invaders, while also offering a strategic vantage point for monitoring river traffic. Elephantine's fortresses, with their commanding views of the Nile, played a crucial role in maintaining the security and stability of the region.

A Hub of Knowledge and Administration

Elephantine was not only a center of trade and defense but also a hub of knowledge and administration. The island housed important governmental offices and served as a base for officials overseeing the region. Records and documents found on the island reveal a well-organized administration that managed trade, taxation, and legal matters, ensuring the smooth functioning of the state.

The island's scribes and scholars contributed to the intellectual life of Egypt, recording astronomical observations, religious texts, and historical events. Elephantine's archives, inscribed on papyrus and stone, provide a rich source of information about the daily life, governance, and spiritual practices of the ancient Egyptians.

The Legacy of Elephantine

Elephantine's legacy is preserved in the ruins and artifacts that remain on the island. Archaeological excavations have uncovered the remnants of its temples, fortresses, and settlements, revealing a complex and vibrant society. The island's Nilometer, still visible today, stands as a testament to the ancient Egyptians' ingenuity and their deep connection to the rhythms of the Nile.

The island's cultural significance endures, with its unique blend of Egyptian and Nubian influences offering insights into the interactions between these ancient civilizations. Elephantine's role as a boundary and a beginning, a place of defense and exchange, continues to captivate historians and archaeologists, shedding light on the dynamics of ancient Egypt's southern frontier.

Key Events

1. **c. 3000 BCE** - Early Settlement: Elephantine is established as a key trading post and administrative center on the Nile.
2. **c. 2000-1800 BCE** - Middle Kingdom: Becomes a significant military and trading hub, with fortifications built to control trade routes.
3. **c. 1550-1070 BCE** - New Kingdom: Continues to be an important military and economic center, with temples dedicated to Khnum.
4. **c. 664-332 BCE** - Late Period: Maintains its strategic importance and serves as a boundary marker for Egypt's southern border.
5. **c. 30 BCE-641 CE** - Roman and Byzantine Periods: Remains a key location for trade and military presence.

Napata: The Jewel of the Nubian Kings

The Sacred Cradle of the Black Pharaohs

Nestled beneath the shadow of the majestic Jebel Barkal, where the desert sands meet the life-giving waters of the Nile, lies Napata, the ancient city that once stood as the heart of the Kushite Kingdom. More than just a city, Napata was a sacred center of power and spirituality, the birthplace of the Black Pharaohs who would come to rule both Nubia and Egypt. With its towering temples, royal pyramids, and the ever-present gaze of the holy mountain, Napata remains a symbol of the resilience and grandeur of the Kushite civilization—a beacon of African heritage that still resonates through the ages.

Jebel Barkal: The Mountain of the Gods

At the heart of Napata's spiritual and political life was Jebel Barkal, a striking sandstone mountain that loomed over the city and was revered as a sacred abode of the gods. The mountain, with its distinctive pinnacle, was believed to be the home of Amun, the chief deity of the Kushites, who was also worshipped across Egypt. Jebel Barkal was more than just a natural landmark; it was a symbol of divine power and legitimacy, a place where heaven and earth were said to meet.

The Kushite kings, known as the Black Pharaohs, saw Jebel Barkal as the source of their divine right to rule, and they built temples at its base to honor Amun and solidify their connection to the gods. These temples, adorned with statues and inscriptions, were places of pilgrimage and ritual, where the kings and their subjects sought the favor of the gods and affirmed their devotion. Jebel Barkal, with its towering presence and sacred aura, was the spiritual anchor of Napata, a constant reminder of the city's connection to the divine and its role as the cradle of kingship.

The Temples of Amun: The Heart of Worship

The temples of Napata, particularly the grand Temple of Amun at Jebel Barkal, were the epicenters of religious life in the Kushite Kingdom. These temples, modeled after their counterparts in Thebes, Egypt, were constructed with massive columns, decorated with intricate carvings, and filled with statues of gods and pharaohs. The Temple of Amun was the largest and most important of these, a place where the Black Pharaohs performed rituals that linked their rule to the divine will of Amun.

The rituals conducted at the Temple of Amun were steeped in symbolism and tradition, reflecting the deep connection between the Kushite rulers and the gods. Festivals, offerings, and oracles were regular features of temple life, ensuring the ongoing favor of the gods and the prosperity of the kingdom. The priests of Amun, who wielded considerable influence, played a key role in advising the king and interpreting the will of the gods. The temples of Napata were not just places of worship; they were centers of political power and cultural identity, embodying the Kushite belief in the sacred nature of kingship.

The Royal Pyramids: The Tombs of the Black Pharaohs

On the west bank of the Nile, at the site of Nuri and later at Meroë, the royal cemeteries of Napata were marked by the distinctive pyramids of the Kushite kings and queens. These pyramids, smaller and steeper than their Egyptian counterparts, were built to house the remains of the Black Pharaohs, who saw themselves as the true heirs to the ancient traditions of Egypt. The pyramids were surrounded by chapels and offering tables, where rituals were performed to ensure the safe passage of the kings to the afterlife.

The royal pyramids of Napata were symbols of both continuity and innovation, reflecting the Kushite rulers' desire to align themselves with the grandeur of Egypt while also asserting their own distinct identity. The pyramids were filled with treasures, including jewelry, weapons, and ceremonial objects, all intended to accompany the king in the afterlife. The burial practices of Napata were a blend of Egyptian and Nubian traditions, illustrating the cultural synthesis that defined the Kushite Kingdom. The royal pyramids stood as enduring monuments to the power and piety of the Black Pharaohs, their sharp silhouettes cutting against the desert sky.

The Coronation City: Where Kings Were Made

Napata was not only a city of temples and tombs; it was the coronation city, where the Black Pharaohs were crowned and received the blessings of the gods. The coronation rituals, conducted at Jebel Barkal and in the temples of Amun, were elaborate ceremonies that reaffirmed the king's divine right to rule and his role as the earthly representative of the gods. The king would receive the crown of Upper and Lower Egypt, symbolizing his dominion over both lands, and would be anointed with sacred oils, marking him as the chosen of Amun.

The coronation of a new king was a moment of great significance for the people of Napata and the wider Kushite Kingdom. It was a time of celebration and renewal, when the bonds between the king, the gods, and the people were reaffirmed. The city would be filled with processions, music, and offerings, as the new king took his place at the head of the kingdom. The coronation city of Napata was a place where the past, present, and future of the Kushite people were united, where the sacred and the temporal were woven together in the fabric of kingship.

The Rise and Fall of Napata: The Legacy of the Black Pharaohs

Napata's prominence as the center of the Kushite Kingdom began in the 8th century BCE, when the Black Pharaohs extended their rule over Egypt, establishing the 25th Dynasty. During this period, Napata became the heart of a vast empire that stretched from the Nile Delta to the heart of Africa. The Black Pharaohs, such as Piye, Taharqa, and Shabaka, left a lasting legacy in both Egypt and Nubia, revitalizing the traditions of the New Kingdom and restoring the grandeur of the Nile Valley.

However, the fortunes of Napata waned in the 7th century BCE, as the Assyrian Empire expanded into Egypt, eventually pushing the Kushite rulers back to Nubia. Despite these setbacks, Napata remained a vital center of culture and religion for centuries, even as the political capital shifted south to Meroë. The legacy of Napata endured in the memory of its sacred sites, its royal pyramids, and its role as the birthplace of the Black Pharaohs.

In modern times, the ruins of Napata, with its temples, pyramids, and the sacred mountain of Jebel Barkal, continue to inspire awe and reverence. Archaeologists and historians have uncovered the remains of this once-great city, shedding light on the rich cultural and religious life of the Kushite Kingdom. Napata's legacy lives on as a symbol of African resilience, creativity, and the enduring power of a civilization that once stood at the crossroads of two great cultures.

Key Events

1. **c. 1000 BCE** - Founding of Napata: Napata is established as a major religious and political center in Nubia, near the Fourth Cataract of the Nile.

2. **c. 750-656 BCE** - Kingdom of Kush: Napata becomes the capital of the Kingdom of Kush, with its rulers, known as the "Black Pharaohs," conquering and ruling Egypt as the 25th Dynasty.

3. **c. 656 BCE** - Decline and Shift to Meroë: Napata declines in importance as the Kushite capital is moved to Meroë, though it remains a significant religious site.

4. **c. 300 BCE** - Continued Religious Significance: Napata remains the religious heart of the Kingdom of Kush, with the Jebel Barkal temple complex serving as a major pilgrimage site.

5. **c. 350 CE** - Final Decline: Napata declines further after the rise of the

Aksumite Kingdom, which conquers and absorbs much of Kush.

Amarna: The City of the Sun's Horizon

The Dawn of a New Era

In the heart of ancient Egypt, along the banks of the Nile River, a city rose from the desert sands as a beacon of innovation and spiritual revolution: Amarna. Founded by the pharaoh Akhenaten around 1350 BCE, Amarna was not just a city; it was a vision, a radical departure from the traditions of old Egypt. Known as Akhetaten, "Horizon of the Aten," this city was dedicated to the worship of a single deity, the Aten, the sun disk. Amarna stands as a testament to one of history's most intriguing and transformative periods, where art, religion, and society were reshaped under the rays of the Egyptian sun.

The Sun God's Sanctuary

At the heart of Amarna lay the Great Temple of the Aten, an architectural marvel open to the sky, reflecting the new monotheistic faith of Akhenaten. Unlike traditional Egyptian temples, which were enclosed and filled with shadows, the Great Temple was bathed in sunlight, with vast open courtyards where priests and worshippers could directly commune with the Aten. The temple's altars and offering tables were scattered throughout the expansive space, allowing the sun's rays to touch the sacred offerings, symbolizing the Aten's direct connection with the people.

The city itself was meticulously planned to align with the religious and ideological principles of the new faith. The Royal Road, a grand avenue, ran through the city, connecting the Great Temple with the Northern and Southern Palaces, reflecting the unity of religious and political power under Akhenaten's reign.

The Royal Visionaries

Amarna was the residence of Akhenaten and his queen, Nefertiti, whose reigns were marked by unprecedented artistic and cultural change. Akhenaten, often depicted with elongated features and a serene expression, was not just a ruler but a spiritual leader who believed himself to be the living embodiment of the Aten. Nefertiti, renowned for her beauty and depicted in iconic busts, played a crucial role in religious ceremonies and state affairs, embodying the new artistic styles and ideals.

The art of Amarna broke away from the rigid conventions of previous Egyptian art, embracing realism and fluidity. Scenes from daily life, intimate family portraits, and depictions of the royal family in informal settings became prevalent. This new artistic style, known as the Amarna art, emphasized naturalism and emotion, capturing the essence of the revolutionary spirit that defined the city.

A City of Light and Life

Amarna was a vibrant urban center, bustling with activity and innovation. Its streets were lined with workshops, homes, and markets, where artisans, traders, and laborers contributed to the city's dynamic economy. The city's layout, with its distinct residential and administrative districts, reflected a well-organized and forward-thinking society.

The city's residents lived in well-constructed houses made of mudbrick, often adorned with painted walls and courtyards filled with greenery. The homes of the wealthy featured spacious layouts with gardens and pools, while the more modest dwellings of the artisans and workers were functional and comfortable. The city was designed to be a model of harmony and efficiency, reflecting the ideals of the Aten faith.

The Spiritual Heartbeat

The religious life of Amarna was centered around the daily worship of the Aten. Unlike the traditional pantheon of gods, the Aten was depicted as a radiant sun disk, whose rays extended down to the earth, ending in hands that held symbols of life. This imagery permeated the city, reinforcing the idea that the Aten's life-giving energy was directly bestowed upon the people and the land.

Religious rituals were conducted in the open air, under the direct gaze of the sun. Hymns and prayers to the Aten, such as the "Great Hymn to the Aten," composed by Akhenaten himself, celebrated the sun god's creation and sustenance of life. These hymns, inscribed on the walls of the temples and palaces, are some of the most profound expressions of the new religious ideology.

The Legacy and Fall

Despite its initial grandeur and visionary aspirations, Amarna's existence was brief. Following Akhenaten's death, the city was abandoned, and the traditional religious practices and capital of Egypt were restored by his successors. The city fell into ruin, its revolutionary ideals buried under the sands of time.

Archaeological excavations in the 19th and 20th centuries uncovered the remains of Amarna, revealing its unique architecture, art, and inscriptions. These discoveries provided invaluable insights into a period of profound change and highlighted the fleeting yet impactful legacy of Akhenaten's vision.

Key Events

1. **c. 1353 BCE** - Founding by Akhenaten: Established as the new capital city dedicated to the worship of the Aten, the sun disk.
2. **c. 1346 BCE** - Construction: Rapid development of temples, palaces,

and residential areas under Akhenaten's orders.

3. **c. 1336 BCE** - Abandonment: Abandoned shortly after Akhenaten's death and the return to traditional religious practices under Tutankhamun.

4. **c. 1336-1300 BCE** - Decline: Gradual decline as it is deserted and its buildings fall into ruin.

Avaris: The Enigmatic Capital of the Hyksos

The Crossroads of Cultures

In the northeastern Delta of ancient Egypt, where the Nile's waters mingle with the sands of the Sinai, there once thrived a city that stood as a beacon of cultural fusion and strategic brilliance: Avaris. Known to the ancient Egyptians as Hut-waret, Avaris was the capital of the enigmatic Hyksos, a people whose origins remain shrouded in mystery. This city, vibrant with the life of multiple cultures, served as a gateway between Egypt and the Near East, blending traditions, technologies, and ideas from across the ancient world.

The Fortress City

Avaris was strategically located on the eastern edge of the Nile Delta, making it a crucial defensive stronghold and a hub of trade. The city's fortifications were formidable, with massive walls and towers designed to protect against invaders and control the vital trade routes that passed through the region. These defenses, combined with the city's bustling harbors, ensured that Avaris was both a shield and a gateway for Egypt.

The city's layout reflected its dual purpose of defense and commerce. The streets were lined with workshops, markets, and warehouses filled with goods from across the Mediterranean and Near East. Merchants and traders from as far afield as Crete, Cyprus, and the Levant brought their wares to Avaris, creating a vibrant, cosmopolitan atmosphere.

The Hyksos Legacy

The Hyksos, who ruled Avaris and much of Lower Egypt during the Second Intermediate Period, brought with them innovations that transformed Egyptian society. They introduced advanced technologies, such as horse-drawn chariots and composite bows, which revolutionized Egyptian warfare. The Hyksos also brought new agricultural techniques, metalworking skills, and artistic styles, blending them with local traditions to create a unique cultural synthesis.

Despite their foreign origins, the Hyksos adopted many aspects of Egyptian culture, worshipping Egyptian gods and even building temples in their honor. The Temple of Seth, the Hyksos' chief deity, was one of the most significant religious structures in Avaris, symbolizing their integration into the spiritual fabric of Egypt. The city's religious life was a blend of Egyptian and Near Eastern traditions, reflecting the Hyksos' dual heritage.

The Palace Complex: A Seat of Power

Avaris was home to an impressive palace complex, the seat of Hyksos power. This palace, with its grand halls, administrative offices, and luxurious living quarters, was the heart of the city's political and economic life. The palace's architecture was a fusion of Egyptian and Near Eastern styles, featuring colonnaded courtyards, elaborate frescoes, and intricate mosaics that showcased the wealth and artistic prowess of the Hyksos rulers.

The palace was not just a center of governance but also a hub of cultural exchange. Dignitaries and emissaries from neighboring regions frequented the palace, bringing with them gifts, news, and knowledge. This flow of information and goods contributed to the city's prosperity and its role as a melting pot of ideas and innovations.

The Tombs of Avaris: Echoes of a Bygone Era

The necropolis of Avaris, located just outside the city, offers a glimpse into the lives and beliefs of its inhabitants. The tombs, adorned with a blend of Egyptian and Near Eastern funerary practices, reflect the city's diverse cultural heritage. Richly decorated burial chambers, filled with grave goods such as pottery, weapons, and jewelry, attest to the wealth and status of the city's elite.

One of the most intriguing discoveries in Avaris is the presence of Minoan frescoes, indicating cultural and possibly diplomatic connections with the Minoan civilization of Crete. These frescoes, depicting scenes of nature, animals, and religious rituals, add to the enigmatic allure of the city and its cosmopolitan character.

The Fall and Rediscovery

The decline of Avaris began with the rise of the Theban princes in Upper Egypt, who eventually expelled the Hyksos and unified Egypt under the New Kingdom. The city fell into obscurity, its grandeur buried under the sands of time. However, its legacy endured, influencing the cultural and technological landscape of ancient Egypt.

The rediscovery of Avaris in the 20th century by archaeologists such as Manfred Bietak has unveiled the city's lost splendor. Excavations have uncovered the remains of its palaces, temples, and fortifications, revealing a city that was once a beacon of innovation and cultural fusion. The artifacts and inscriptions found in Avaris provide invaluable insights into the lives and achievements of the Hyksos and their impact on Egyptian history.

Key Events

1. **c. 1800 BCE** - Early Settlement: Avaris is established in the Nile Delta, becoming a significant trade and military center.
2. **c. 1650-1550 BCE** - Hyksos Period: Becomes the capital of the Hyksos, a foreign dynasty that rules northern Egypt.
3. **c. 1550 BCE** - Conquest by Ahmose I: Avaris is captured by the founder of the New Kingdom, leading to the expulsion of the Hyksos.
4. **c. 1550-1070 BCE** - New Kingdom: Remains a significant site but declines in political importance.
5. **c. 1300 BCE** - Decline: Gradually abandoned and falls into obscurity.

Meroë: The Black Jewel of the Nile

The Nubian Kingdom of Gold and Iron

Nestled between the Nile and the harsh deserts of northern Sudan, where the sands whisper ancient secrets and the river brings life to the arid land, lies Meroë, the dazzling capital of the Kingdom of Kush. Flourishing from around 800 BCE to 350 CE, Meroë was more than just a city; it was the heart of a powerful African civilization, renowned for its wealth, iron production, and its enigmatic pyramids. With its royal tombs, bustling workshops, and temples dedicated to gods both Nubian and Egyptian, Meroë remains a symbol of African resilience, ingenuity, and cultural synthesis—a black jewel on the banks of the Nile.

The Pyramids of Meroë: A Desert of Royal Tombs

The most iconic feature of Meroë is its sprawling necropolis, where over 200 pyramids rise from the sands, their steep, narrow forms distinct from those of their Egyptian neighbors to the north. These pyramids served as the tombs of Kushite royalty, their pointed shapes and elegant designs reflecting a unique architectural style that blended indigenous African traditions with Egyptian influences. The pyramids of Meroë, smaller but more numerous than those of Giza, were monuments to the power and continuity of the Kushite dynasty, each one marking the resting place of a king, queen, or noble.

At the base of these pyramids, chapels adorned with reliefs and inscriptions tell the stories of the rulers buried within, depicting them in the presence of gods such as Amun, Isis, and Osiris. The pyramids were not just tombs; they were gateways to the afterlife, where the Kushite kings and queens would join their divine ancestors in the eternal realm. The necropolis of Meroë, with its silent sentinels of stone, stands as a testament to the enduring legacy of a civilization that revered its past while carving out a distinct identity in the ancient world.

The Iron Workshops: The Forge of an Empire

Meroë was renowned as a center of iron production, a craft that gave the city its economic strength and helped sustain its empire. The city's workshops, located on the outskirts of the settlement, were bustling with activity, as blacksmiths and artisans smelted iron ore and forged weapons, tools, and ornaments. The iron industry of Meroë was not only a source of wealth but also a symbol of the city's technological prowess and self-sufficiency.

Iron from Meroë was traded across the ancient world, from the heart of Africa to the Mediterranean, making the city a vital hub in regional trade networks. The skill of Meroë's blacksmiths was renowned, and their products were sought after for their quality and durability. The iron industry was the backbone of Meroë's economy, fueling its military might and enabling the city to flourish as a powerful and independent kingdom.

The Temples of Meroë: A Fusion of Cultures

Meroë's temples, dedicated to a pantheon of gods that blended Nubian and Egyptian traditions, were the spiritual heart of the city. The most prominent of these was the Temple of Amun, the chief deity of the Kushites, whose worship was a direct continuation of the religious practices of their Egyptian predecessors. This temple, with its grand pylons and sanctuaries, was a place of pilgrimage and devotion, where priests performed rituals to ensure the favor of the gods and the prosperity of the kingdom.

Alongside Amun, Meroë also honored Isis, the mother goddess, and Apedemak, the lion-headed warrior god who symbolized the strength and ferocity of the Kushite kings. The fusion of Egyptian and Nubian religious practices in Meroë's temples reflected the city's role as a cultural crossroads, where different traditions met and merged to create a unique spiritual landscape. These temples were more than just places of worship; they were symbols of the city's identity, representing its connection to the divine and its place in the broader cultural and religious world of antiquity.

The Royal Palace: The Seat of Power

The royal palace of Meroë was the center of political and administrative power in the kingdom, a sprawling complex where the kings of Kush ruled over their vast territories. The palace, built from stone and brick, was adorned with frescoes, carvings, and inscriptions that celebrated the achievements of the Kushite rulers and their divine right to govern. Within its walls, the king held court, received emissaries, and directed the affairs of state, ensuring the stability and prosperity of his kingdom.

The palace was not only a symbol of royal authority but also a center of culture and learning. It was here that scribes recorded the deeds of the kings, chronicling their victories in battle, their religious offerings, and their contributions to the kingdom's prosperity. The royal palace of Meroë was a microcosm of the kingdom itself—a place where power, culture, and religion converged to create a thriving and dynamic society.

The Trade Routes: Lifeblood of the Kingdom

Meroë's strategic location along the Nile and near major trade routes made it a vital link between sub-Saharan Africa, Egypt, and the Mediterranean world. The city was a bustling trade center, where goods from across Africa—gold, ivory, ebony, and exotic animals—were exchanged for luxury items from the north, such as fine textiles, wine, and jewelry. The wealth generated by this trade fueled the city's growth and allowed the Kushite kings to maintain their power and influence.

Meroë's role as a trade hub also brought cultural exchange, as merchants, travelers, and artisans from different regions converged in the city. This exchange enriched Meroë's culture, introducing new ideas, technologies, and artistic styles that were adapted and incorporated into the city's own traditions. The trade routes were the lifeblood of Meroë, sustaining its economy and connecting it to the broader ancient world.

The Decline and Legacy of Meroë

The decline of Meroë began in the 4th century CE, as external pressures from rival powers, environmental changes, and shifts in trade routes weakened the kingdom. By the mid-4th century, the city was abandoned, its once-thriving workshops and temples falling silent as the sands of the desert slowly reclaimed the land. However, the legacy of Meroë endured, preserved in the ruins of its pyramids, temples, and palaces, and in the memories of the people who lived there.

In modern times, the city of Meroë has been recognized as a UNESCO World Heritage site, drawing archaeologists and visitors from around the world who come to explore its ruins and uncover the stories of its past. The city's enduring legacy is evident in its contributions to African history, its role in the ancient world, and its unique blend of cultures and traditions.

Meroë remains a symbol of the power, resilience, and creativity of the Kingdom of Kush, a black jewel on the banks of the Nile that continues to inspire awe and admiration.

Key Events

1. **c. 800 BCE** - Founding and Early Development: Meroë is established as an important city in the Kingdom of Kush, known for its strategic location near iron ore deposits.

2. **c. 590 BCE** - Rise as the Capital: Meroë becomes the capital of the Kingdom of Kush after the decline of Napata, flourishing as a center of iron production, trade, and culture.

3. **c. 300 BCE-300 CE** - Golden Age of Meroë: Meroë reaches its peak, known for its distinctive pyramids, advanced ironworking technology, and extensive trade networks with Egypt, Rome, and other regions.

4. **c. 350 CE** - Conquest by the Kingdom of Aksum: Meroë is conquered by the Aksumite Kingdom, marking the end of the Kingdom of Kush and the decline of Meroë as a major urban center.

5. **c. 4th-5th centuries CE** - Abandonment: Meroë gradually declines and is abandoned, though its legacy endures through its archaeological remains.

Alexandria: The Shimmering Jewel of the Mediterranean

The City of Conquests and Knowledge

In the confluence of the Mediterranean Sea's azure waters and the Nile River's fertile embrace lies Alexandria, a city that sparkles with the brilliance of history, culture, and intellect. Founded by Alexander the Great in 331 BCE, Alexandria was destined to become a beacon of Hellenistic civilization, a crossroads where East met West, and a repository of the ancient world's collective wisdom. This metropolis, steeped in the allure of conquest and the pursuit of knowledge, stood as a testament to human ambition and the thirst for enlightenment.

The Lighthouse of Pharos: Beacon of the Ancient World

One of Alexandria's most iconic landmarks was the Lighthouse of Pharos, a marvel of engineering that guided sailors safely to the city's bustling harbor. Standing approximately 100 meters tall, this towering structure was one of the Seven Wonders of the Ancient World. Built by the architect Sostratus of Cnidus during the reign of Ptolemy II Philadelphus, the lighthouse was a symbol of Alexandria's status as a gateway to the Mediterranean and a hub of maritime trade.

The lighthouse's beacon, fueled by a constant fire, could be seen for miles, a shining guide through treacherous waters. At its pinnacle, a statue of Zeus or Poseidon gazed out over the sea, a guardian of travelers and a testament to the city's architectural grandeur. The Lighthouse of Pharos not only ensured safe passage but also proclaimed Alexandria's brilliance to the far corners of the known world.

The Great Library: A Sanctuary of Knowledge

At the heart of Alexandria's intellectual legacy stood the Great Library, the most famous repository of knowledge in antiquity. Founded by Ptolemy I Soter and expanded by his successors, the library aimed to collect all the world's knowledge under one roof. Scholars from across the globe, including Euclid, Archimedes, and Eratosthenes, were drawn to Alexandria, making it a vibrant center of learning and discovery.

The library housed hundreds of thousands of scrolls, encompassing works of literature, science, philosophy, and history. Its scribes meticulously copied and preserved texts, ensuring the transmission of knowledge across generations. The adjacent Mouseion, a research institute, provided scholars with the resources and environment to conduct their studies, fostering an atmosphere of intellectual collaboration and innovation.

The Serapeum: Temple of Syncretism

The Serapeum of Alexandria was a grand temple dedicated to Serapis, a deity created by the Ptolemaic dynasty to unify Greek and Egyptian religious traditions. This majestic sanctuary, with its towering columns and lavish decorations, symbolized the fusion of cultures that defined Alexandria. Serapis, depicted as a combination of Greek and Egyptian gods, embodied the city's spirit of syncretism and its role as a melting pot of beliefs.

The Serapeum was not only a place of worship but also a center of learning, housing an annex of the Great Library. Its subterranean passages, lined with sacred texts and statues, were a testament to the city's dedication to both spirituality and knowledge. Pilgrims and scholars alike visited the Serapeum, seeking divine guidance and intellectual enrichment.

A Cosmopolitan Melting Pot

Alexandria was a city where cultures, languages, and peoples converged, creating a vibrant and cosmopolitan atmosphere. The city's layout, with its grid-like streets and grand public spaces, reflected the Hellenistic ideals of urban planning. The Canopic Way, Alexandria's main thoroughfare, was lined with shops, temples, and public buildings, bustling with the activity of merchants, scholars, and citizens.

Alexandria's diverse population included Greeks, Egyptians, Jews, and people from across the Mediterranean and beyond. This cultural mosaic was reflected in the city's art, architecture, and daily life. The blending of traditions and ideas fostered an environment of tolerance and innovation, making Alexandria a beacon of progress and creativity.

The Tomb of Alexander: A Monument to Greatness

The city's founder, Alexander the Great, was entombed in Alexandria, and his mausoleum became a focal point of reverence and legend. The precise location of his tomb has long been a mystery, adding to the city's enigmatic allure. Alexander's legacy lived on in the city he founded, inspiring generations with his vision of a world united by knowledge and culture.

The Decline and Enduring Legacy

Despite its splendor, Alexandria faced periods of turmoil and decline. The city suffered from political upheavals, natural disasters, and the gradual waning of its maritime dominance. The Great Library, a symbol of Alexandria's intellectual might, was destroyed in a series of tragic events, marking the end of an era.

Yet, Alexandria's legacy endures. The city's contributions to science, philosophy, and culture laid the foundations for the Renaissance and the modern world. The discoveries made by its scholars, the architectural marvels it built, and the spirit of inquiry it fostered continue to inspire and captivate.

Key Events

1. **c. 331 BCE** - Founding by Alexander the Great: Established as a new city in Egypt, designed to be a major cultural and economic hub.
2. **c. 300-30 BCE** - Ptolemaic Period: Alexandria flourishes under the Ptolemaic dynasty, becoming a center of learning and culture with the famous Library of Alexandria and the Lighthouse of Alexandria.
3. **c. 30 BCE** - Roman Period: Alexandria becomes a major city of the Roman Empire after Cleopatra's defeat by Augustus.
4. **c. 30 BCE-300 CE** - Roman Period: Continues to thrive as a major center of commerce, learning, and culture.
5. **c. 300-641 CE** - Byzantine Period: Alexandria remains a significant city, although it faces periods of conflict and decline.

Carthage: The Phoenix of the Mediterranean

The City of Traders and Warriors

Perched on the sun-drenched coast of North Africa, where the azure waters of the Mediterranean kiss the shores of modern-day Tunisia, lies Carthage, a city that once rivaled Rome itself. Founded around 800 BCE by Phoenician settlers from Tyre, Carthage was more than just a city; it was a formidable maritime power, a hub of trade and culture, and a beacon of resilience. With its vast harbors, grand temples, and bustling markets, Carthage remains a symbol of ancient ingenuity, ambition, and the relentless pursuit of greatness.

The Double Harbors: A Maritime Masterpiece

Carthage's most striking feature was its ingenious double harbor system—one for commercial trade and the other for its mighty navy. The circular military harbor, known as the Cothon, was a marvel of ancient engineering, designed to house and protect the city's powerful fleet. At its center stood a round island with ship sheds, where vessels could be quickly launched or repaired, ready to defend the city or set sail on expeditions across the Mediterranean.

The commercial harbor, bustling with activity, was the lifeblood of Carthage's economy. Here, merchant ships from across the known world—laden with goods such as spices from Arabia, gold from Africa, and silver from Spain—docked to trade their wares. The harbors of Carthage were more than just functional; they were a symbol of the city's dominance over the seas, reflecting its role as the linchpin of a vast and far-reaching trade network that connected civilizations across three continents.

The Tophet: A Sacred and Somber Place

Amidst the bustling life of Carthage, there existed a place of deep religious significance and mystery—the Tophet. This sacred precinct, dedicated to the deities Baal Hammon and Tanit, was both a temple and a cemetery, where the Carthaginians practiced rituals that have intrigued and puzzled historians for centuries. According to ancient sources, the Tophet was the site of child sacrifices, offered to appease the gods and secure the city's prosperity and protection.

Rows of stelae, inscribed with prayers and dedications, marked the graves of those sacrificed, often infants or young children. Whether these sacrifices were voluntary offerings or a grim response to dire circumstances, the Tophet stood as a testament to the Carthaginians' profound piety and the lengths to which they would go to ensure their city's survival. The Tophet remains one of the most enigmatic aspects of Carthaginian religion, reflecting a complex society where devotion and duty intertwined with the harsh realities of life in a fiercely competitive world.

The Byrsa: The Citadel of Strength

Overlooking the harbors and the sprawling city below was the Byrsa, the citadel of Carthage, where the city's elite resided and where its political and military decisions were made. The Byrsa, with its fortified walls and commanding view of the surrounding landscape, was the heart of Carthage's power. Within its precincts stood grand palaces, temples, and administrative buildings, where the ruling oligarchy, known as the Council of Elders, governed the city-state with a mix of pragmatism and ambition.

The Byrsa was also the site of the Temple of Eshmun, the god of healing, where citizens sought divine favor and protection. The citadel's strategic location and imposing architecture reflected Carthage's determination to defend itself against its many rivals, most notably Rome. The Byrsa was more than just a fortress; it was a symbol of Carthage's enduring strength and resilience, a place where the city's leaders planned its expansion and prepared for the inevitable conflicts that would shape its destiny.

The Punic Wars: A Clash of Titans

Carthage's rivalry with Rome is one of the most famous and dramatic chapters in ancient history. The Punic Wars, a series of three brutal conflicts fought between 264 and 146 BCE, pitted the two superpowers of the Mediterranean against each other in a struggle for dominance. Carthage, with its superior navy and wealth from trade, initially held the upper hand, but Rome's relentless military discipline and strategic ingenuity eventually turned the tide.

The legendary Carthaginian general Hannibal, known for his audacious crossing of the Alps with war elephants, brought Rome to its knees during the Second Punic War, winning numerous victories on Italian soil. However, despite Hannibal's brilliance, Carthage was ultimately defeated, culminating in the city's destruction at the hands of the Roman general Scipio Aemilianus in 146 BCE.

The Punic Wars were more than just a military conflict; they were a clash of cultures, ideologies, and visions for the future of the Mediterranean world. Carthage's fall marked the end of an era, but its legacy lived on, influencing Roman culture, economy, and military strategy. The memory of Carthage's strength, resilience, and innovation became a touchstone for future generations, both in Rome and beyond.

The Agora: A Melting Pot of Cultures

The Agora of Carthage was the city's vibrant public square, where traders, artisans, and citizens gathered to conduct business, exchange ideas, and socialize. The Agora was a microcosm of Carthage's cosmopolitan nature, reflecting its role as a melting pot of cultures from across the Mediterranean and beyond. Here, one could hear a babel of languages— Punic, Greek, Berber, Egyptian, and more—as people from different backgrounds interacted, traded, and shared their knowledge.

The goods sold in the Agora were as diverse as the people: fine textiles from the East, glassware from Phoenicia, grain from Sicily, and precious metals from Iberia. The Agora was not just an economic center; it was also a cultural crossroads, where the artistic, philosophical, and religious traditions of the ancient world mingled and influenced one another. Carthage's openness to different cultures and ideas was a key factor in its success, allowing it to adapt, innovate, and thrive in a constantly changing world.

The Rebirth of Carthage: A Phoenix from the Ashes

After its destruction by Rome, Carthage rose again, much like the mythical phoenix, as a Roman colony under Julius Caesar in 44 BCE. The new Carthage was rebuilt with Roman architecture, including baths, amphitheaters, and forums, yet it retained its strategic importance as a hub of trade and agriculture in the Roman Empire. The city's fertile lands produced olive oil, grain, and wine, which were exported throughout the empire, contributing to Carthage's renewed prosperity.

Roman Carthage became one of the empire's most important cities in North Africa, a center of learning, culture, and commerce. The city's new life as a Roman metropolis did not erase its Punic past; instead, it layered Roman culture atop the deep foundations of its Phoenician heritage, creating a unique blend that continued to influence the region for centuries. The rebirth of Carthage as a Roman city was a testament to its resilience and the enduring appeal of its strategic location and fertile lands.

Key Events

1. **c. 814 BCE** - Founding of Carthage: According to tradition, Carthage is founded by Phoenician settlers from Tyre under Queen Dido.
2. **c. 650-500 BCE** - Phoenician Colonization: Carthage expands its influence across the western Mediterranean, establishing colonies and trade networks.

3. **c. 264-146 BCE** – Punic Wars: Carthage engages in three major wars with Rome, ultimately leading to its destruction.

4. **c. 146 BCE** – Destruction by Rome: Carthage is destroyed at the end of the Third Punic War, with its population enslaved and the city razed.

5. **c. 29 BCE** – Roman Rebuilding: Carthage is rebuilt as a Roman colony and becomes a major city in the Roman Empire.

6. **c. 439-533 CE** – Vandal Kingdom: Carthage is captured by the Vandals and becomes the capital of their kingdom.

7. **c. 533 CE** – Byzantine Reconquest: Carthage is recaptured by the Byzantine Empire, marking the beginning of a new era of prosperity until its eventual decline.

III

Levant

Jerusalem: The Eternal City of Faith and Strife

The Pinnacle of Devotion

Nestled among the rugged hills of Judea, where the arid landscape gives way to sacred stone, lies Jerusalem, a city that has stood as a testament to faith, conflict, and endurance. Known as Yerushalayim in Hebrew and Al-Quds in Arabic, Jerusalem is more than just a city; it is a spiritual epicenter revered by Jews, Christians, and Muslims alike. Its streets and stones are steeped in millennia of history, echoing with the prayers, battles, and dreams of countless generations.

The Temple Mount: Heart of Holiness

At the core of Jerusalem's sacred geography is the Temple Mount, a site of profound religious significance. For the Jewish people, it is the location of the First and Second Temples, the holiest places in Judaism. The First Temple, built by King Solomon, was a magnificent structure housing the Ark of the Covenant. After its destruction by the Babylonians, the Second Temple rose from its ashes, only to be later destroyed by the Romans in 70 CE. The Western Wall, a remnant of the Second Temple, remains a focal point for Jewish prayer and pilgrimage.

For Muslims, the Temple Mount is known as Haram al-Sharif, home to the Al-Aqsa Mosque and the Dome of the Rock. The Dome, with its striking golden dome, enshrines the rock from which the Prophet Muhammad is believed to have ascended to heaven during his Night Journey. This makes Jerusalem the third holiest city in Islam, after Mecca and Medina.

Christians revere Jerusalem for its association with the life, crucifixion, and resurrection of Jesus Christ. The Church of the Holy Sepulchre, believed to be the site of Jesus' crucifixion, burial, and resurrection, is a pilgrimage destination for millions of Christians worldwide.

A City of Kings and Prophets

Jerusalem's history is intertwined with the lives of great kings and prophets. King David established Jerusalem as the capital of Israel, and his son Solomon built the First Temple, solidifying the city's status as the religious and political heart of the Jewish people. The prophets of Israel, from Isaiah to Jeremiah, walked its streets, proclaiming messages of faith, justice, and repentance.

The city's strategic location made it a coveted prize for empires throughout history. It fell under the sway of the Babylonians, Persians, Greeks, and Romans, each leaving their mark on its character and architecture. Despite its turbulent history, Jerusalem's spiritual significance remained undiminished, a beacon of hope and devotion for its people.

The Walled City: Fortress of Faith

Jerusalem's Old City, encircled by ancient walls, is a labyrinth of narrow streets and historic sites. The walls, built by Sultan Suleiman the Magnificent in the 16th century, enclose the city's most sacred precincts. Entering through one of its seven gates, such as the Damascus Gate or the Jaffa Gate, is like stepping back in time.

The Old City is divided into four quarters: Jewish, Christian, Muslim, and Armenian, each with its unique character and heritage. The Jewish Quarter, with its narrow alleys and synagogues, is centered around the Western Wall. The Christian Quarter is dominated by the Church of the Holy Sepulchre, where pilgrims trace the final steps of Jesus along the Via Dolorosa. The Muslim Quarter, with its bustling markets and the majestic Dome of the Rock, is the largest and most populous. The Armenian Quarter, though small, boasts the ancient St. James Cathedral and a rich cultural heritage.

A Tapestry of Cultures

Jerusalem's streets are a vibrant tapestry of cultures, languages, and traditions. The city's markets, such as the famous Mahane Yehuda Market, buzz with activity, offering a sensory feast of sights, sounds, and smells. Here, vendors sell everything from fresh produce and spices to handmade crafts and religious artifacts. The blending of different cultures creates a unique and dynamic atmosphere, where ancient traditions coexist with modern life.

The city's festivals and religious celebrations reflect its diverse heritage. Passover, Easter, and Ramadan are observed with fervor, bringing together communities in a shared spirit of devotion and celebration. Despite the tensions that have marked its history, Jerusalem remains a place where different faiths and cultures intersect, each contributing to the city's rich mosaic.

The Valley of Kings

Just outside the walls of Jerusalem lies the Kidron Valley, a place of ancient tombs and sacred significance. The valley is home to the Tomb of Absalom, the Tomb of Zechariah, and the Tomb of the Sons of Hezir, monumental rock-cut structures that stand as silent witnesses to the city's ancient past. The Mount of Olives, overlooking the Kidron Valley, is a site of pilgrimage and prophecy, offering panoramic views of the city and its holy sites.

The valley is also the setting for the Jewish cemetery on the Mount of Olives, the oldest continuously used cemetery in the world. For centuries, Jews have sought to be buried here, believing it to be the place where the resurrection of the dead will begin when the Messiah comes.

A Legacy of Resilience

Jerusalem's history is one of resilience and renewal. Despite being besieged, conquered, and destroyed multiple times, the city has always risen from its ruins, a testament to the enduring spirit of its people. The modern city of Jerusalem, with its vibrant cultural scene, high-tech innovation, and thriving communities, stands as a continuation of its ancient legacy.

The city's archaeological sites, such as the City of David and the Herodian Quarter, reveal layers of history, offering glimpses into the lives of its ancient inhabitants. These discoveries not only enrich our understanding of Jerusalem's past but also underscore its significance as a living testament to human perseverance and faith.

Key Events

1. **c. 3000 BCE** – Early Settlement: Earliest settlements in the area that would become Jerusalem.
2. **c. 1000 BCE** – Davidic Kingdom: King David captures Jerusalem and establishes it as the capital of Israel.
3. **c. 960 BCE** – Solomon's Temple: King Solomon builds the First Temple, making Jerusalem the religious center of the Jewish people.
4. **c. 586 BCE** – Babylonian Exile: Jerusalem is conquered by Nebuchad-nezzar II, and the First Temple is destroyed.
5. **c. 516 BCE** – Second Temple: Rebuilding of the Temple after the return from Babylonian exile.
6. **c. 70 CE** – Roman Destruction: The Second Temple is destroyed by the Romans during the First Jewish-Roman War.

Sidon: The Ancient Mariner's Haven

The Jewel of the Phoenician Coast

On the sun-kissed shores of the eastern Mediterranean, where the waves whisper tales of ancient voyages, lies Sidon, a city that was once the heart of maritime prowess and cultural exchange. Known as Sidonia in the classical world, this ancient Phoenician city was a haven for sailors, traders, and craftsmen. Sidon was more than just a bustling port; it was a crucible of innovation, where the sea met the land and cultures intertwined.

The Harbor of Voyages

Sidon's harbors were the lifeblood of the city, bustling with activity as ships from across the Mediterranean and beyond docked to unload their exotic cargoes. These harbors, naturally protected by rocky outcrops and fortified by human ingenuity, were a testament to Sidon's strategic importance and maritime expertise. The city's shipyards were renowned for producing the finest vessels of the ancient world, crafted from the cedars of nearby Lebanon.

From Sidon, Phoenician sailors embarked on daring voyages, navigating the treacherous waters of the Mediterranean to establish trade routes and colonies as far afield as Carthage and the Iberian Peninsula. These seafarers brought back not only goods but also stories and knowledge, enriching Sidon's cultural tapestry.

The Purple City

Sidon was famed for its production of Tyrian purple, a dye so precious that it was worth its weight in gold. Extracted from the murex shellfish found along the coast, this vibrant purple dye became a symbol of royalty and wealth throughout the ancient world. Sidonian craftsmen perfected the art of dyeing textiles with this luxurious color, and their fabrics were sought after by kings and emperors.

The city's economy thrived on the trade of purple textiles, glassware, and other luxury goods. Sidon's markets were a kaleidoscope of colors and scents, filled with merchants hawking spices, perfumes, and intricate glassware. The city's artisans were masters of their craft, producing glass that was famed for its clarity and beauty, and pioneering techniques that would influence glassmaking for centuries.

Temples and Sanctuaries

Sidon was a city of diverse beliefs and religious practices, reflecting its cosmopolitan nature. The city's temples and sanctuaries, dedicated to a pantheon of gods and goddesses, were centers of worship and community life. The Temple of Eshmun, the Phoenician god of healing, was one of the most significant religious sites in Sidon. Situated on the outskirts of the city, this sanctuary, with its lush gardens and sacred spring, was a place of pilgrimage and reverence.

The city's devotion extended to other deities, such as Astarte, the goddess of fertility and war, and Baal, the storm god. These temples were not only spiritual centers but also social hubs where festivals and rituals strengthened communal bonds and celebrated the city's divine favor.

A City of Innovation and Learning

Sidon's contributions to science, literature, and art were profound. The city's scholars and craftsmen were known for their innovation and expertise. Phoenician scribes in Sidon played a crucial role in the development of the Phoenician alphabet, which would become the foundation for many modern alphabets, including Greek and Latin. This alphabet revolutionized communication, making writing more accessible and spreading literacy across the Mediterranean.

The city's intellectual life was vibrant, with schools and libraries fostering a culture of learning and inquiry. Sidonian poets and philosophers engaged with ideas from across the ancient world, contributing to a rich intellectual tradition that influenced their Greek and Roman counterparts.

The City's Enduring Legacy

Despite facing conquests and occupations by empires such as the Assyrians, Babylonians, Persians, and eventually the Greeks and Romans, Sidon retained its resilience and cultural significance. Each wave of conquerors left their mark on the city, adding to its rich tapestry of history and heritage.

In the modern era, the ruins of Sidon, from its ancient harbors to its grand temples, continue to tell the story of a city that was once a beacon of maritime power and cultural exchange. Archaeological excavations have unearthed treasures that provide insights into Sidonian life and achievements, from intricately crafted glassware to inscribed tablets that shed light on the city's economic and social structures.

Key Events

1. **c. 3000 BCE** - Early Settlement: Sidon is established as one of the oldest Phoenician cities.
2. **c. 1500 BCE** - Egyptian Influence: Sidon comes under Egyptian control and influence.

3. **c. 1200 BCE** - Phoenician Peak: Sidon becomes a major center of trade and maritime activity in the Mediterranean.

4. **c. 875 BCE** - Assyrian Domination: Sidon is conquered by the Assyrian Empire but retains some autonomy as a trade hub.

5. **c. 539 BCE** - Persian Period: Sidon flourishes under Persian rule, continuing its role as a major port city.

6. **c. 333 BCE** - Conquest by Alexander the Great: Sidon surrenders to Alexander and becomes part of the Hellenistic world.

Byblos: The Timeless Cradle of Civilization

The Birthplace of the Written Word

In the heart of the Levant, where the cedar forests of Lebanon meet the azure waters of the Mediterranean Sea, lies Byblos, one of the oldest continuously inhabited cities in the world. Known to the ancient Phoenicians as Gebal and to the Greeks as Byblos, this city is not just a relic of antiquity but a living testament to the dawn of human civilization. Byblos is where history, myth, and innovation converge, creating a tapestry that has captivated historians and adventurers for millennia.

The Port of Ages

Byblos's strategic coastal location made it a bustling hub of maritime trade and cultural exchange. Its harbors were the lifeblood of the city, where ships laden with goods from across the Mediterranean docked. Byblos was renowned for exporting cedar wood, a precious resource used for constructing palaces, temples, and ships. The city's timber trade was so integral that it is believed the very name "Byblos" is derived from the Greek word for papyrus, which was shipped to Greece from this port.

The markets of Byblos buzzed with activity, offering everything from timber and papyrus to finely crafted jewelry and pottery. Merchants and traders from Egypt, Mesopotamia, and beyond mingled in its streets, creating a cosmopolitan atmosphere that was a melting pot of ideas, languages, and cultures.

The Temples of Byblos: Echoes of Eternity

Byblos was a city deeply rooted in spirituality, with its sacred sites and temples serving as the heart of religious life. The Temple of Baalat Gebal, dedicated to the city's patron goddess, was one of the most important religious centers. Baalat Gebal, also known as the "Lady of Byblos," was revered as a goddess of the city and the sea, reflecting the city's maritime heritage.

Adjacent to the temple of Baalat Gebal stood the Temple of Resheph, the god of plague and war, emphasizing the city's diverse religious practices. These temples, with their grand columns and intricate carvings, were not only places of worship but also centers of communal life, where festivals and rituals celebrated the divine and strengthened social bonds.

The Birth of the Alphabet

Byblos's most profound contribution to human civilization is undoubtedly the development of the alphabet. The city's scribes created a simple, yet revolutionary system of writing that used a limited set of symbols to represent sounds. This innovation laid the foundation for the Phoenician alphabet, the precursor to Greek, Latin, and ultimately, modern alphabets. This breakthrough democratized writing, making literacy more accessible and transforming communication across the ancient world.

The legacy of Byblos's alphabet is etched into the annals of history. Inscriptions on stone tablets, pottery shards, and temple walls provide a window into the lives, beliefs, and transactions of its people. These ancient texts are treasures of historical knowledge, offering insights into the daily life, trade, and governance of Byblos.

The Citadel of Byblos: A Fortress of Time

Perched on a hill overlooking the city, the Byblos Citadel stands as a testament to the city's strategic importance and resilience. This formidable fortress, built by the Crusaders in the 12th century on the ruins of earlier structures, offers panoramic views of the Mediterranean and the surrounding landscape. The citadel's thick walls and imposing towers symbolize the city's enduring strength and its ability to withstand the tides of history.

The layers of the citadel reveal a palimpsest of civilizations—from the Bronze Age to the Phoenician, Roman, and Crusader periods—each leaving its mark on the city's architecture and culture. Walking through its ancient corridors, one can almost hear the echoes of past inhabitants and the clamor of battles fought to protect this storied city.

A City of Legends and Myths

Byblos is steeped in legend and myth, with stories that intertwine with the city's history. According to ancient Egyptian mythology, Byblos was the place where the god Osiris was buried after being slain by his brother Set. The tale of Isis, who journeyed to Byblos to retrieve her husband's body, reflects the deep connections between Byblos and Egypt, both culturally and commercially.

The city's legendary status is further cemented by its association with the epic of Gilgamesh. In this Mesopotamian tale, the hero Gilgamesh travels to Byblos in search of the secrets of immortality, highlighting the city's symbolic role as a place of ancient wisdom and divine mysteries.

The Resilient Legacy

Despite the passage of millennia and the rise and fall of empires, Byblos has remained a vibrant and enduring city. Its ancient ruins, including the well-preserved city walls, the Roman theater, and the medieval castle, attract scholars, archaeologists, and tourists alike. Each discovery in Byblos adds a new layer to our understanding of human history and the city's pivotal role in the development of civilization.

The modern city of Byblos, with its charming old town, lively souks, and picturesque harbor, continues to celebrate its rich heritage while embracing the future. Festivals, cultural events, and educational programs keep the spirit of Byblos alive, ensuring that its legacy as the cradle of civilization is passed on to future generations.

Key Events

1. **c. 5000 BCE** - Early Settlement: Byblos is established as one of the oldest continuously inhabited cities in the world.
2. **c. 3000 BCE** - Rise as a Trade Center: Byblos becomes a major center for the trade of papyrus and other goods.
3. **c. 2500 BCE** - Egyptian Influence: Byblos develops strong trade ties with Egypt, becoming a key exporter of cedar wood.
4. **c. 1200 BCE** - Phoenician Peak: Byblos thrives as a leading Phoenician city, known for its production of the earliest known alphabet.
5. **c. 539 BCE** - Persian Period: Byblos continues to prosper under Persian rule.
6. **c. 332 BCE** - Hellenistic Period: Byblos is incorporated into the Hellenistic world following the conquests of Alexander the Great.

Tyre: The Sapphire of the Sea

A City Born from the Waves

In the heart of the Eastern Mediterranean, where the azure waters kiss the rugged coastline, lies Tyre, an ancient city that emerged from the sea like a jewel. Known to its inhabitants as Tyrus, this Phoenician stronghold was not just a city; it was a maritime marvel, a beacon of trade and culture that shone brightly across the ancient world. Tyre's twin harbors, its bustling bazaars, and its ingenious architecture made it a symbol of resilience and prosperity, earning it the moniker "The Sapphire of the Sea."

The Island Fortress

Tyre was uniquely situated on an island, about a kilometer from the mainland, making it a natural fortress. This island location, coupled with formidable walls and intricate defenses, made Tyre nearly impregnable. The city's harbors, one facing Egypt to the south and the other facing Sidon to the north, were engineering marvels, designed to accommodate the largest ships of the ancient world and to facilitate the thriving maritime trade that was the lifeblood of Tyre.

The island city was connected to the mainland by a narrow causeway, which was often submerged by the tides, adding an additional layer of defense. This ingenious design protected Tyre from invasions and ensured its dominance as a maritime power for centuries.

The Purple Dye: Tyre's Royal Legacy

Tyre was famously known for producing Tyrian purple, a dye so valuable that it became synonymous with royalty and prestige. This rich, deep purple dye was extracted from the murex shellfish found in the waters around Tyre. The dyeing process was labor-intensive and costly, making Tyrian purple a luxury item reserved for the elite and the powerful. The association of purple with royalty in ancient times can be traced back to Tyre's mastery of this craft.

The wealth generated from the trade of Tyrian purple, along with other luxury goods such as glassware and fine textiles, contributed to the city's prosperity. Tyre's markets were a kaleidoscope of colors, scents, and sounds, with merchants from all corners of the Mediterranean and beyond bringing their wares to trade.

The Temple of Melqart: The Divine Protector

At the heart of Tyre stood the grand Temple of Melqart, the city's patron god, often equated with the Greek Heracles. Melqart was revered as the protector of Tyre and the god of the sea, commerce, and colonization. The temple, with its imposing columns and intricate carvings, was a center of worship and a testament to the city's religious devotion and architectural prowess.

Melqart's temple was also a symbol of Tyre's far-reaching influence. The cult of Melqart spread to Tyre's colonies across the Mediterranean, including the famous city of Carthage. Pilgrims and traders would visit the temple, seeking the god's favor for safe voyages and prosperous ventures.

A Cradle of Colonies

Tyre was not just a city but the mother of cities. Its sailors and merchants established colonies throughout the Mediterranean, spreading Phoenician culture and influence far and wide. The most famous of these colonies was

Carthage, which would later become a powerful empire in its own right. From Cyprus to Sicily, from North Africa to Spain, Tyre's colonies thrived, connected by their shared heritage and loyalty to the mother city.

These colonies facilitated trade networks that brought immense wealth to Tyre, allowing it to flourish as a cultural and economic hub. The city's influence extended beyond commerce; it played a pivotal role in the dissemination of the Phoenician alphabet, which laid the foundation for many modern writing systems.

A City of Legends and Resilience

Tyre's strategic importance and wealth made it a coveted prize for empires throughout history. It withstood numerous sieges, the most famous being the prolonged siege by Alexander the Great in 332 BCE. Using innovative siege tactics, Alexander eventually breached the city's defenses by constructing a causeway from the mainland to the island, transforming Tyre's geography forever.

Despite the devastation wrought by the siege, Tyre rose from the ashes, demonstrating its resilience and capacity for renewal. The city's spirit of innovation and adaptation allowed it to continue thriving under various rulers, from the Greeks to the Romans and beyond.

The Enduring Legacy

Tyre's legacy endures in the annals of history as a symbol of maritime prowess, economic ingenuity, and cultural influence. Its ruins, including the remnants of the ancient harbor, the impressive columns of the Temple of Melqart, and the echoes of its bustling bazaars, offer a glimpse into a city that was once a beacon of the ancient world.

Archaeological discoveries in Tyre continue to reveal the richness of its history and the complexity of its society. The city's contributions to commerce, navigation, and culture have left an indelible mark on the Mediterranean and the world.

Key Events

1. **c. 2750 BCE** - Early Settlement: Tyre is established as a significant Phoenician city.
2. **c. 1200 BCE** - Phoenician Peak: Tyre becomes a leading maritime and commercial center, famous for its production of purple dye.
3. **c. 814 BCE** - Founding of Carthage: Tyrian settlers found the city of Carthage in North Africa.
4. **c. 586 BCE** - Babylonian Siege: Tyre withstands a lengthy siege by Babylonian king Nebuchadnezzar II.
5. **c. 332 BCE** - Conquest by Alexander the Great: Tyre is besieged and captured by Alexander, marking the end of its independence.
6. **c. 64 BCE** - Roman Period: Tyre becomes part of the Roman Empire, continuing to thrive as a trade hub.

Gaza: The Coastal Gateway of the Near East

The Eternal Threshold of Empires and Trade

Where the arid sands of the Sinai Peninsula meet the azure waves of the Mediterranean, lies Gaza—an ancient city that has served as a gateway between Africa and Asia for millennia. More than just a city, Gaza has been a vibrant crossroad of cultures, a bustling hub of commerce, and a strategic prize coveted by empires from Egypt to Rome. With its bustling ports, resilient walls, and cosmopolitan streets, Gaza remains a symbol of endurance and adaptability—a city that has weathered the storms of history while maintaining its place as a vital link between East and West.

The Ports of Gaza: The Lifeline of Commerce

The heart of Gaza's ancient power lay in its thriving ports, which served as key transit points for goods flowing between the civilizations of the Near East, Egypt, and the Mediterranean world. These ports, bustling with activity, were gateways through which caravans of spices, textiles, grain, and precious metals passed, linking distant markets and facilitating the exchange of both goods and ideas.

Gaza's ports were more than just centers of trade; they were the lifeblood of the city, fueling its economy and connecting it to the wider world. Ships from Phoenicia, Greece, and beyond docked in Gaza's harbors, their holds filled with goods destined for the markets of Egypt, Mesopotamia, and beyond. The docks were lined with warehouses, where goods were stored and merchants haggled over prices, creating a vibrant atmosphere of commerce and exchange. The ports of Gaza were a symbol of the city's cosmopolitan nature, where people from different lands and cultures came together in the pursuit of trade and prosperity.

The Walls of Gaza: Guardians of the Gateway

Gaza's strategic location made it a target for invaders throughout its long history, from the Pharaohs of Egypt to the armies of Alexander the Great. To protect itself, Gaza was fortified with strong walls, designed to withstand sieges and keep the city's enemies at bay. These walls, with their sturdy gates and imposing towers, were not just physical barriers; they were symbols of the city's resilience and determination to maintain its independence in the face of external threats.

The walls of Gaza bore witness to many battles and sieges, as successive empires sought to control this vital gateway to the Near East. Despite being conquered and reconquered multiple times, Gaza's walls stood firm, a testament to the city's enduring spirit and its strategic importance. The walls were more than just fortifications; they were the guardians of Gaza's legacy, protecting the city's people, its wealth, and its role as a key player in the ancient world's power dynamics.

The Cosmopolitan Streets: A Melting Pot of Cultures

Gaza's streets were a microcosm of the ancient world, where the languages, customs, and beliefs of different cultures mingled in a vibrant tapestry of human life. The city was home to Egyptians, Canaanites, Philistines, Greeks, and later Romans, each leaving their mark on Gaza's culture, architecture, and way of life. This diversity was reflected in the city's markets, where traders from across the Mediterranean and the Near East sold their wares, and in its temples, where gods from different pantheons were worshipped side by side.

The cosmopolitan nature of Gaza made it a center of learning and culture, where ideas flowed as freely as goods. The city's schools and libraries were places where scholars from different traditions exchanged knowledge and debated philosophy, contributing to the intellectual vibrancy of the region. Gaza's streets were not just thoroughfares; they were the arteries of a city that pulsed with the energy of cultural exchange and the blending of traditions. This melting pot of cultures made Gaza a unique and dynamic place, where the East met the West in a fusion of art, religion, and commerce.

The Temples of Gaza: Sanctuaries of the Sacred

Gaza was a city of deep religious significance, home to numerous temples dedicated to a variety of deities worshipped by its diverse population. Among the most important was the temple of Dagon, a god revered by the Philistines, who were one of the city's most prominent inhabitants during the Iron Age. The temple of Dagon, with its imposing architecture and sacred rituals, was a center of religious life, where priests performed sacrifices and the people of Gaza sought the favor of the gods.

The city also had temples dedicated to gods from Egypt, Greece, and later Rome, reflecting its role as a crossroads of cultures. These temples were more than just places of worship; they were symbols of Gaza's spiritual diversity and its openness to different beliefs and practices. The temples of Gaza were sanctuaries of the sacred, where the city's inhabitants could connect with the divine and seek guidance in a world that was often unpredictable and tumultuous.

The Fall and Endurance of Gaza

Gaza's strategic importance made it a prize for successive empires, from the Pharaohs of Egypt to the Assyrians, Babylonians, Persians, and finally the Greeks and Romans. Each of these powers left their mark on the city, contributing to its rich and complex history. Despite being conquered and reconquered, Gaza endured, its spirit unbroken by the tides of history.

In the Hellenistic and Roman periods, Gaza became a thriving city once again, known for its production of wine and its role as a key stop on the trade routes connecting the Mediterranean to the East. The city's endurance in the face of adversity is a testament to the resilience of its people and its ability to adapt to changing circumstances. Gaza's fall at various points in history was never total; each time, the city rose again, drawing strength from its strategic location and its role as a gateway between worlds.

In modern times, Gaza's ancient history continues to be a source of fascination and study, with archaeologists uncovering the layers of its past and piecing together the story of a city that has played a pivotal role in the history of the Near East. The legacy of Gaza is one of survival and adaptation, a reminder of the enduring power of a city that has stood at the crossroads of history for millennia.

Key Events

1. **c. 3000 BCE** - Early Settlement: Gaza is established as an important trading port along the Mediterranean coast, serving as a crossroads for various civilizations.

2. **c. 1500 BCE** - Egyptian Rule: Gaza comes under Egyptian control, becoming a key administrative and military outpost in the region.

3. **c. 1200 BCE** - Philistine Settlement: Gaza becomes one of the five cities of the Philistine Pentapolis, known for its strategic and commercial importance.

4. **c. 734 BCE** - Assyrian Conquest: Gaza is captured by the Neo-Assyrian Empire under Tiglath-Pileser III, marking the beginning of a long period of foreign domination.

5. **c. 332 BCE** - Conquest by Alexander the Great: Gaza falls to Alexander the Great after a fierce siege, becoming part of the Hellenistic world.

6. **c. 63 BCE** - Roman Period: Gaza is integrated into the Roman Empire, continuing to serve as a vital trade hub linking the Mediterranean and the Near East.

Aleppo: The Timeless Crossroads of Civilizations

The Eternal City of Traders and Scholars

Nestled at the heart of the ancient Near East, where the Silk Road met the Mediterranean, lies Aleppo, a city that has stood the test of time as a beacon of commerce, culture, and resilience. Known to its ancient inhabitants as Halab, Aleppo is one of the oldest continuously inhabited cities in the world. Its storied past is woven with threads of trade, conflict, and intellectual pursuit, making it a living testament to the enduring spirit of human civilization.

The Citadel: A Fortress of History

Dominating the skyline of Aleppo is its majestic Citadel, a massive fortress that has withstood the ravages of time and war. Perched atop a natural hill, the Citadel of Aleppo is a symbol of the city's strength and strategic importance. Its thick walls and imposing gates have protected the city from countless invasions, from the days of the Hittites and the Assyrians to the Crusaders and the Ottomans.

Inside the Citadel, the echoes of history come alive. The grand halls, ancient mosques, and secret passages tell tales of sieges and sultans, of triumphs and tragedies. The Citadel was not only a military stronghold but also a center of administration and culture, where rulers governed and scholars gathered to exchange ideas.

The Souks: Heartbeat of Commerce

Aleppo's souks, or marketplaces, are legendary for their labyrinthine alleys and vibrant energy. The city's strategic location made it a key trading hub where merchants from across the world converged. The Great Souk of

Aleppo, with its vaulted stone ceilings and bustling stalls, was a melting pot of goods and cultures. Spices from India, silks from China, and precious metals from Persia were traded alongside local products such as olive oil, soap, and textiles.

The souks were not just places of commerce but also centers of social life. Here, merchants haggled over prices, travelers shared stories from distant lands, and locals gathered to exchange news and gossip. The fragrance of exotic spices, the clamor of bargaining, and the sight of colorful wares created a sensory feast that captured the essence of Aleppo's cosmopolitan spirit.

A Hub of Intellectual Pursuit

Aleppo was renowned for its intellectual and cultural contributions. The city was home to numerous schools, libraries, and religious institutions that fostered learning and scholarship. Scholars from diverse backgrounds gathered in Aleppo to study subjects ranging from theology and philosophy to science and medicine.

One of Aleppo's most famous intellectual landmarks was the Madrasa al-Halawiyya, an educational institution that attracted scholars from across the Islamic world. The city's libraries housed vast collections of manuscripts, preserving the knowledge of ancient civilizations and contributing to the advancement of learning in the medieval period.

The Great Mosque: A Spiritual Beacon

The Great Mosque of Aleppo, also known as the Umayyad Mosque, is one of the city's most significant religious sites. Built in the 8th century by the Umayyad Caliph al-Walid I, the mosque is an architectural masterpiece that reflects the city's rich Islamic heritage. Its grand courtyard, towering minaret, and intricate mosaics create a serene and majestic atmosphere, inviting worshippers and visitors alike to contemplate and connect.

The mosque served not only as a place of worship but also as a community center where religious and social activities took place. It was a symbol of the city's unity and faith, a beacon that guided the spiritual life of Aleppo's inhabitants through the centuries.

The Resilient Spirit of Aleppo

Throughout its long history, Aleppo has faced numerous challenges, from natural disasters to wars and invasions. Despite these hardships, the city has always risen from the ashes, rebuilding and renewing itself with remarkable resilience. The spirit of Aleppo's people, their ingenuity and determination, have ensured that the city remains a vibrant and enduring symbol of human endurance.

In recent times, Aleppo has once again faced devastating conflict, but the hope for its restoration and revival remains strong. The city's historical sites, cultural heritage, and the indomitable spirit of its people continue to inspire hope for a brighter future.

Key Events

1. **c. 3000 BCE** - Early Settlement: Aleppo is established, becoming an important trade center due to its strategic location.
2. **c. 2000-1600 BCE** - Amorite Period: Aleppo flourishes as a major city in the kingdom of Yamhad.
3. **c. 1600 BCE** - Hittite Conquest: Aleppo is captured by the Hittites, integrating it into their empire.
4. **c. 1000 BCE** - Neo-Hittite Period: Aleppo becomes a significant city in the Neo-Hittite states following the collapse of the Hittite Empire.
5. **c. 333 BCE** - Hellenistic Period: Aleppo is influenced by Greek culture following the conquests of Alexander the Great.
6. **c. 64 BCE** - Roman Period: Aleppo is incorporated into the Roman Empire, continuing to be a key trading hub.

Damascus: The Eternal City of the Levant

The Crossroads of History and Civilization

Nestled in the fertile basin of the Barada River, where the vast desert meets the lush oasis, lies Damascus, one of the oldest continuously inhabited cities in the world. As ancient as the sands that surround it, Damascus has stood as a sentinel of civilization for millennia, witnessing the rise and fall of empires, the spread of religions, and the flow of countless caravans along the Silk Road. Founded over 4,000 years ago, Damascus was more than just a city; it was a living chronicle of the human experience, a place where cultures converged and history was etched into every stone. With its winding streets, grand mosques, and vibrant markets, Damascus remains a symbol of resilience, continuity, and the enduring spirit of the Levant.

The Ancient City Walls: Guardians of Memory

The ancient walls of Damascus, built and rebuilt over the centuries, have seen the passage of time like few other places on earth. These walls, constructed from massive stone blocks, encircled the old city, protecting it from invaders while preserving the rich tapestry of cultures within. The gates of Damascus—Bab Sharqi, Bab al-Salam, and Bab al-Jabiya, among others—were more than just entry points; they were thresholds between worlds, where traders, scholars, and pilgrims from all corners of the known world passed through, bringing with them goods, ideas, and stories.

The walls of Damascus were not merely physical barriers; they were guardians of memory, holding within them the echoes of Canaanites, Arameans, Greeks, Romans, Byzantines, and Umayyads. Each layer of stone told a story of conquest, resilience, and renewal, making Damascus a living palimpsest of human history. The city's walls stood as a testament to its enduring role as a crossroads of civilization, where the ancient and the new, the East and the West, met and mingled.

159

The Umayyad Mosque: A Temple of Faith and Empire

At the heart of Damascus stands the magnificent Umayyad Mosque, one of the oldest and most revered sites of worship in the Islamic world. Built on the foundations of a Roman temple dedicated to Jupiter and later converted into a Christian basilica, the mosque was constructed in the early 8th century by the Umayyad Caliph al-Walid I. The Umayyad Mosque was more than just a place of prayer; it was a symbol of the Islamic Golden Age and the cultural and religious fusion that defined Damascus.

The mosque's grandeur, with its expansive courtyard, towering minarets, and intricate mosaics, reflected the Umayyad dynasty's ambition to create a center of Islamic power and learning. The prayer hall, adorned with elaborate mosaics depicting paradisiacal gardens and flowing rivers, was a place where the faithful gathered to connect with the divine and contemplate the eternal. The Umayyad Mosque was not only a spiritual center but also a symbol of Damascus's central role in the Umayyad Caliphate, which stretched from Spain to India, making the city one of the most important capitals of the ancient world.

The Straight Street: The Artery of Commerce and Culture

Running through the heart of Damascus is the legendary Straight Street, or Via Recta, a thoroughfare that has been the lifeblood of the city since Roman times. The street, which cuts through the old city from east to west, was a bustling artery of commerce, where merchants from across the Mediterranean, Arabia, and beyond traded spices, textiles, glassware, and precious metals. The sounds of haggling, the scents of exotic spices, and the vibrant colors of silks and carpets filled the air, creating a sensory tapestry that reflected the city's cosmopolitan nature.

The Straight Street was more than just a market; it was a cultural melting pot, where languages, traditions, and ideas flowed freely. Along its length stood temples, churches, and mosques, symbolizing the religious diversity that has characterized Damascus for millennia. The street was a living symbol of the city's role as a crossroads of cultures, where East met West, and where the ancient world's great civilizations left their mark.

The Citadel: A Fortress of Resilience

Dominating the northwestern corner of the old city, the Citadel of Damascus was a formidable fortress that stood as a symbol of the city's resilience and strategic importance. Built by the Seljuks in the 11th century and later expanded by the Ayyubids, the Citadel was a military stronghold designed to protect Damascus from invaders and to assert the authority of its rulers. The fortress's massive walls, crenellated towers, and deep moats made it nearly impregnable, a bulwark against the tides of conquest that swept across the Levant.

Within the Citadel, rulers and generals plotted campaigns, defended the city against Crusaders and Mongols, and maintained their grip on power. The fortress was not just a military installation; it was a symbol of the city's determination to endure and thrive in the face of adversity. The Citadel of Damascus, with its commanding view of the surrounding landscape, stood as a guardian of the city and a reminder of its long history of survival and adaptation.

The Old Souks: A Labyrinth of Life

The souks of Damascus, with their narrow, winding alleys and vaulted ceilings, were the beating heart of the city's economy and social life. These ancient markets, such as Souk al-Hamidiyah and Souk al-Bzouriyah, were places where commerce and culture intersected, where traders sold everything from fragrant spices and handcrafted jewelry to textiles and perfumes. The souks were more than just places of trade; they were vibrant social spaces where people from all walks of life gathered to exchange news, gossip, and ideas.

The labyrinthine layout of the souks, with their maze-like alleys and hidden courtyards, reflected the organic growth of the city over the

161

centuries. The bustling markets were a microcosm of Damascus itself—complex, diverse, and full of life. The souks were also places of cultural transmission, where artisans and craftsmen passed down their skills and traditions from generation to generation, ensuring the continuity of Damascus's rich cultural heritage.

The Ghouta Oasis: The Lungs of the City

Surrounding Damascus was the Ghouta Oasis, a verdant belt of orchards, gardens, and farmland that provided the city with food, water, and a respite from the harsh desert climate. The Ghouta was more than just an agricultural hinterland; it was the lifeline of Damascus, sustaining its population and ensuring its prosperity. The oasis's fertile soil, nourished by the waters of the Barada River, produced an abundance of fruits, vegetables, and grains that were sold in the city's markets and exported to distant lands.

The Ghouta was also a place of leisure and retreat for the city's inhabitants, who sought refuge in its cool, shaded groves and fragrant gardens. The oasis's natural beauty and productivity were celebrated in poetry and song, reflecting its importance to the life and culture of Damascus. The Ghouta was the lungs of the city, a symbol of its connection to the land and its ability to thrive in a challenging environment.

The Legacy of Damascus: A City Eternal

Damascus's history is a tapestry woven from the threads of countless civilizations, each leaving its mark on the city's fabric. From the Arameans to the Romans, from the Umayyads to the Ottomans, Damascus has been a city of continuity and change, adapting to the ebb and flow of history while retaining its unique identity. Its streets, walls, and buildings are living monuments to the city's resilience, creativity, and enduring spirit.

In modern times, Damascus continues to be a center of culture, learning, and spirituality, drawing visitors from around the world who come to explore its ancient sites and experience its vibrant traditions. The city's enduring legacy is evident in its role as a cultural crossroads, a place where the past and present coexist, and where the spirit of the Levant is embodied in every corner. Damascus remains the eternal city of the Levant, a shining example of the enduring legacy of human civilization and the quest to preserve and celebrate our shared heritage.

Key Events

1. **c. 3000 BCE** - Early Settlement: Damascus is established as one of the oldest continuously inhabited cities in the world, benefiting from its strategic location at the crossroads of trade routes.

2. **c. 1500-1200 BCE** - Amorite and Aramean Periods: Damascus becomes a significant city-state under the Amorites and later the Arameans, who establish it as their capital.

3. **c. 732 BCE** - Assyrian Conquest: Damascus is captured by the Neo-Assyrian Empire under Tiglath-Pileser III, marking the end of its independence as a kingdom.

4. **c. 605-539 BCE** - Babylonian and Persian Rule: Damascus falls under the control of the Neo-Babylonian and later the Achaemenid Persian Empires, continuing to thrive as a key city.

5. **c. 332 BCE** - Conquest by Alexander the Great: Damascus becomes part of the Hellenistic world after the conquests of Alexander, integrating Greek culture into its fabric.

6. **c. 64 BCE** - Roman Period: Damascus is incorporated into the Roman Empire, becoming an important administrative and commercial center in the province of Syria.

Ugarit: The Gateway to the Ancient World

The Melodic Crossroads

Perched on the Mediterranean coast of modern-day Syria, Ugarit was an ancient city that served as a vibrant nexus of culture, commerce, and innovation. Known for its bustling ports and cosmopolitan spirit, Ugarit was more than just a city; it was a gateway to the ancient world, where the rhythms of diverse civilizations converged in a harmonious blend. From its invention of one of the earliest alphabets to its sophisticated urban planning, Ugarit was a place where the pulse of progress beat strong, echoing through the annals of history.

The Port of Prosperity

Ugarit's strategic coastal location made it a vital hub for maritime trade. Its harbors teemed with ships from across the Mediterranean, bringing goods and ideas from Egypt, Anatolia, Cyprus, Mesopotamia, and beyond. The city's markets buzzed with activity, where traders exchanged exotic goods such as copper, gold, textiles, and spices. This vibrant trade network not only fueled Ugarit's economy but also facilitated cultural exchanges that enriched the city's diverse tapestry.

The wealth generated by this bustling trade allowed Ugarit to flourish, funding the construction of grand palaces, temples, and public buildings. The city's prosperity was reflected in its well-planned streets, impressive fortifications, and sophisticated infrastructure, making it one of the most advanced urban centers of its time.

The Birthplace of the Alphabet

One of Ugarit's most significant contributions to human civilization was the creation of one of the earliest known alphabets. The Ugaritic script, developed around 1400 BCE, was a groundbreaking innovation that used a cuneiform writing system to represent sounds. This simplified form of writing revolutionized communication, making literacy more accessible and influencing subsequent alphabets, including Phoenician, Greek, and Latin.

The discovery of clay tablets inscribed with Ugaritic texts in the ruins of Ugarit has provided invaluable insights into the city's administrative, religious, and literary life. These texts include diplomatic correspondence, trade records, mythological narratives, and hymns, offering a glimpse into the intellectual and cultural vibrancy of Ugarit.

The Temples of Ugarit: Sanctuaries of the Divine

Ugarit was a city deeply rooted in spirituality, with its religious life centered around grand temples dedicated to a pantheon of gods. The most prominent of these were the temples of Baal, the storm god, and Dagon, the god of fertility. These temples were architectural marvels, adorned with intricate carvings and sculptures that depicted scenes of divine myths and rituals.

The religious practices of Ugarit reflected the city's cosmopolitan nature, incorporating elements from neighboring cultures and creating a unique syncretism. Festivals and ceremonies dedicated to the gods were grand public events that brought the community together, reinforcing social bonds and cultural identity.

The Palace of Ugarit: Seat of Power

The royal palace of Ugarit was a sprawling complex that served as the political and administrative heart of the city. This grand structure, with its vast courtyards, audience halls, and residential quarters, was a testament to the city's wealth and influence. The palace was not only the residence of the king but also a center of governance, where officials managed the city's affairs and foreign envoys were received.

The archives discovered within the palace walls contain a wealth of information about Ugarit's diplomatic relations, trade agreements, and legal matters. These records reveal a highly organized society with sophisticated systems of administration and governance.

A Cultural Mosaic

Ugarit's location at the crossroads of civilizations made it a melting pot of cultures, languages, and traditions. The city's art, architecture, and literature reflected this rich diversity, blending influences from Egypt, Mesopotamia, the Hittite Empire, and the Aegean world. This cultural mosaic fostered an environment of creativity and innovation, making Ugarit a center of artistic and intellectual achievement.

The city's theaters and public spaces were venues for performances, debates, and communal gatherings, where the people of Ugarit engaged in cultural and intellectual exchanges. This vibrant cultural life contributed to the city's dynamic and progressive character.

The Fall and Legacy

Despite its prosperity and cultural achievements, Ugarit faced destruction around 1200 BCE, likely due to invasions by the Sea Peoples and internal strife. The city's fall marked the end of a golden era, but its legacy endured through the ages. The innovations and cultural contributions of Ugarit left an indelible mark on the ancient world, influencing subsequent civilizations and shaping the course of history.

Archaeological excavations have unearthed the ruins of Ugarit, revealing its grandeur and complexity. The artifacts and texts discovered in Ugarit provide a window into a civilization that was at the forefront of human progress, a city that was a true gateway to the ancient world.

Key Events

1. **c. 6000 BCE** - Early Settlement: Ugarit is established as one of the earliest known cities in the region.
2. **c. 1900-1200 BCE** - Bronze Age Flourish: Ugarit becomes a major port city and trade hub, known for its extensive commercial networks.
3. **c. 1400 BCE** - Peak of Ugarit: Reaches its height as a cosmopolitan center with a sophisticated writing system, one of the earliest alphabets.
4. **c. 1200 BCE** - Destruction: Ugarit is destroyed, likely due to the invasions of the Sea Peoples and the collapse of Bronze Age civilizations.
5. **c. 1200 BCE** - Abandonment: Ugarit is abandoned and never reoccupied as a major urban center.

Qatna: The Enchanted Crossroads of Kings and Mystics

The Oasis of Majesty

In the heart of ancient Syria, where the fertile plains meet the arid expanse of the desert, lies Qatna, a city that shimmered like a mirage amidst the sands. Known for its opulence, strategic significance, and spiritual aura, Qatna was more than just a settlement; it was an enchanted crossroads where kings met mystics, and cultures converged. This ancient city, nestled near the Orontes River, served as a vital link between the great civilizations of Mesopotamia, Anatolia, and Egypt.

The Citadel of Splendor

The centerpiece of Qatna was its grand citadel, an architectural marvel that stood as a testament to the city's wealth and power. This fortified palace complex, perched on a hill, offered sweeping views of the surrounding landscape. Within its walls, the citadel housed vast halls, ornate chambers, and lush gardens, all adorned with intricate frescoes and mosaics that depicted scenes of myth and royal grandeur.

The citadel was not only a royal residence but also a political and administrative hub. Here, the kings of Qatna held court, forging alliances and negotiating treaties with emissaries from distant lands. The palace archives, filled with clay tablets inscribed in cuneiform, recorded the city's diplomatic endeavors, trade agreements, and legal matters, revealing a sophisticated and cosmopolitan society.

The Tombs of the Ancients

Beneath the citadel lay the royal necropolis, a labyrinth of tombs and burial chambers that held the remains of Qatna's elite. These tombs, carved deep into the bedrock, were filled with treasures—gold jewelry, finely crafted pottery, and luxurious textiles—intended to accompany the deceased into the afterlife. The grandeur of these burials reflected the city's wealth and the high status of its rulers.

One of the most significant discoveries in Qatna's necropolis was the tomb of a royal couple, their remains surrounded by a wealth of grave goods and artifacts. This tomb provided invaluable insights into the burial practices, beliefs, and material culture of ancient Qatna, highlighting the city's connection to both the terrestrial and the divine.

The Temple of the Divine Oracle

Qatna was a city deeply steeped in spirituality and mysticism. At its heart stood the Temple of the Divine Oracle, a sacred sanctuary dedicated to the gods. This temple, with its towering pillars and sacred precincts, was a place where priests and priestesses communed with the divine, offering prayers and sacrifices to seek guidance and favor.

The oracle of Qatna was famed throughout the ancient world. Pilgrims and leaders from distant lands journeyed to the city to consult the oracle, seeking prophecies and divine insight. The temple's priests, believed to possess the power to interpret the will of the gods, played a crucial role in shaping the city's religious and political decisions.

A Nexus of Trade and Culture

Qatna's strategic location made it a bustling hub of trade and cultural exchange. The city's markets were teeming with merchants from across the ancient world, trading goods such as olive oil, wine, metals, and exotic spices. Caravans laden with precious commodities traversed the desert routes, connecting Qatna to the major trade networks of the Near East.

The cultural landscape of Qatna was a rich tapestry woven from diverse influences. Art, music, and literature flourished in the city, reflecting a blend of Anatolian, Mesopotamian, and Egyptian traditions. Qatna's artisans were renowned for their craftsmanship, producing exquisite jewelry, statuary, and textiles that were highly prized in distant lands.

The Enigma of the Underground Palace

One of Qatna's most intriguing features was its underground palace, a subterranean complex discovered beneath the city's ruins. This hidden palace, with its labyrinthine corridors and secret chambers, has puzzled archaeologists and historians alike. The purpose of this underground structure remains a mystery, fueling speculation about its role in the city's life.

Some theories suggest that the underground palace served as a refuge during times of conflict, while others propose it was a ceremonial center for secret rituals and rites. The discovery of this enigmatic complex adds an air of mystery to Qatna, highlighting the city's multifaceted character and its enduring allure.

The Fall and Rediscovery

Qatna's prominence waned with the rise of new powers and shifting trade routes. The city was eventually abandoned, its grand citadel and temples falling into ruin. However, the sands of time could not erase Qatna's legacy. In the early 20th century, archaeologists uncovered the remains of this once-great city, bringing to light its splendor and significance.

Excavations have revealed a wealth of artifacts, from the luxurious grave goods in the royal necropolis to the everyday items found in the city's homes and workshops. These discoveries have provided a deeper understanding of Qatna's role in the ancient world and its contributions to the cultural and historical tapestry of the Near East.

Key Events

1. **c. 2800 BCE** - Early Settlement: Qatna is established as an important city-state in the region of modern-day Syria.
2. **c. 1800-1600 BCE** - Middle Bronze Age: Qatna flourishes as a significant kingdom, known for its wealth and extensive trade connections.
3. **c. 1400 BCE** - Hittite Conquest: Qatna is conquered by the Hittites, becoming part of their empire.
4. **c. 1300 BCE** - Mitanni Influence: Qatna falls under the influence of the Mitanni kingdom.
5. **c. 1300-1200 BCE** - Decline and Abandonment: Qatna declines in importance and is eventually abandoned.

Antioch: The Radiant Crown of the East

The City of Light and Splendor

Nestled along the banks of the Orontes River, where the fertile plains of Syria give way to the rugged terrain of the Anatolian plateau, lies Antioch, a city that gleamed like a jewel in the ancient world. Known as "Antioch on the Orontes," this illustrious metropolis was founded by Seleucus I Nicator, one of Alexander the Great's generals, around 300 BCE. Antioch quickly rose to prominence as a center of commerce, culture, and cosmopolitanism, earning it the title "The Radiant Crown of the East."

The Heart of Hellenistic Culture

Antioch was the embodiment of Hellenistic culture, blending Greek traditions with the local Semitic influences and the vibrant cultures of the East. The city's wide, colonnaded streets, public baths, and grand theaters reflected the architectural and cultural ethos of the Hellenistic world. The Great Colonnade, a grand avenue lined with columns and adorned with statues, served as the city's main thoroughfare, bustling with merchants, scholars, and citizens from all walks of life.

The city's theaters and gymnasiums were hubs of social and cultural life, where dramatic performances, athletic contests, and philosophical debates took place. Antioch's blend of Greek and Eastern traditions fostered a unique cultural environment that attracted artists, philosophers, and intellectuals from across the known world.

The Garden City

Antioch was renowned for its luxurious gardens, which were an integral part of the city's charm and splendor. The famed Daphne Gardens, located just outside the city, were a paradise on earth, filled with lush greenery, exotic flowers, and flowing fountains. These gardens were named after the nymph Daphne from Greek mythology and were said to be the site where Apollo pursued her. The gardens provided a serene escape from the bustling city, a place where residents and visitors could relax, meditate, and enjoy the natural beauty.

The city itself was adorned with public parks and garden squares, enhancing its aesthetic appeal and providing communal spaces for recreation and gatherings. The presence of such verdant spaces amidst the urban landscape underscored Antioch's reputation as a city of luxury and refinement.

The Crossroads of Commerce

Strategically located at the crossroads of major trade routes linking the Mediterranean with the Near East and beyond, Antioch was a bustling commercial hub. Its markets were legendary, offering a dazzling array of goods from distant lands. Silk from China, spices from India, precious metals from Persia, and fine wines from the Aegean all found their way to Antioch's bustling bazaars.

The city's harbor, connected to the Mediterranean Sea via the Orontes River, facilitated maritime trade, while its position along the Silk Road ensured a steady flow of caravans bringing exotic goods and travelers. The wealth generated by this trade fueled Antioch's growth and prosperity, making it one of the richest cities of the ancient world.

The Beacon of Early Christianity

Antioch holds a special place in the history of Christianity. It was here that the followers of Jesus were first called "Christians." The city became a major center of early Christianity, playing a crucial role in the spread of the faith throughout the Roman Empire. The Church of St. Peter, one of the earliest Christian communities, was founded in Antioch, and the city served as a base for missionary journeys by apostles such as Paul and Barnabas.

The vibrant Christian community in Antioch contributed to the city's diverse religious landscape, which included temples and shrines dedicated to various Greco-Roman and Eastern deities. This religious pluralism fostered an environment of theological debate and spiritual exploration.

The Walls of Antioch

Antioch was a city of impressive fortifications, with walls that stood as a testament to its strength and strategic importance. The city's walls, stretching for kilometers, were punctuated by towers and gates that provided both defense and grandeur. The walls were designed to protect against invasions and to showcase the city's might.

One of the most remarkable features of Antioch's fortifications was the Iron Gate, a massive and formidable entrance that controlled access to the city. The walls and gates of Antioch not only provided security but also symbolized the city's status as a powerful and impregnable urban center.

The Earthquake of 115 AD

Despite its splendor, Antioch was not immune to natural disasters. In 115 AD, a devastating earthquake struck the city, causing widespread destruction and loss of life. The emperor Trajan, who was in the city at the time, narrowly escaped with his life. The earthquake left a profound impact on Antioch, but the city's resilience and the determination of its inhabitants ensured its recovery and rebuilding.

The disaster also highlighted the city's strategic and economic importance, as significant resources were allocated for its reconstruction. Antioch rose from the ruins, continuing to thrive as a beacon of culture and commerce.

The Legacy of Antioch

The legacy of Antioch endures through its contributions to culture, commerce, and religion. Its role as a center of early Christianity, its status as a major trade hub, and its rich cultural heritage have left an indelible mark on history. The ruins of Antioch, including the remnants of its grand colonnades, theaters, and fortifications, offer a glimpse into the city's glorious past.

Archaeological discoveries in Antioch have revealed a wealth of artifacts, from intricate mosaics and sculptures to everyday items that provide insights into the lives of its inhabitants. These findings continue to enrich our understanding of the city's significance and its role in shaping the ancient world.

Key Events

1. **c. 300 BCE** - Founding by Seleucus I Nicator: Antioch is established as a major city of the Seleucid Empire.
2. **c. 200 BCE** - Hellenistic Period: Antioch flourishes as a center of Hellenistic culture and learning.
3. **c. 64 BCE** - Roman Period: Antioch becomes one of the major cities of the Roman Empire, known for its beauty and cosmopolitan nature.
4. **c. 37-50 CE** - Early Christianity: Antioch becomes a key center for the early Christian community.
5. **c. 330-641 CE** - Byzantine Period: Antioch remains an important city within the Byzantine Empire.

IV

Anatolia

Hattusa: The Stone Heart of the Hittite Empire

The City Carved from Granite

Amid the rugged highlands of Anatolia, where the winds whisper tales of ancient glory and the terrain is as challenging as it is majestic, lies Hattusa, the impregnable capital of the Hittite Empire. Known for its formidable fortifications, grand temples, and sophisticated urban planning, Hattusa was not merely a city; it was the indomitable stone heart of a powerful civilization. Rising from the rock and etched into the landscape, Hattusa stood as a testament to the Hittites' engineering prowess, military might, and spiritual depth.

The Lion's Gate: Guardians of the Realm

The Lion's Gate, one of Hattusa's most iconic entrances, stood as a symbol of strength and protection. Flanked by imposing stone lions, this gateway was not just a means of entry but a statement of the city's power. The lions, carved from solid rock, exuded an aura of vigilance and guardianship, warding off any threats to the city. Passing through this gate, one could feel the weight of history and the watchful eyes of these ancient sentinels.

The Great Walls: A Fortress of Granite

Hattusa's walls, stretching for kilometers and punctuated by towers and gates, were a marvel of ancient military architecture. Constructed from massive stone blocks, these walls were designed to withstand any siege and deter invaders. The fortifications included cleverly designed gates and complex defensive structures, such as the Sphinx Gate and the King's Gate, each adorned with intricate carvings and symbols of protection.

Within these walls, Hattusa was a labyrinth of strategic and sacred spaces. The city's layout was meticulously planned, with residential areas, administrative buildings, and religious complexes seamlessly integrated into the rugged terrain. The defensive prowess of Hattusa was a testament to the Hittites' ingenuity and their understanding of the importance of security in sustaining their empire.

The Temples of Hattusa: Sanctuaries of the Gods

Hattusa was a city deeply connected to the divine, with numerous temples dedicated to the gods of the Hittite pantheon. The Great Temple, dedicated to the storm god Teshub and the sun goddess Arinna, was the spiritual heart of the city. This massive complex, with its towering columns, sacred courtyards, and intricate reliefs, was a center of worship and pilgrimage. Priests conducted elaborate rituals and ceremonies to honor the gods, seeking their favor and guidance.

The city was also home to smaller temples and shrines, each serving different deities and reflecting the rich tapestry of Hittite religion. These sacred spaces were adorned with statues, inscriptions, and offerings, creating an environment where the divine and mortal realms intertwined.

The Royal Palace: The Seat of Power

At the heart of Hattusa stood the royal palace, the administrative and political center of the Hittite Empire. This sprawling complex, built on a series of terraces, overlooked the city and the surrounding landscape. The palace was a hive of activity, where the king and his court conducted the affairs of state, received foreign dignitaries, and planned military campaigns.

The palace's architecture reflected the grandeur and authority of the Hittite rulers. Grand halls, residential quarters, and administrative offices were interconnected by corridors and courtyards. The walls of the palace were decorated with murals and carvings that depicted scenes of royal life, military victories, and religious rituals, underscoring the king's role as both a warrior and a spiritual leader.

The Yazilikaya Sanctuary: The Open-Air Temple

Just outside the city lies the Yazilikaya Sanctuary, an extraordinary open-air temple carved into the living rock. This sacred site features a series of rock-cut reliefs depicting the Hittite gods, kings, and warriors in intricate detail. The sanctuary was a place of pilgrimage and religious observance, where rituals were performed under the open sky.

The reliefs of Yazilikaya are a testament to the artistic and spiritual achievements of the Hittites. The depictions of the divine procession, with the gods and goddesses arranged in orderly rows, convey a sense of cosmic order and divine hierarchy. The sanctuary's serene and otherworldly atmosphere offers a glimpse into the spiritual life of the Hittites and their connection to the natural world.

The Tablets of Hattusa: A Legacy of Knowledge

Hattusa was not only a center of power and religion but also a hub of knowledge and administration. The city's archives, discovered in the ruins of the royal palace and other buildings, contained thousands of clay tablets inscribed in cuneiform. These tablets recorded everything from legal decrees and diplomatic correspondence to religious texts and literary works.

The discovery of the Hittite archives has provided invaluable insights into the political, economic, and cultural life of the Hittite Empire. The tablets reveal a highly organized society with complex legal systems, extensive trade networks, and a rich literary tradition. The preservation of these texts has allowed modern scholars to reconstruct the history and achievements of this ancient civilization.

The Fall and Rediscovery

The decline of Hattusa began in the 12th century BCE, as the Hittite Empire faced internal strife and external threats. The city was eventually abandoned, its grand temples and fortifications falling into ruin. For centuries, the remnants of Hattusa lay hidden beneath the earth, forgotten by history.

In the early 20th century, archaeological excavations brought Hattusa back to light. The ruins of the city, including its impressive walls, temples, and palaces, have been painstakingly uncovered and studied, revealing the grandeur of this ancient capital. The artifacts and inscriptions found at Hattusa have provided a deeper understanding of the Hittite civilization and its contributions to the ancient world.

Key Events

1. **c. 2000 BCE** - Early Settlement: Hattusa is established as a small settlement in central Anatolia.
2. **c. 1700 BCE** - Conquest by Hattusili I: Hattusa is captured and made the capital of the Hittite Empire by Hattusili I.
3. **c. 1600-1200 BCE** - Hittite Empire: Hattusa becomes a major political, military, and religious center of the Hittite Empire.
4. **c. 1250 BCE** - Construction of the Great Walls: Massive stone fortifications are built around Hattusa, showcasing its importance.
5. **c. 1200 BCE** - Destruction: Hattusa is abandoned and partially destroyed, likely due to the invasions of the Sea Peoples and the collapse of the Hittite Empire.
6. **c. 1200 BCE** - Abandonment: The city is left in ruins and never reestablished as a major urban center.

Troy: The City of Legends and Lament

The Eternal Stage of Heroic Epics

On the windswept plains of northwest Anatolia, where the Dardanelles meet the Aegean Sea, lies Troy, a city shrouded in myth and legend. Known to the ancient Greeks as Ilion, Troy is not just a historical site but a timeless stage where the greatest heroes and tragic fates of ancient lore played out. Immortalized in Homer's "Iliad," Troy is the city of Helen and Paris, Achilles and Hector, a place where the boundary between history and mythology blurs into the mists of time.

The Walls of Immortality

The walls of Troy, towering and impenetrable, were said to be built by the gods Poseidon and Apollo, making them an enduring symbol of divine craftsmanship and human resilience. These formidable fortifications encircled the city, providing both protection and a dramatic backdrop for the epic battles that would define its legend. The gates, particularly the Scaean Gate, were the settings for countless confrontations and heroic feats, their stone arches echoing with the clamor of war and the cries of warriors.

The city's walls also enclosed a bustling urban center, with winding streets, bustling marketplaces, and grand palaces. The fortifications were not merely defensive structures but also symbols of Troy's power, wealth, and divine favor.

The Palace of Priam: A Royal Sanctuary

At the heart of Troy stood the majestic palace of King Priam, the aging yet noble ruler of the city. This sprawling complex, with its grand halls, courtyards, and living quarters, was a place of regal splendor and political intrigue. Here, Priam held court, surrounded by his numerous sons and daughters, including the valiant Hector and the prophetic Cassandra.

The palace was also a place of tragedy and sorrow, as Priam and his family faced the relentless siege and the impending doom that would befall their beloved city. The walls of the palace witnessed both the celebrations of royal banquets and the laments of a family torn apart by war and loss.

The Sanctuary of Athena: A Divine Refuge

Troy was a city deeply connected to the divine, with temples and sanctuaries dedicated to the gods who watched over its fate. The Sanctuary of Athena, the goddess of wisdom and war, was one of the most significant religious sites in Troy. This sacred precinct, with its towering statue of the goddess and its altar, was a place of worship and refuge.

The Trojans believed that Athena's favor would protect their city and guide them through the trials of war. The sanctuary was a focal point of religious life, where priests conducted rituals and offered sacrifices to seek the goddess's blessing and guidance.

The Trojan Horse: A Tale of Deception

One of the most enduring legends of Troy is the story of the Trojan Horse, a masterful ruse devised by the Greeks to breach the city's impregnable walls. According to myth, the Greeks constructed a massive wooden horse, concealing a select force of warriors within its hollow belly. They left the horse at the gates of Troy as a supposed offering to Athena and then feigned a retreat.

The Trojans, believing they had won, brought the horse into the city as a trophy. That night, while the city slept in celebration, the Greek warriors emerged from the horse, opened the gates to their returning comrades, and launched a devastating assault that led to Troy's downfall. This tale of cunning and betrayal has become one of the most famous episodes in ancient literature, symbolizing the themes of trust, deception, and the tragic consequences of war.

The Layers of Time: A City Reborn

Troy is a city of many layers, both literally and metaphorically. Archaeological excavations have revealed multiple layers of habitation, each corresponding to different periods of the city's long history. From the early Bronze Age settlement to the grand city of Priam, and later the Roman and Byzantine periods, Troy's ruins tell a story of continuity and change, destruction and rebirth.

These layers reflect the city's resilience and its ability to rise from the ashes of war and disaster. Each stratum of Troy's ruins holds clues to its past, offering insights into the lives, struggles, and achievements of its inhabitants.

The Heroic Legacy

The legacy of Troy extends far beyond its physical ruins. The city has inspired countless works of art, literature, and music, from ancient times to the present day. The epic tales of the Trojan War have been retold and reimagined by poets, playwrights, and authors, each adding their own interpretation to the enduring myth.

Troy's influence can be seen in the works of Homer, Virgil, Shakespeare, and many others. The themes of heroism, honor, love, and tragedy that are central to the story of Troy continue to resonate with audiences around the world, making it a timeless source of inspiration and reflection.

Key Events

1. **c. 3000 BCE** - Early Settlement: Troy (Hisarlik) is established as a fortified settlement in northwestern Anatolia.
2. **c. 2500-2000 BCE** - Troy I-V: Troy evolves through various phases, becoming a significant trade and cultural center.
3. **c. 1700-1200 BCE** - Troy VI-VII: Troy reaches its peak as a wealthy and powerful city, likely the setting for the events later immortalized in the *Iliad*.
4. **c. 1200 BCE** - Trojan War: The legendary Trojan War, as described by Homer, is believed to have taken place during this period.
5. **c. 1180 BCE** - Destruction of Troy VII: The city is destroyed, possibly by earthquake or conflict, marking the end of its most prosperous era.
6. **c. 700 BCE** - Greek Rebuilding: Troy is rebuilt and inhabited by Greek settlers, maintaining its significance as a cultural and religious site.
7. **c. 85 BCE** - Roman Period: Troy becomes a Roman city and continues to be revered for its legendary past.

Alalakh: The Forgotten Crossroads of Kings

The Gateway of Empires and the Silent Witness of Time

In the fertile plains of the ancient Near East, where the Orontes River meanders through a landscape once rich with the echoes of caravans and the clang of swords, lies Alalakh—a city that once thrived as a crucial link between the great civilizations of Mesopotamia, Anatolia, and the Levant. More than just a city, Alalakh was a thriving hub of diplomacy, trade, and culture, a place where the ambitions of kings and the lives of ordinary people intertwined in the grand tapestry of history. With its palatial ruins, intricate cuneiform tablets, and layers of forgotten splendor, Alalakh remains a symbol of the transient nature of power—a city that rose, flourished, and fell, only to be buried by the sands of time.

The Royal Palace: The Seat of Power and Intrigue

At the heart of Alalakh was its royal palace, a sprawling complex that served as the administrative and ceremonial center of the city. This palace, with its grand halls, storerooms, and private chambers, was not just the residence of the city's kings; it was the nerve center of a small but influential kingdom that played a pivotal role in the politics of the ancient Near East. The palace was where treaties were signed, alliances forged, and the fate of nations decided, making it a place of both power and intrigue.

The palace's walls were adorned with frescoes and reliefs that depicted scenes of royal life, battles, and religious rituals, reflecting the wealth and sophistication of Alalakh's rulers. The storerooms held treasures from distant lands—gold from Egypt, lapis lazuli from Afghanistan, and textiles from Anatolia—testifying to the city's role as a crossroads of trade and culture. The royal palace of Alalakh was more than just a building; it was a symbol of the city's status as a regional power, a place where the ambitions of kings were played out on the grand stage of history.

The Cuneiform Tablets: Voices of the Past

One of the most remarkable discoveries at Alalakh is its vast collection of cuneiform tablets, which provide a detailed record of the city's administration, diplomacy, and daily life. These tablets, inscribed with the wedge-shaped script of Mesopotamia, offer a glimpse into the lives of the people of Alalakh—kings and merchants, farmers and craftsmen—whose voices have echoed down through the millennia. The tablets record everything from legal disputes and trade agreements to letters exchanged between rulers, revealing a complex society that was deeply connected to the wider world.

The cuneiform tablets of Alalakh are not just historical documents; they are a window into the minds and hearts of a long-vanished people. Through these tablets, we learn about the city's trade networks, which stretched across the ancient Near East, its religious practices, and its interactions with powerful neighbors like the Hittites, Egyptians, and Babylonians. The tablets also tell stories of everyday life—of marriages and births, debts and disputes, hopes and fears—painting a rich and nuanced picture of a city that was once a thriving center of culture and commerce.

The Sacred Temples: The Home of the Gods

Alalakh was not only a center of political power but also a place of deep religious significance. The city's temples, dedicated to a pantheon of gods and goddesses, were the spiritual heart of the city, where priests performed rituals and sacrifices to ensure the favor of the divine. The most important of these was the Temple of the Storm God, the chief deity of Alalakh, who was believed to control the weather, fertility, and the fortunes of the city.

The temples were not just places of worship; they were also centers of economic activity, where offerings of grain, wine, and livestock were brought by the city's inhabitants. The temples were richly decorated with statues, altars, and inscriptions, reflecting the city's wealth and the devotion of its people. The priests of Alalakh, who served as intermediaries between the gods and the people, wielded considerable influence, advising the king and playing a key role in the city's governance. The temples of Alalakh were more than just buildings; they were the earthly homes of the gods, places where the divine and the mortal worlds intersected.

The Fall of Alalakh: The Silence of the Forgotten City

Alalakh's prosperity made it a target for more powerful neighbors, and the city was eventually sacked and destroyed, most likely by the Sea Peoples or the Hittites. The city's palaces and temples were reduced to ruins, its people scattered, and its name gradually faded from memory. By the time of the Iron Age, Alalakh had been largely forgotten, its once-grand buildings buried beneath layers of earth and time.

The fall of Alalakh was part of the broader collapse of the Bronze Age civilizations, a period marked by the decline of great empires, the movement of peoples, and the rise of new powers. Yet, the memory of Alalakh lived on in the ruins and artifacts that remained, waiting to be rediscovered by modern archaeologists. The rediscovery of Alalakh in the 20th century, through the excavations led by Sir Leonard Woolley, brought to light the city's rich history and its role in the ancient world. The fall of Alalakh is a reminder of the fragility of human achievements, and the ways in which even the mightiest cities can be forgotten, only to be rediscovered and remembered once again.

The Legacy of Alalakh: A City Reborn in Memory

Today, the ruins of Alalakh offer a glimpse into a world that was once vibrant and full of life. The city's palaces, temples, and cuneiform tablets have provided invaluable insights into the history of the ancient Near East, revealing the complex interplay of power, culture, and religion that shaped the region. Alalakh's legacy endures not only in the physical remains that have been uncovered but also in the stories and memories that continue to inspire those who study its past.

The rediscovery of Alalakh has also contributed to our understanding of the broader history of the ancient Near East, shedding light on the connections between different civilizations and the ways in which they influenced one another. The city's legacy is a testament to the enduring power of human creativity, ambition, and resilience, even in the face of the inevitable passage of time. Alalakh, once forgotten, has been reborn in memory, a symbol of the enduring legacy of a city that once stood at the crossroads of history.

Key Events

1. **c. 2000 BCE** - Founding of Alalakh: Alalakh is established in the region of modern-day Turkey, becoming a significant city-state in the Amorite Kingdom.

2. **c. 1800-1600 BCE** - Peak under the Amorites: Alalakh flourishes as a major city-state during the Amorite period, serving as a political and commercial hub in the region.

3. **c. 1600 BCE** - Conquest by the Hittites: Alalakh is captured by the Hittite king Hattusili I, but later rebuilt and continues to be an important city under Hittite influence.

4. **c. 1350 BCE** - Decline and Destruction: Alalakh is destroyed, possibly by invading forces or internal strife, leading to its decline as a major urban center.

5. **c. 1200 BCE** - Abandonment: The city is finally abandoned during the widespread collapse of Bronze Age civilizations, leaving behind ruins that would later be rediscovered by archaeologists.

Sardis: The Golden Gateway of Lydia

The Radiant Metropolis of Wealth and Innovation

Nestled at the foot of Mount Tmolus and beside the fertile plains of the Hermus River, Sardis stands as a gleaming testament to the ingenuity and opulence of the ancient world. As the capital of the ancient kingdom of Lydia, Sardis was a city of immense wealth and influence, famed for its gold-rich riverbeds and its pioneering spirit. The city's legacy, etched in gold and stone, tells a tale of prosperity, innovation, and cultural fusion.

The Pactolus River: The Source of Gold

Legend has it that the Pactolus River, which flowed through Sardis, was imbued with gold by King Midas, whose touch turned everything into the precious metal. This riverbed was indeed rich with gold deposits, making Sardis synonymous with unimaginable wealth. The gold of Sardis funded the city's grandeur, enabling the construction of magnificent buildings, temples, and monuments.

The wealth generated by this natural bounty laid the foundation for Sardis's prosperity and its emergence as a major economic and cultural hub. The city's artisans and jewelers became renowned for their craftsmanship, creating intricate gold jewelry and luxurious items that were highly prized across the ancient world.

The Acropolis: The Crown of Sardis

High above the city, the acropolis of Sardis stood as a symbol of power and protection. This fortified citadel, perched on a rugged hill, offered commanding views of the surrounding plains and served as a refuge in times of conflict. The acropolis housed royal palaces, administrative buildings, and military barracks, reflecting the city's strategic and political significance.

The steep slopes of the acropolis were dotted with terraces and fortifications, creating an impressive and formidable skyline. From this vantage point, one could see the sprawling city below, with its bustling streets, grand temples, and the shimmering waters of the Pactolus River.

The Temple of Artemis: A Sanctuary of Splendor

Sardis was home to one of the grandest temples of the ancient world, the Temple of Artemis. This magnificent sanctuary, dedicated to the goddess of the hunt and the moon, was a marvel of Hellenistic architecture. With its towering columns and ornate decorations, the temple was a center of religious worship and a testament to the city's artistic and architectural prowess.

The temple complex was not only a place of worship but also a social and cultural hub, where festivals, ceremonies, and gatherings took place. The annual festival of Artemis, marked by processions, feasting, and athletic competitions, drew participants from far and wide, reinforcing Sardis's status as a cultural and religious center.

The Royal Road: A Highway of Commerce

Sardis was strategically located at the western terminus of the Royal Road, an ancient highway that stretched across the Persian Empire. This road facilitated the movement of goods, people, and ideas, linking Sardis with distant cities such as Susa and Babylon. As a result, Sardis became a melting pot of cultures, where merchants, diplomats, and travelers converged, bringing with them a diverse array of influences.

The markets of Sardis were vibrant centers of trade, offering goods from across the empire and beyond. Textiles, spices, precious metals, and exotic luxuries filled the stalls, creating a cosmopolitan atmosphere that reflected the city's importance as a commercial hub.

The Gymnasium and Baths: Centers of Learning and Leisure

The gymnasium of Sardis was a grand complex that served as a center of education, physical training, and social interaction. With its expansive courtyards, lecture halls, and athletic facilities, the gymnasium was a place where young men were trained in the arts of rhetoric, philosophy, and sports. This institution embodied the Greek ideal of a sound mind in a sound body, blending intellectual and physical pursuits.

Adjacent to the gymnasium were the Roman baths, another architectural marvel that provided a space for relaxation and socializing. The baths, with their elaborate heating systems, mosaic floors, and marble-lined pools, offered a luxurious respite from the demands of daily life. These public spaces were vital to the social fabric of Sardis, fostering community and camaraderie.

The Fall and Transformation

The decline of Sardis began with its capture by the Persian Empire in the 6th century BCE, yet the city continued to thrive under Persian rule, serving as an important administrative center. Later, under Alexander the Great and his successors, Sardis experienced a resurgence, becoming a key city in the Hellenistic world. The Romans further developed the city, enhancing its infrastructure and integrating it into their vast empire.

Despite earthquakes and invasions, Sardis persisted as a vibrant urban center, adapting to the changing tides of history. Its ruins, including the remnants of the temple, the gymnasium, and the acropolis, bear witness to its enduring legacy.

The Legacy of Sardis

Today, the ruins of Sardis stand as a testament to its historical grandeur and significance. Archaeological excavations have uncovered a wealth of artifacts, from gold jewelry and coins to inscriptions and architectural fragments, offering insights into the city's illustrious past. The discovery of the synagogue, one of the largest of its kind from antiquity, underscores the city's cultural and religious diversity.

Sardis's innovations in metallurgy, urban planning, and cultural integration continue to be celebrated, reflecting the city's role as a beacon of ancient ingenuity and prosperity.

Key Events

1. **c. 1200 BCE** - Early Settlement: Sardis is established as a prominent city in western Anatolia.
2. **c. 680-547 BCE** - Lydian Empire: Sardis becomes the capital of Lydia under the Mermnad dynasty, reaching its height under King Croesus, famous for his immense wealth.
3. **c. 547 BCE** - Conquest by Cyrus the Great: Sardis falls to the Persian Empire, ending Lydian independence.
4. **c. 334 BCE** - Alexander the Great: Sardis is captured by Alexander, marking the beginning of Hellenistic influence.
5. **c. 133 BCE** - Roman Period: Sardis becomes part of the Roman Empire, continuing as an important administrative and cultural center.
6. **c. 17 CE** - Earthquake and Rebuilding: Sardis is devastated by a massive earthquake but is rebuilt by Emperor Tiberius.

Miletus: The Beacon of Philosophy and Exploration

The Harbor of Minds

On the edge of the Aegean Sea, where the azure waters lap against the shores of western Anatolia, lies Miletus, an ancient city that radiated the light of intellect and innovation across the ancient world. Known as the "City of Thinkers," Miletus was not just a bustling port but a cradle of philosophy, science, and exploration. This vibrant city, with its strategic harbors and sophisticated urban planning, was a beacon of human curiosity and ingenuity.

The Four Harbors: Gateways to the World

Miletus was uniquely blessed with four harbors, making it a vital center for maritime trade and cultural exchange. These harbors, bustling with ships from across the Mediterranean and beyond, were the lifeblood of the city. Merchants and explorers from Egypt, Phoenicia, and the wider Hellenic world converged here, bringing goods, ideas, and innovations.

The city's markets were a mosaic of cultures, filled with the sounds of bargaining in multiple languages and the scents of exotic spices. From the harbors of Miletus, goods flowed into the city, and knowledge flowed out, spreading the city's influence far and wide.

The Birthplace of Philosophy

Miletus holds a special place in the annals of intellectual history as the birthplace of Western philosophy. It was here that Thales, often regarded as the first philosopher, sought to explain the natural world through rational thought rather than mythology. Thales and his successors, Anaximander and Anaximenes, founded the Milesian school of philosophy, which laid the groundwork for scientific inquiry and empirical observation.

These early thinkers dared to question the nature of the cosmos, the origin of life, and the fundamental principles of existence. Their pioneering efforts in mathematics, astronomy, and physics were revolutionary, and their legacy endures as a cornerstone of scientific and philosophical thought.

The Theatre: Stage of Democracy and Drama

The grand theatre of Miletus, carved into the slopes of a hill, was a testament to the city's cultural and political life. This impressive structure could accommodate thousands of spectators, who gathered to watch dramatic performances, civic debates, and public assemblies. The theatre was a place where the democratic ideals of the city were enacted, where citizens could voice their opinions and participate in decision-making processes.

The performances held in the theatre were not just entertainment but also reflections of societal values and human experience. Tragedies and comedies by playwrights like Thespis and Phrynichus explored themes of fate, justice, and the human condition, resonating deeply with the audience.

The Milesian Grid: A Model of Urban Planning

Miletus was renowned for its sophisticated urban planning, attributed to the architect Hippodamus, who is often called the "father of urban planning." The city was laid out in a grid pattern, a revolutionary design that maximized efficiency and aesthetics. Wide streets intersected at right angles, dividing the city into orderly blocks that housed residential, commercial, and public buildings.

This grid system, known as the "Milesian plan," became a model for future cities throughout the Greek and Roman worlds. The logical and harmonious layout of Miletus reflected the city's dedication to order, beauty, and functionality.

The Sanctuary of Apollo Delphinios: A Divine Connection

Miletus was home to several grand temples and sanctuaries, the most prominent being the Sanctuary of Apollo Delphinios. This sacred precinct, dedicated to Apollo in his aspect as the god of sailors and colonizers, was a center of worship and oracular consultation. Pilgrims from across the Mediterranean came to seek Apollo's guidance, offering sacrifices and participating in religious festivals.

The sanctuary's serene courtyards and grand altars provided a space for reflection and communion with the divine. The oracles delivered here were revered, guiding the decisions of individuals and city leaders alike, reinforcing Miletus's spiritual and cultural significance.

The Lighthouse: Guiding Explorers Home

At the entrance to Miletus's harbors stood a towering lighthouse, a beacon guiding sailors safely to shore. This lighthouse symbolized the city's role as a guide for explorers and thinkers, illuminating the way forward with knowledge and innovation. The lighthouse, with its powerful beam cutting through the night, was a metaphor for Miletus's intellectual light, which shone brightly across the ancient world.

The Legacy of Exploration

Miletus was not only a center of intellectual and cultural life but also a launching pad for exploration and colonization. Milesian adventurers established colonies along the coasts of the Black Sea, the Mediterranean, and even as far as the shores of the Nile. These colonies spread the influence of Miletus, creating a network of trade and cultural exchange that extended the city's reach far beyond its geographical boundaries.

The legacy of these explorers is evident in the archaeological remains of

Milesian colonies, which reflect the architectural and cultural hallmarks of their mother city. The spirit of curiosity and adventure that drove these explorers continues to inspire modern-day scholars and adventurers.

The Rise and Fall

Miletus thrived for centuries, reaching its zenith during the 6th century BCE under the Lydian and Persian empires. However, the city's fortunes declined after repeated conflicts, including its rebellion against Persian rule and subsequent destruction by the Persian king Darius. Despite its decline, Miletus continued to be a significant cultural and intellectual center, influencing the Hellenistic and Roman periods.

Archaeological excavations have uncovered the ruins of Miletus, revealing the grandeur of its public buildings, temples, and theaters. These ruins, along with the rich literary and historical records, provide a window into the life and achievements of this remarkable city.

Key Events

1. **c. 1400 BCE** - Early Settlement: Miletus is established as a significant port city in Ionia, Anatolia.
2. **c. 800-600 BCE** - Flourishing as a Trade Hub: Miletus becomes one of the wealthiest and most powerful Greek cities, with extensive colonies around the Mediterranean and Black Sea.
3. **c. 600-500 BCE** - Birthplace of Philosophy: Miletus is home to the Milesian school of philosophy, with figures like Thales, Anaximander, and Anaximenes laying the foundations of Western philosophy and science.
4. **c. 494 BCE** - Destruction by Persians: Miletus is sacked by the Persians after the Ionian Revolt but later rebuilt.
5. **c. 334 BCE** - Hellenistic Period: Miletus falls under the influence of Alexander the Great, continuing as a significant cultural and economic center.

6. **c. 133 BCE** - Roman Period: Miletus becomes part of the Roman Empire, remaining an important city in the region.

Ephesus: The Luminous Crossroads of the Ancient World

The City of Artemis and Innovation

On the sun-drenched shores of the Aegean Sea, cradled between the fertile valleys and rolling hills of Asia Minor, lies Ephesus, a city that sparkled with the brilliance of ancient civilization. Known as one of the most influential cities of the Greek and Roman worlds, Ephesus was more than just a bustling metropolis; it was a beacon of culture, religion, and commerce. This vibrant city, with its grand temples, bustling markets, and innovative spirit, stood at the crossroads of the ancient world, illuminating the path of history with its achievements and legacy.

The Temple of Artemis: A Wonder of the Ancient World

At the heart of Ephesus stood the Temple of Artemis, one of the Seven Wonders of the Ancient World. This colossal sanctuary, dedicated to the goddess of the hunt and fertility, was a masterpiece of Hellenistic architecture. Its immense marble columns soared into the sky, and its richly decorated facades were adorned with intricate sculptures and reliefs depicting mythological scenes.

The Temple of Artemis was not only a religious center but also a symbol of the city's wealth and artistic achievement. Pilgrims and tourists from across the ancient world flocked to Ephesus to marvel at its splendor and seek the blessings of the goddess. The temple served as a hub of activity, where festivals, rituals, and markets brought the community together in celebration of their patron deity.

The Library of Celsus: A Repository of Knowledge

Ephesus was a city that celebrated learning and culture, and nowhere was this more evident than in the Library of Celsus. Built in the 2nd century CE in honor of the Roman senator Tiberius Julius Celsus Polemaeanus, this magnificent library housed thousands of scrolls and texts. Its grand facade, with its towering columns and statues representing the virtues of wisdom, knowledge, and intelligence, was a testament to the city's dedication to intellectual pursuits.

The library was a center of scholarship and learning, attracting scholars, philosophers, and students from across the empire. Within its walls, ideas were exchanged, and knowledge was preserved and disseminated, contributing to the rich intellectual tapestry of Ephesus.

The Great Theater: Stage of Drama and Democracy

The Great Theater of Ephesus, carved into the slopes of Mount Pion, was one of the largest and most impressive theaters of the ancient world. With a seating capacity of over 24,000, it was a venue for dramatic performances, gladiatorial contests, and public assemblies. The theater's grand stage and sweeping tiers provided a dramatic setting for the city's cultural and political life.

Here, the works of playwrights such as Sophocles, Euripides, and Aristophanes were brought to life, exploring themes of human nature, morality, and society. The theater also served as a forum for civic engagement, where citizens gathered to discuss and debate issues of public concern, reflecting the democratic spirit of Ephesus.

The Agora: Heartbeat of Commerce

The Agora of Ephesus was the bustling heart of the city's commercial life. This expansive marketplace was filled with shops, stalls, and workshops, offering a dazzling array of goods from across the Mediterranean and beyond. Merchants traded in spices, textiles, precious metals, and exotic luxuries, creating a vibrant and cosmopolitan atmosphere.

The Agora was more than just a marketplace; it was a social and cultural hub where people from diverse backgrounds mingled, exchanged ideas, and forged connections. The lively interactions in the Agora reflected the city's role as a major center of trade and cultural exchange.

The Sacred Way: Path of Pilgrims and Patrons

The Sacred Way, a grand marble-paved avenue, connected the Temple of Artemis with the heart of Ephesus. This ceremonial road was lined with statues, monuments, and fountains, creating a majestic pathway for processions and pilgrimages. Along the Sacred Way, pilgrims made their journey to the temple, participating in religious festivals and rituals that honored the goddess.

The road also served as a symbol of the city's prosperity and devotion, showcasing the architectural and artistic achievements of Ephesus. The Sacred Way was a testament to the city's spiritual and cultural vitality, drawing visitors from far and wide to witness its splendor.

The Terrace Houses: Homes of the Elite

Nestled on the slopes of the city, the Terrace Houses of Ephesus were the luxurious residences of the city's elite. These multi-storied homes, with their opulent mosaics, frescoes, and marble-lined courtyards, reflected the wealth and sophistication of their inhabitants. The Terrace Houses were equipped with advanced amenities, including private baths, underfloor heating, and elaborate plumbing systems.

These homes provide a glimpse into the daily lives of Ephesus's affluent citizens, revealing their tastes, lifestyles, and social customs. The preservation of the Terrace Houses offers invaluable insights into the domestic architecture and interior design of the ancient world.

The Christian Legacy

Ephesus also holds a significant place in Christian history. The city was home to one of the earliest and most influential Christian communities, and it is traditionally believed to be the place where the Apostle John wrote his Gospel. The Basilica of St. John, built over his reputed burial site, became an important pilgrimage destination.

The city's Christian heritage is further highlighted by its association with the Virgin Mary. According to tradition, Mary spent her last years in Ephesus, and her house, now a revered shrine, attracts pilgrims from around the world. The Council of Ephesus, held in 431 CE, was a pivotal event in early Christian history, shaping the doctrine of the church.

The Rise and Fall

Ephesus experienced periods of great prosperity and cultural flourishing under various rulers, from the Lydians and Persians to the Greeks and Romans. However, the city also faced challenges, including natural disasters, shifting trade routes, and invasions. By the Byzantine period, the harbor had silted up, diminishing the city's importance as a trading hub.

Despite its decline, the legacy of Ephesus endures. The ruins of the city, including the magnificent theater, the Library of Celsus, and the Temple of Artemis, continue to captivate visitors and scholars alike. These remnants of a glorious past offer a window into the life and achievements of one of the ancient world's most remarkable cities.

Key Events

1. **c. 1000 BCE** - Early Settlement: Ephesus is founded by Ionian Greeks, becoming an important city in Anatolia.
2. **c. 560 BCE** - Temple of Artemis: The construction of the Temple of Artemis, one of the Seven Wonders of the Ancient World, solidifies Ephesus as a major religious center.

3. **c. 356 BCE** - Destruction and Rebuilding: The Temple of Artemis is destroyed by arson but is later rebuilt on an even grander scale.

4. **c. 133 BCE** - Roman Period: Ephesus becomes a major city of the Roman Empire, known for its wealth, grandeur, and as a center of early Christianity.

5. **c. 52-53 CE** - Paul the Apostle: Ephesus becomes an important center for the early Christian church, with Paul the Apostle spending time there.

6. **c. 262 CE** - Gothic Raid: Ephesus is sacked by the Goths but continues to thrive under Roman rule.

Pergamon: The Pinnacle of Knowledge and Power

The City on the Hill

Perched atop a commanding hill in the heart of ancient Anatolia, Pergamon stood as a beacon of intellectual and cultural prowess. Known for its strategic acropolis, monumental architecture, and legendary library, Pergamon was not just a city; it was a symbol of Hellenistic ambition and enlightenment. Overlooking the Caicus River valley, this city seamlessly blended power and knowledge, crafting a legacy that would echo through the corridors of history.

The Acropolis: The Throne of the Gods

The acropolis of Pergamon, towering over the landscape, was a marvel of ancient engineering and urban planning. This fortified hilltop, surrounded by massive walls, was the heart of the city, housing the royal palaces, temples, and administrative buildings. The most striking feature of the acropolis was the Great Altar of Zeus, a monumental structure adorned with a frieze depicting the epic battle between the gods and the giants. This altar, a masterpiece of Hellenistic art, symbolized the city's divine favor and its cultural zenith.

From the acropolis, one could gaze down upon the sprawling city below, with its neatly laid-out streets, public buildings, and lush gardens. The view extended to the fertile plains and distant mountains, a testament to Pergamon's strategic and aesthetic brilliance.

The Library of Pergamon: A Sanctuary of Knowledge

Pergamon's library was one of the most renowned repositories of knowledge in the ancient world, rivaling even the legendary Library of Alexandria. Founded by the Attalid dynasty, this library housed hundreds of thousands of scrolls and texts, attracting scholars, philosophers, and scientists from across the Mediterranean.

The library was a center of learning and innovation, where intellectual giants such as Galen, the famous physician, studied and taught. Pergamon's library also played a crucial role in the development of parchment, a durable writing material that would revolutionize the preservation of knowledge. The invention of parchment, attributed to Pergamon, was a response to the Ptolemaic embargo on papyrus, showcasing the city's resilience and ingenuity.

The Asclepeion: The Healing Sanctuary

Pergamon was also a center of medical knowledge and healing, epitomized by the Asclepeion, a renowned sanctuary dedicated to Asclepius, the god of medicine. This healing complex, located just outside the city, was a place where patients sought cures through a combination of medical treatment, religious rituals, and holistic therapies.

The Asclepeion featured temples, baths, and therapeutic gardens, creating a serene environment conducive to healing. The most advanced medical practices of the time, including surgeries and herbal remedies, were performed here, making Pergamon a beacon of medical science in the ancient world.

The Theater: A Stage of Grandeur

Pergamon's theater, carved into the steep slope of the acropolis, was one of the most impressive structures of its kind. With a seating capacity of over 10,000, this theater provided a breathtaking view of the city and the surrounding landscape. The theater was a venue for dramatic performances, musical events, and public gatherings, reflecting the city's vibrant cultural life.

The steepness of the seating tiers created a sense of intimacy and engagement, allowing spectators to fully immerse themselves in the performances. The acoustics were meticulously designed to ensure that the voices of actors and musicians reached every corner of the theater, enhancing the overall experience.

The Gymnasium and the Agora: Centers of Civic Life

The gymnasium of Pergamon was a grand complex that served as a hub of education, physical training, and social interaction. With its spacious courtyards, lecture halls, and athletic facilities, the gymnasium embodied the Greek ideal of a balanced education that nurtured both the body and the mind.

The agora, or marketplace, was the economic and social heart of Pergamon. This bustling square was lined with shops, temples, and public buildings, creating a vibrant space where citizens conducted business, debated politics, and celebrated festivals. The agora was a microcosm of Pergamon's diverse and dynamic society, reflecting the city's prosperity and cultural richness.

The Legacy of Innovation

Pergamon was a city that thrived on innovation and creativity. Its advancements in architecture, art, and science set new standards for the ancient world. The city's inventors and craftsmen were renowned for their skill, producing everything from exquisite sculptures and mosaics to advanced medical instruments and scientific devices.

The legacy of Pergamon's innovation extended beyond its borders, influencing other cities and cultures. The city's commitment to knowledge, art, and healing made it a center of learning and inspiration that attracted scholars and artists from across the Mediterranean.

The Rise and Fall

Pergamon's rise to prominence began under the Attalid dynasty, which transformed the city into a cultural and intellectual powerhouse. The Attalids were patrons of the arts and sciences, investing in grand building projects and fostering a vibrant cultural scene. Pergamon reached its zenith in the 2nd century BCE, becoming one of the most influential cities of the Hellenistic world.

However, the city's fortunes declined after it was bequeathed to the Roman Empire in 133 BCE. While Pergamon continued to thrive under Roman rule, it eventually faced the same challenges as other ancient cities, including invasions, earthquakes, and economic decline. Despite these challenges, the legacy of Pergamon endures, preserved in its ruins and the lasting impact of its contributions to culture and knowledge.

Key Events

1. **c. 300 BCE** - Rise of Pergamon: Pergamon is established as the capital of the Attalid dynasty, becoming a major cultural and political center in Hellenistic Anatolia.
2. **c. 241-197 BCE** - Expansion and Prosperity: Pergamon flourishes under the Attalid kings, who build the famous Altar of Zeus and establish the Great Library of Pergamon, rivaling Alexandria's library.
3. **c. 133 BCE** - Bequeath to Rome: The last Attalid king, Attalus III, bequeaths Pergamon to Rome, making it the capital of the Roman province of Asia.
4. **c. 150-200 CE** - Roman Flourish: Pergamon remains an important city under Roman rule, known for its monumental architecture and cultural significance.
5. **c. 262 CE** - Gothic Raid: Pergamon suffers during the Gothic invasions but continues to be an important city.

6. **c. 330 CE** - Byzantine Period: Pergamon remains significant during the early Byzantine period but gradually declines as Constantinople rises.

Tarsus: The Bridge Between East and West

The River Gateway

Nestled along the banks of the Cydnus River in southeastern Anatolia, Tarsus was a city that thrived as a vital link between the Eastern and Western worlds. Known for its vibrant culture, strategic significance, and intellectual vigor, Tarsus was more than a mere trading hub; it was a bridge connecting diverse civilizations. With its rich history and legacy of innovation, Tarsus stands as a testament to the enduring power of cultural exchange and adaptation.

The Port of Encounters

Tarsus's location along the Cydnus River, which flowed into the Mediterranean Sea, made it a bustling port city and a critical point of connection for traders, travelers, and conquerors. The city's harbors were filled with ships from across the Mediterranean, bringing goods, ideas, and people from distant lands. Tarsus's markets were a tapestry of colors, sounds, and scents, offering everything from silks and spices to precious metals and exotic animals.

The port was not just a place of commerce but also a melting pot of cultures. Merchants from Greece, Egypt, Persia, and Rome mingled in Tarsus's busy streets, exchanging stories and knowledge, creating a cosmopolitan atmosphere that was unique in the ancient world.

The Birthplace of Legends

Tarsus is renowned as the birthplace of Saul of Tarsus, better known as Saint Paul, one of the most influential figures in the spread of Christianity. Born in this diverse and dynamic city, Paul's upbringing in Tarsus provided him with a unique perspective that would later influence his mission to spread the Christian faith across the Roman Empire.

Paul's letters, many of which were written during his travels, reflect the multicultural influences of his home city, blending Jewish traditions with Greek philosophy and Roman pragmatism. Tarsus's legacy as the birthplace of Saint Paul continues to resonate, drawing pilgrims and scholars alike to explore its rich spiritual and historical heritage.

The Cultural Crossroads

Tarsus was a city where East met West, a place where Greek, Roman, and Eastern influences merged to create a unique cultural landscape. The city's schools and academies were renowned centers of learning, attracting students and philosophers from across the ancient world. The blend of Hellenistic and Eastern philosophies fostered a vibrant intellectual climate, where ideas were debated and knowledge was shared.

The city's theaters and public spaces were venues for dramatic performances, philosophical debates, and civic gatherings. The amphitheater of Tarsus, a grand structure that could seat thousands, hosted everything from gladiatorial contests to musical performances, reflecting the city's rich cultural life.

The Meeting of Cleopatra and Mark Antony

One of the most famous events in Tarsus's history was the meeting of Cleopatra VII of Egypt and Mark Antony of Rome. According to legend, Cleopatra sailed up the Cydnus River on a gilded barge, its sails purple and its oars of silver, to meet Antony. The splendor of her arrival dazzled the

221

citizens of Tarsus and left a lasting impression on Antony, marking the beginning of one of history's most famous love affairs.

This meeting was more than just a romantic encounter; it was a political alliance that would shape the fate of the ancient world. The grandeur and drama of this moment reflect the city's status as a stage for significant historical events and its role in the broader geopolitical landscape.

The Innovations of Tarsus

Tarsus was not only a center of commerce and culture but also a hub of innovation and technological advancement. The city was known for its production of high-quality textiles, particularly a type of cloth known as "cilicium," made from goat hair and used for making tents and garments. The skill and craftsmanship of Tarsus's weavers were renowned throughout the ancient world.

The city's engineers and architects also made significant contributions, designing advanced irrigation systems, public baths, and aqueducts that showcased the city's ingenuity and commitment to improving the quality of life for its inhabitants.

The Rise and Fall

Throughout its history, Tarsus experienced periods of great prosperity and influence, as well as times of conquest and decline. The city thrived under various empires, including the Hittites, Assyrians, Persians, Greeks, and Romans. Each of these civilizations left their mark on Tarsus, contributing to its rich cultural and historical tapestry.

Despite facing challenges such as invasions, natural disasters, and political upheavals, Tarsus maintained its significance as a cultural and economic hub. The city's ability to adapt and integrate diverse influences is a testament to its resilience and enduring legacy.

The Legacy of Tarsus

Today, the ruins of Tarsus offer a glimpse into its glorious past. Archaeological excavations have uncovered remnants of ancient buildings, roads, and artifacts that tell the story of a city that was once a beacon of cultural exchange and innovation. The ancient road of Tarsus, with its well-preserved pavement and columns, and the remains of the ancient gymnasium and baths, reflect the city's grandeur and architectural achievements.

Tarsus's legacy continues to inspire scholars, historians, and visitors, drawing them to explore its rich heritage and to reflect on the enduring impact of cultural and intellectual exchange.

Key Events

1. **c. 2000 BCE** - Early Settlement: Tarsus is established in Cilicia, becoming an important crossroads between Mesopotamia and the Mediterranean.
2. **c. 700 BCE** - Neo-Assyrian Period: Tarsus becomes an important city under the Assyrians, known for its strategic location.
3. **c. 333 BCE** - Alexander the Great: Tarsus is captured by Alexander during his conquest of the Persian Empire.
4. **c. 64 BCE** - Roman Period: Tarsus becomes part of the Roman Empire and is made the capital of the province of Cilicia.
5. **c. 5 CE** - Birth of Paul the Apostle: Tarsus is the birthplace of Paul the Apostle, making it an important city in the history of Christianity.
6. **c. 100-300 CE** - Roman Prosperity: Tarsus flourishes as a major cultural and intellectual center, bridging the eastern and western parts of the Roman Empire.
7. **c. 300-500 CE** - Byzantine Period: Tarsus remains important during the early Byzantine period, serving as a key military and trade hub.

Gordion: The Knot of Destiny

The Crossroads of Legend and Empire

In the heart of Anatolia, where the plains stretch out under a vast sky and the echoes of ancient footsteps linger in the air, lies Gordion, a city steeped in legend and history. Once the capital of the powerful Phrygian Kingdom, Gordion was more than just a city; it was a place where myths were born, where kings were crowned, and where the fates of empires were intertwined. With its rich burial mounds, fabled knot, and strategic location at the crossroads of ancient trade routes, Gordion remains a symbol of the enigmatic and the eternal—a place where history and legend are inseparably knotted together.

The Gordian Knot: A Puzzle for the Ages

The most famous symbol of Gordion is the Gordian Knot, a seemingly impossible tangle of ropes that, according to legend, held the yoke of an ancient chariot. This knot was said to be so intricate that no one could untie it, and it became a symbol of complex problems that defied easy solutions. The legend held that whoever could unravel the Gordian Knot would become the ruler of all Asia.

This prophecy attracted many ambitious figures, but it was Alexander the Great who, in 333 BCE, famously cut through the knot with his sword, declaring that he had solved the problem in his own way. This bold act at Gordion marked Alexander as a man of destiny and set the stage for his conquests that would reshape the ancient world. The Gordian Knot was more than just a physical challenge; it was a metaphor for destiny, authority, and the power to transcend the ordinary through decisive action.

The Midas Mound: A Tomb of Kings

Just outside the ancient city lies the Midas Mound, also known as the Great Tumulus, a massive burial mound that is believed to be the final resting place of King Midas, the most famous ruler of Phrygia. According to legend, Midas was the king with the golden touch, cursed with the ability to turn everything he touched into gold—a gift that became a curse when it threatened his very life.

The Midas Mound is one of the largest burial mounds in the ancient world, towering over the surrounding landscape. Inside, archaeologists have discovered a wooden tomb containing rich grave goods, including bronze vessels, furniture, and ornaments, all testifying to the wealth and power of the Phrygian kings. The mound itself, with its monumental scale and ancient artifacts, serves as a reminder of the grandeur and mystery of the Phrygian Kingdom and its legendary rulers. It is a place where myth and reality converge, where the echoes of ancient power still resonate in the earth.

The Citadel of Gordion: A Stronghold of Power

At the heart of Gordion stood its mighty citadel, a fortified complex that served as the political and military center of the Phrygian Kingdom. The citadel was strategically located on a hill overlooking the Sangarius River, providing a commanding view of the surrounding plains and controlling the vital trade routes that passed through the region. The fortifications, with their thick stone walls and defensive towers, were a testament to the city's importance as a stronghold in the ancient world.

Within the citadel, the Phrygian kings ruled over their lands, overseeing a prosperous kingdom that was known for its skilled artisans, metalwork, and textiles. The palace within the citadel was adorned with intricate carvings and vibrant frescoes, reflecting the wealth and cultural achievements of the Phrygians. The citadel of Gordion was more than just a fortress; it was a symbol of the kingdom's power and resilience, a place where the threads of politics, culture, and military might were tightly woven together.

The Trade Routes: Lifeblood of the Kingdom

Gordion's strategic location made it a key hub in the network of ancient trade routes that crisscrossed Anatolia. The city was situated at the crossroads of important routes connecting the Aegean, the Black Sea, and the heart of the Near East, making it a vital center for commerce and cultural exchange. Merchants from distant lands brought goods such as textiles, metals, spices, and luxury items to Gordion, turning its markets into bustling centers of trade.

This flow of goods also brought new ideas, technologies, and cultural influences, which the Phrygians incorporated into their own traditions. Gordion's wealth and prosperity were built on this vibrant trade, and the city's influence extended far beyond its walls, shaping the cultural and economic landscape of the entire region. The trade routes were the lifeblood of Gordion, sustaining its economy and connecting it to the wider ancient world.

The Phrygian Culture: A Blend of Innovation and Tradition

The people of Gordion were known for their unique culture, which blended indigenous traditions with influences from neighboring civilizations, such as the Hittites, Greeks, and Lydians. This cultural fusion was reflected in the city's art, architecture, and religious practices, which were both distinctive and cosmopolitan.

Phrygian artisans were renowned for their skill in metalwork, particularly in the crafting of elaborate fibulae (brooches), jewelry, and weapons. The Phrygian cap, a distinctive peaked hat worn by both men and women, became a symbol of freedom and was later adopted by other cultures, including the Romans. The Phrygians also had a rich musical tradition, with the aulos (a double-reeded instrument) and the lyre being popular instruments.

The city's religious practices were deeply connected to the natural world, with the worship of the Mother Goddess Cybele playing a central role. Cybele, often depicted as a powerful, nurturing figure, was the protector of the Phrygian people and the embodiment of the earth's fertility. The Phrygian culture was a tapestry of innovation and tradition, reflecting the dynamic and multifaceted nature of Gordion itself.

The Decline and Legacy of Gordion

Gordion's decline began in the 7th century BCE, as the kingdom faced invasions from the Cimmerians and later the expansion of the Persian Empire. Despite these challenges, the city remained an important regional center for centuries, though its political power waned. By the time of Alexander the Great's arrival in 333 BCE, Gordion was a shadow of its former glory, but its legacy as a city of legend and history was already secure.

In modern times, archaeological excavations have uncovered the remains of Gordion's citadel, tombs, and artifacts, revealing the richness of its culture and the complexity of its history. The story of Gordion continues to captivate historians, archaeologists, and visitors, who are drawn to the city's legendary past and its enduring place in the annals of ancient history.

Key Events

1. **c. 1200 BCE** - Founding of Gordion: Gordion is established as the capital of Phrygia, located in central Anatolia.
2. **c. 8th-7th centuries BCE** - Phrygian Peak: Gordion becomes the political and cultural heart of Phrygia, ruled by the legendary King Midas, known for his wealth and the famous "Midas touch."
3. **c. 7th century BCE** - Cimmerian Invasion: Gordion is sacked by the Cimmerians, leading to the decline of Phrygian power, though the city continues to be inhabited.
4. **c. 333 BCE** - Alexander the Great: Gordion becomes famous for the "Gordian Knot," which Alexander the Great famously cuts, symboliz-

ing his destiny to conquer Asia.

5. **c. 3rd century BCE** - Hellenistic Period: Gordion continues to be an important city under various Hellenistic rulers, including the Seleucids and the Attalids.

6. **c. 189 BCE** - Roman Influence: Gordion comes under Roman control, though it gradually declines in importance and influence over the following centuries.

V

Greece

Knossos: The Labyrinthine Heart of Minoan Civilization

The Palace of Myths and Majesty

Nestled amid the rolling hills and fertile plains of Crete, where the Mediterranean breeze whispers through olive groves and vineyards, lies Knossos, a city that stands as the vibrant heart of the ancient Minoan civilization. More than just a city, Knossos was a cultural and political powerhouse, a place where mythology and history intertwined to create a rich tapestry of human achievement. Known for its sprawling palace complex, advanced infrastructure, and artistic brilliance, Knossos was a beacon of innovation and splendor in the ancient world.

The Labyrinth of Legends

At the core of Knossos was the legendary Palace of Knossos, an architectural marvel that inspired the myth of the Labyrinth and the Minotaur. According to legend, the labyrinth was a vast, intricate maze built by the master craftsman Daedalus to contain the fearsome Minotaur, a creature with the body of a man and the head of a bull. The palace itself, with its complex network of rooms, corridors, and staircases, seemed to embody the essence of the labyrinthine myth.

The palace was a center of administration, worship, and daily life, with its grand halls, storage rooms, workshops, and living quarters. The Throne Room, with its ceremonial chair and frescoes depicting griffins, was the seat of power, where the ruler of Knossos would conduct affairs of state and hold court.

Frescoes and Artistry: Walls of Color and Life

Knossos was renowned for its vibrant frescoes, which adorned the walls of the palace with scenes of nature, religious rituals, and everyday life. These frescoes, painted with vivid colors and dynamic compositions, captured the essence of Minoan society and its connection to the natural world. The famous "Bull-Leaping Fresco" depicts the athletic prowess and ceremonial significance of bull-leaping, a sport and ritual central to Minoan culture.

The "Prince of the Lilies" fresco, with its elegant depiction of a young man wearing a crown of lilies, reflects the artistry and sophistication of Minoan portraiture. The frescoes of Knossos not only showcased the artistic skills of the Minoans but also provided insights into their religious practices, societal norms, and daily activities.

The Central Court: A Stage for Ritual and Festivity

The Central Court of the palace was a grand open space where religious ceremonies, public gatherings, and festivals took place. This expansive courtyard was the heart of social and religious life in Knossos, a place where the community came together to celebrate, worship, and share in the collective experience.

The court was surrounded by colonnades and chambers, creating a majestic setting for rituals and performances. The presence of large storage jars, or pithoi, around the court indicated the palace's role as a center of economic activity, where goods were collected, stored, and distributed.

Advanced Infrastructure: A City of Innovation

Knossos was a city ahead of its time, with advanced infrastructure that included sophisticated plumbing and drainage systems. The palace featured elaborate water management systems, including aqueducts, cisterns, and terracotta pipes that provided fresh water and sanitation. The presence of flushing toilets and baths in the palace highlighted the Minoans' commitment to hygiene and public health.

The architectural innovations of Knossos extended to its multi-story buildings, complex staircases, and the use of natural light and ventilation to create comfortable living spaces. These advancements reflected the ingenuity and technical prowess of the Minoan civilization.

The Hall of the Double Axes: A Symbol of Power

The Hall of the Double Axes, named after the symbolic double axe, or labrys, that adorned its walls, was another significant area within the palace. The double axe was a sacred symbol in Minoan culture, associated with the goddess and used in religious rituals. The hall's grand columns, intricate frescoes, and ceremonial spaces underscored its importance as a place of worship and authority.

The labrys symbol, which gave rise to the term "labyrinth," highlighted the deep connection between the palace, the myth of the Minotaur, and the religious practices of the Minoans. This hall exemplified the blend of political power and spiritual significance that defined Knossos.

The Decline and Rediscovery

The decline of Knossos began around 1450 BCE, likely due to a combination of natural disasters, such as earthquakes and volcanic eruptions, and external invasions. Despite its eventual fall, the legacy of Knossos endured through the myths and legends that continued to captivate imaginations.

The rediscovery of Knossos in the early 20th century by British archaeologist Sir Arthur Evans brought the ancient city back to light. Evans's excavations revealed the grandeur and complexity of the palace and unearthed a wealth of artifacts that provided invaluable insights into Minoan civilization. His work at Knossos transformed our understanding of the Bronze Age Aegean and established Knossos as a key site in the study of ancient history.

Key Events

1. **c. 7000 BCE** – Early Settlement: Knossos is established as one of the earliest known human settlements in the Aegean.
2. **c. 2000–1700 BCE** – First Palace Period: The first palatial complex is built at Knossos, marking the rise of the Minoan civilization.
3. **c. 1700–1450 BCE** – Second Palace Period: Knossos reaches its peak, with the construction of the famous labyrinthine palace complex associated with the myth of King Minos and the Minotaur.
4. **c. 1450 BCE** – Decline and Destruction: Knossos suffers destruction, likely due to natural disasters and possibly Mycenaean invasion.
5. **c. 1400–1200 BCE** – Mycenaean Control: Knossos continues to be occupied, but its influence wanes under Mycenaean control.
6. **c. 1200 BCE** – Abandonment: The palace is abandoned, and Knossos declines as a major center.

Mycenae: The Citadel of Heroes and Legends

The Lion-Guarded Stronghold

Perched on a rocky hill in the Peloponnesian peninsula, Mycenae stood as a fortress of power and a cradle of epic tales. Known as the center of the Mycenaean civilization, this ancient city was more than a mere settlement; it was a realm of warriors, kings, and gods. With its imposing walls, grand tombs, and legendary relics, Mycenae remains a symbol of the heroic age, where myth and history are intertwined in a timeless narrative of human ambition and divine intervention.

The Lion Gate: The Portal of Kings

The entrance to Mycenae is marked by the iconic Lion Gate, a monumental structure that has captivated imaginations for millennia. Carved from massive limestone blocks, the gate is crowned with a relief of two lions standing guard over a central column, symbolizing both royal power and divine protection. Passing through this gate, visitors are transported into a world of myth and grandeur, where the echoes of ancient heroes can still be felt.

The Lion Gate was not merely a defensive structure but a statement of the city's might and sophistication. Its construction required advanced engineering skills and artistic vision, reflecting the Mycenaeans' mastery of both practical and aesthetic realms.

The Citadel: The Heart of Power

The citadel of Mycenae, with its Cyclopean walls, was the heart of the city's power and prestige. These walls, built from enormous stone blocks, were said to be constructed by the Cyclopes, the one-eyed giants of Greek mythology, emphasizing their superhuman scale and strength. Within these walls lay the royal palace, administrative buildings, and residential quarters, forming a self-contained fortress that dominated the surrounding landscape.

The palace, with its grand megaron (main hall), was the center of political and ceremonial life. Here, the king and his court conducted affairs of state, hosted banquets, and performed religious rituals. The richly decorated throne room, with its intricate frescoes and ornate hearth, symbolized the king's divine right to rule and his connection to the gods.

The Treasury of Atreus: A Monumental Tomb

One of the most remarkable structures in Mycenae is the Treasury of Atreus, also known as the Tomb of Agamemnon. This beehive-shaped tholos tomb, built into the hillside, is a marvel of ancient engineering and architectural design. Its massive entrance, framed by monolithic lintels, leads into a circular chamber with a soaring corbelled dome, creating a space of awe and reverence.

The Treasury of Atreus reflects the Mycenaeans' beliefs in the afterlife and their desire to honor their dead with monumental tombs. The tomb's grandeur and scale are a testament to the wealth and power of the Mycenaean elite, who were buried with lavish grave goods to accompany them into the next world.

The Grave Circles: Ancestral Echoes

The grave circles of Mycenae, particularly Grave Circle A, are among the city's most significant archaeological discoveries. These burial sites, located near the Lion Gate, contain the remains of Mycenaean royalty and elite warriors. The richly adorned shaft graves, filled with gold masks, weapons, and jewelry, provide a glimpse into the wealth and sophistication of Mycenaean society.

The famous Mask of Agamemnon, a gold funerary mask discovered in Grave Circle A, is one of the most iconic artifacts from Mycenae. While its attribution to Agamemnon is debated, the mask symbolizes the artistry and craftsmanship of the Mycenaean people and their reverence for their ancestors.

The Myths and Legends

Mycenae is a city steeped in myth and legend, its name forever linked to the tales of the Trojan War and the epic heroes of Homer's "Iliad." According to legend, Mycenae was founded by Perseus, the slayer of Medusa, and later became the seat of King Agamemnon, the leader of the Greek forces at Troy. The tragic stories of Agamemnon's return from Troy, his murder by his wife Clytemnestra, and the subsequent revenge by his children, Orestes and Electra, are central to the mythic legacy of Mycenae.

These tales, immortalized in Greek literature and drama, have kept the memory of Mycenae alive through the ages, blending historical events with divine intervention and human emotion. The city's association with these epic narratives has made it a symbol of heroism, betrayal, and the complex interplay between fate and free will.

The Artistic Heritage

Mycenae was a center of artistic innovation and craftsmanship, known for its intricate goldwork, pottery, and frescoes. The city's artisans created masterpieces that reflected both the natural world and the divine, from the delicate gold ornaments found in the graves to the vibrant frescoes depicting scenes of hunting, warfare, and religious ceremonies.

The Mycenaean Lion Hunt Dagger, with its detailed inlay of gold, silver, and niello, exemplifies the skill and creativity of Mycenaean metalworkers. The city's artistic heritage influenced neighboring cultures and left a lasting legacy in the art and iconography of ancient Greece.

The Decline and Legacy

The decline of Mycenae began around 1200 BCE, possibly due to a combination of natural disasters, internal strife, and external invasions. Despite its eventual fall, the legacy of Mycenae endured through the myths and legends that continued to captivate the ancient Greeks and later civilizations.

Archaeological excavations in the 19th and 20th centuries, led by pioneers such as Heinrich Schliemann, uncovered the ruins of Mycenae and revealed its historical significance. The city's monumental architecture, rich grave goods, and artistic achievements provide invaluable insights into the Mycenaean civilization and its impact on the ancient world.

Key Events

1. **c. 1600 BCE** - Rise of Mycenae: Mycenae emerges as a powerful city-state in mainland Greece, known for its strong citadel.
2. **c. 1400-1200 BCE** - Peak of Mycenaean Civilization: Mycenae becomes the center of a wealthy and powerful kingdom, associated with the legendary King Agamemnon and the events of the Trojan War.
3. **c. 1250 BCE** - Construction of the Lion Gate: The iconic Lion Gate

and the Cyclopean walls of Mycenae are constructed, symbolizing its strength and grandeur.

4. **c. 1200 BCE** - Decline: Mycenae begins to decline, possibly due to internal strife, invasions, and natural disasters.

5. **c. 1100 BCE** - Abandonment: Mycenae is eventually abandoned, marking the end of the Mycenaean civilization.

Athens: The Cradle of Democracy and Enlightenment

The City of Wisdom and Heroes

Perched upon the rocky hills of Attica, where olive groves whisper ancient secrets and the Aegean Sea glistens in the sunlight, lies Athens, a city that stands as the emblem of ancient civilization. Known as the cradle of democracy and the birthplace of philosophy, Athens was more than just a city; it was a beacon of enlightenment, a forge of ideas, and a stage for the timeless drama of human endeavor. With its grand temples, bustling agoras, and iconic acropolis, Athens remains a symbol of intellectual and cultural brilliance.

The Acropolis: The Sacred Rock

Rising majestically above the city, the Acropolis of Athens is a symbol of both spiritual reverence and architectural genius. Dominated by the Parthenon, a temple dedicated to Athena, the goddess of wisdom and the city's patron, the Acropolis served as the religious and cultural heart of Athens. Built under the guidance of the statesman Pericles, the Parthenon epitomized the glory and ambition of Athenian society.

The Parthenon's Doric columns and intricate sculptures, including the famous frieze depicting the Panathenaic procession, showcased the artistic and architectural prowess of ancient Athens. The Erechtheion, with its iconic Caryatids, and the Temple of Athena Nike further adorned the Acropolis, making it a sanctuary of divine beauty and human creativity.

The Agora: The Heartbeat of Democracy

The Agora of Athens was the bustling center of public life, a space where democracy was not just an idea but a lived reality. Here, citizens gathered to discuss politics, philosophy, and commerce, engaging in debates that shaped the course of history. The Stoa of Attalos, a grand colonnaded building, provided shelter for these discussions, while the nearby Bouleuterion housed the council that guided the city's governance.

The Agora was also a marketplace where merchants sold goods from across the known world, from fine pottery and olive oil to exotic spices and silks. This vibrant commercial hub reflected the city's economic vitality and its role as a crossroads of cultures and ideas.

The Theater of Dionysus: The Stage of Tragedy and Comedy

Nestled on the slopes of the Acropolis, the Theater of Dionysus was the birthplace of Western drama, where the works of playwrights such as Aeschylus, Sophocles, Euripides, and Aristophanes came to life. This open-air theater, with its stone seats and grand stage, was a place where Athenians gathered to witness the exploration of human nature, morality, and the divine through the medium of tragedy and comedy.

The theatrical performances, held during the festivals of Dionysia, were more than mere entertainment; they were communal experiences that engaged the audience in the philosophical and ethical questions of their time. The themes explored in these plays, from the inevitability of fate to the complexities of justice, resonated deeply with the citizens of Athens and continue to influence literature and theater to this day.

The Academy and the Lyceum: Schools of Thought

Athens was the intellectual powerhouse of the ancient world, home to the Academy of Plato and the Lyceum of Aristotle. These institutions were more than just schools; they were vibrant centers of philosophical inquiry and scientific investigation. Plato's Academy, situated in a tranquil grove, was a place where students engaged in dialogues about metaphysics, ethics, and politics, laying the foundations for Western philosophy.

Aristotle's Lyceum, with its extensive library and peripatetic teaching style, focused on empirical observation and logical analysis, contributing to a wide range of disciplines from biology to political theory. The intellectual legacy of these schools shaped the course of Western thought, influencing everything from the scientific method to political philosophy.

The Pnyx: The Platform of Democracy

The Pnyx was the hill where the Athenian Assembly, or Ecclesia, gathered to deliberate and vote on matters of state. This open-air platform symbolized the democratic ideals of Athens, where citizens had the right to speak and participate in the decision-making process. The democratic reforms initiated by leaders such as Cleisthenes and Pericles transformed Athens into a model of citizen governance, where power was distributed among the people rather than concentrated in the hands of a few.

Debates on the Pnyx were robust and passionate, reflecting the dynamic nature of Athenian democracy. Decisions made here shaped the policies and direction of the city, from war and peace to economic regulations and legal reforms.

The Legacy of the Philosophers

Athens was a city that revered knowledge and wisdom, producing some of the greatest thinkers in history. Socrates, with his method of questioning and dialogue, challenged Athenians to examine their beliefs and seek truth. His trial and subsequent execution for impiety and corrupting the youth highlighted the tensions between tradition and new ideas.

Plato, a student of Socrates, founded the Academy and wrote dialogues that explored justice, beauty, and the ideal state. Aristotle, Plato's student, contributed to numerous fields of knowledge, from logic and ethics to biology and politics. The philosophical contributions of these thinkers laid the groundwork for Western intellectual tradition and continue to be studied and revered.

The Panathenaic Festival: Celebration of the Goddess

One of the most important religious and cultural events in Athens was the Panathenaic Festival, held in honor of Athena. This grand festival included athletic competitions, musical contests, and a grand procession that culminated at the Acropolis with the offering of a peplos, a richly embroidered robe, to the statue of Athena.

The festival was a celebration of Athenian identity and pride, showcasing the city's achievements in arts, athletics, and religious devotion. The procession, depicted in the frieze of the Parthenon, was a symbol of civic unity and the shared reverence for the city's patron goddess.

The Persian Wars: Defense of Freedom

Athens played a crucial role in the defense of Greece during the Persian Wars, particularly at the battles of Marathon and Salamis. The courage and strategic brilliance of Athenian leaders and soldiers, such as Themistocles and Miltiades, were instrumental in securing victories against the Persian Empire.

These victories were celebrated as triumphs of democracy and freedom over tyranny, enhancing Athens's reputation as a leader of the Greek world. The stories of heroism and sacrifice from these wars became part of the city's proud heritage, inspiring future generations.

Key Events

1. **c. 3000 BCE** - Early Settlement: Athens is established as a small Mycenaean community on the Acropolis.
2. **c. 800-600 BCE** - Archaic Period: Athens grows in power and influ-

ence, laying the foundations for its future democratic institutions.

3. **c. 508 BCE** – Birth of Democracy: Cleisthenes introduces democratic reforms, establishing Athens as the world's first known democracy.

4. **c. 490-479 BCE** – Persian Wars: Athens plays a key role in the defeat of the Persian invasions, securing its leadership in the Greek world.

5. **c. 447-432 BCE** – Golden Age: The Parthenon and other iconic structures are built under the leadership of Pericles, marking the height of Athenian cultural and political power.

6. **c. 431-404 BCE** – Peloponnesian War: Athens fights a protracted war against Sparta, leading to its eventual defeat and decline.

7. **c. 338 BCE** – Conquest by Macedon: Athens is conquered by Philip II of Macedon, marking the end of its independence.

Sparta: The Warrior's Citadel

The Iron-Hearted City

Nestled in the fertile valley of the Eurotas River, flanked by the rugged mountains of Taygetus and Parnon, lies Sparta, a city that stood as a bastion of discipline, strength, and austere simplicity. Known for its unmatched military prowess and rigorous social system, Sparta was more than just a city; it was a living embodiment of the warrior ethos. With its legendary soldiers, austere lifestyle, and unyielding principles, Sparta remains a symbol of martial excellence and communal solidarity.

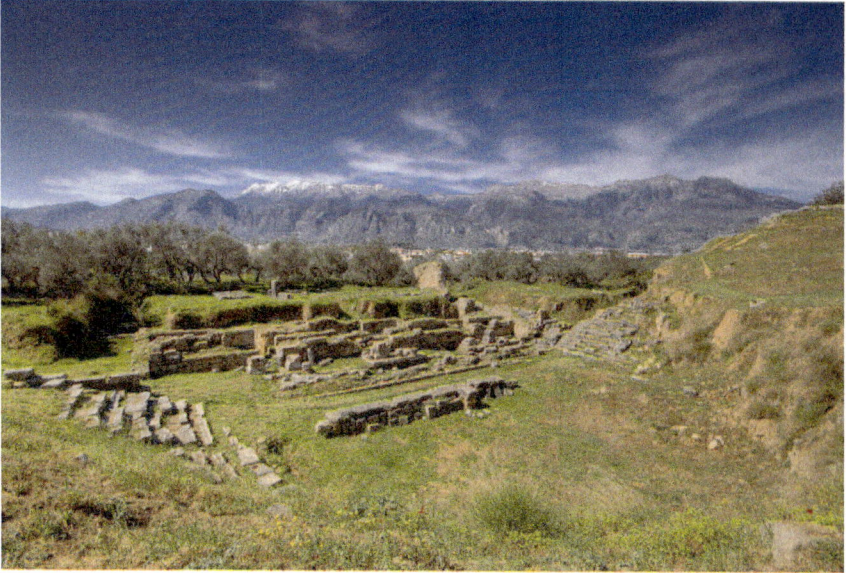

The Agoge: The Forge of Warriors

The beating heart of Spartan society was the agoge, an education and training system designed to cultivate the perfect soldier. From a young age, Spartan boys were taken from their families and subjected to rigorous physical training, discipline, and survival skills. They learned to endure pain, hunger, and hardship, fostering a spirit of resilience and camaraderie.

The agoge emphasized not just physical prowess but also loyalty, obedience, and cunning. Boys were encouraged to engage in competitive games and combat, honing their skills and learning to work as a cohesive unit. This relentless training produced warriors of unparalleled ability and discipline, whose valor and skill were feared and respected throughout the ancient world.

The Syssitia: The Brotherhood of Equals

Central to Spartan life was the syssitia, communal meals shared among male citizens. These dining groups, composed of about fifteen members, fostered equality, solidarity, and mutual support. The syssitia was a place where bonds were forged, and loyalty was tested, reinforcing the collective identity of the Spartan warrior.

Participation in the syssitia was a mark of full citizenship, and the austere meals reflected the Spartan ideal of simplicity and self-restraint. Here, stories of heroism were shared, strategies discussed, and the Spartan ethos reinforced, creating a brotherhood bound by shared experiences and common purpose.

The Spartan Women: Guardians of Strength

Spartan women, unlike their counterparts in other Greek city-states, were afforded considerable freedom and responsibility. They were expected to maintain physical fitness, manage households, and uphold Spartan values. Educated and outspoken, Spartan women played a crucial role in society, instilling discipline and strength in their children and supporting their husbands.

The saying, "Spartan women give birth to real men," underscored their role in perpetuating the warrior culture. Spartan mothers were known for their stoic resolve, famously telling their sons to return with their shield or on it, reflecting the uncompromising values of duty and honor.

The Battle of Thermopylae: A Stand of Legend

One of the most enduring symbols of Spartan valor is the Battle of Thermopylae, where King Leonidas and his 300 Spartans made a legendary stand against the vast Persian army. Despite being vastly outnumbered, the Spartans' courage and tactical brilliance became the stuff of legend, epitomizing the Spartan ideal of fighting to the death for their homeland

and comrades.

This heroic last stand, immortalized in history and popular culture, showcased the Spartan commitment to duty and sacrifice. Thermopylae became a rallying cry for Greek resistance against Persian invasion and cemented Sparta's reputation as a bastion of unwavering resolve and martial excellence.

The Dual Kingship: Balance of Power

Sparta's unique political system featured a dual kingship, with two kings from separate royal families ruling simultaneously. This system provided balance and stability, ensuring that no single ruler could dominate the city's affairs. The kings shared religious, military, and judicial responsibilities, often leading the army in battle and presiding over important ceremonies.

The dual kingship was complemented by a council of elders, the Gerousia, and an assembly of citizens, the Apella. This blend of monarchy, oligarchy, and democracy created a robust governance structure that upheld Spartan values and maintained social order.

The Helots: The Subjugated Class

Integral to Spartan society were the helots, an enslaved population primarily composed of conquered Messenians. The helots worked the land and provided the economic foundation that allowed the Spartan citizens to focus on military training and governance. Despite their crucial role, helots were treated harshly and kept under constant surveillance to prevent rebellion.

Periodic purges, known as the Krypteia, were conducted to instill fear and maintain control over the helots. This oppressive system underscored the stark divide between the Spartan warrior elite and the subjugated classes, reflecting the harsh realities of Spartan life.

The Peloponnesian League: A Sphere of Influence

Sparta's influence extended beyond its borders through the Peloponnesian League, an alliance of city-states united under Spartan leadership. This league was a formidable military coalition that played a crucial role in the Greek world, particularly during the Peloponnesian War against Athens.

Sparta's leadership in the league was characterized by its military dominance and strategic diplomacy. The alliance allowed Sparta to project its power and protect its interests, while also fostering a sense of shared purpose among its allies.

The Spartan Mirage: A Legacy of Paradoxes

The legacy of Sparta, often referred to as the "Spartan Mirage," is a complex tapestry of paradoxes. While celebrated for their discipline and martial prowess, the Spartans' rigid social structure and harsh treatment of helots paint a darker picture of their society. The Spartan way of life, with its emphasis on austerity, military excellence, and communal solidarity, has been both idealized and criticized through the ages.

Sparta's decline began in the 4th century BCE, as it struggled to adapt to changing political and military landscapes. Despite this decline, the legend of Sparta endured, influencing later cultures and inspiring admiration and debate.

Key Events

1. **c. 900 BCE** - Founding of Sparta: Sparta is established in the region of Laconia, becoming known for its militaristic society.
2. **c. 650 BCE** - Lycurgus' Reforms: Sparta undergoes significant social and political reforms, creating a rigidly organized society focused on military excellence.
3. **c. 490-479 BCE** - Persian Wars: Sparta plays a key role in the Greek victories, particularly at the Battle of Thermopylae and the Battle of

Plataea.

4. **c. 431-404 BCE** - Peloponnesian War: Sparta defeats Athens, establishing itself as the dominant power in Greece.

5. **c. 371 BCE** - Battle of Leuctra: Sparta suffers a significant defeat at the hands of Thebes, marking the beginning of its decline.

6. **c. 146 BCE** - Roman Conquest: Sparta is incorporated into the Roman Empire, losing its autonomy but retaining some of its unique social practices.

Corinth: The Shimmering Jewel of the Isthmus

The City of Commerce and Culture

Perched on the narrow Isthmus of Corinth, where the Aegean and Ionian Seas nearly kiss, lies the ancient city of Corinth, a thriving metropolis that dazzled with wealth, innovation, and cultural fusion. Corinth was not merely a city; it was a bustling crossroads of trade, a center of artistic excellence, and a beacon of political power. Known for its strategic location, Corinth played a pivotal role in the ancient Greek world, linking mainland Greece with the Peloponnese and the wider Mediterranean.

The Diolkos: The Pathway of Trade

One of Corinth's most remarkable innovations was the Diolkos, a paved trackway that allowed ships to be transported overland across the narrow isthmus, bypassing the perilous journey around the Peloponnesian peninsula. This ingenious engineering feat not only saved time and reduced risk but also cemented Corinth's status as a major hub of commerce.

The Diolkos enabled Corinth to control trade routes and collect tolls, filling its coffers with wealth from across the Mediterranean. The bustling ports of Lechaion and Cenchreae, connected by the Diolkos, teemed with activity as merchants and sailors from Egypt, Phoenicia, and beyond exchanged goods, ideas, and stories.

The Acrocorinth: The Watchful Guardian

Towering above the city, the Acrocorinth was a formidable fortress and acropolis that offered both sanctuary and strategic advantage. This massive rock outcrop, fortified with imposing walls and dotted with temples and springs, served as the ultimate refuge in times of war and a vantage point for monitoring the surrounding seas and lands.

The Temple of Aphrodite, perched atop the Acrocorinth, was a renowned sanctuary dedicated to the goddess of love and beauty. It was said that the temple housed courtesans who played a significant role in Corinthian society and economy. The Acrocorinth's commanding presence symbolized the city's strength and its connection to the divine.

The Corinthian Order: Architectural Elegance

Corinth was a city of architectural splendor, famed for the Corinthian order of columns, characterized by their ornate capitals adorned with acanthus leaves. This architectural style, epitomized by the Temple of Apollo, showcased the city's artistic innovation and influence. The elegant columns of the Corinthian order became a hallmark of classical architecture, admired and emulated throughout the ancient world.

The Temple of Apollo, with its stately columns and commanding presence, was a center of religious life and a testament to the city's devotion to the gods. The theater and the odeon of Corinth further reflected the city's cultural vibrancy, hosting performances, festivals, and gatherings that enriched the communal life of its citizens.

The Isthmian Games: Celebrations of Strength and Skill

Every two years, Corinth hosted the Isthmian Games, one of the Panhellenic Games of ancient Greece. These athletic and musical competitions, held in honor of Poseidon, attracted participants and spectators from all over the Greek world. The games included chariot races, wrestling, and poetry contests, celebrating both physical prowess and artistic excellence.

The Isthmian Games were more than just a sporting event; they were a celebration of Hellenic unity and shared culture. The games fostered a sense of identity and pride among the Greek city-states, with Corinth at the center of this grand festival.

The Agora: The Heart of Civic Life

The Agora of Corinth was the bustling heart of the city, a vibrant market-place and civic center where citizens gathered to trade, debate, and socialize. The Agora was lined with stoas, public buildings, and temples, creating a dynamic space where economic, political, and religious life intersected.

The Bema, a prominent platform in the Agora, was used for public speeches and legal proceedings. It was here that the Apostle Paul is said to have been brought before the Roman proconsul Gallio, reflecting the city's significance in the early spread of Christianity. The Agora was a microcosm of Corinthian society, reflecting its diversity and dynamism.

The Wealth of Corinth: A Beacon of Prosperity

Corinth's strategic location and innovative spirit made it one of the wealthiest cities of the ancient world. Its craftsmen were renowned for producing high-quality pottery, bronze work, and textiles. The city's wealth was also evident in its luxurious public baths, ornate fountains, and grand villas, which showcased the opulence and refinement of Corinthian society.

The economic prosperity of Corinth attracted a diverse population, including Greeks, Romans, Phoenicians, and others, creating a cosmopolitan atmosphere. The city's markets offered goods from across the Mediterranean, making it a melting pot of cultures and ideas.

The Decline and Resurgence

Corinth's fortunes fluctuated over the centuries, with periods of decline and resurgence. The city was famously destroyed by the Roman general Lucius Mummius in 146 BCE but was later rebuilt by Julius Caesar in 44 BCE as a Roman colony. This rebirth marked a new era of prosperity and significance, with Corinth becoming an important center of Roman Greece.

The Roman influence brought new architectural styles, infrastructure, and cultural practices, blending with the city's Hellenic heritage to create a unique and vibrant urban landscape. Despite its turbulent history, Corinth's resilience and strategic importance ensured its enduring legacy.

Key Events

1. **c. 800 BCE** - Founding of the Corinthian Polis: Corinth becomes a major city-state, known for its wealth, trade, and strategic location on the Isthmus of Corinth.
2. **c. 700-600 BCE** - Tyranny of Cypselus and Periander: Corinth flourishes under the rule of its tyrants, becoming a cultural and economic powerhouse.
3. **c. 580 BCE** - Establishment of the Isthmian Games: Corinth establishes the Isthmian Games, a major panhellenic festival.
4. **c. 431-404 BCE** - Peloponnesian War: Corinth plays a crucial role in the conflict, allied with Sparta against Athens.
5. **c. 146 BCE** - Destruction by Rome: Corinth is destroyed by the Romans after a revolt, but is later rebuilt as a major Roman colony.
6. **c. 44 BCE** - Roman Rebuilding: Julius Caesar refounds Corinth as a Roman colony, leading to a new period of prosperity.

Olympia: The Sacred Grove of Champions

The Sanctuary of Gods and Heroes

Nestled in the verdant valley of the Alpheus River in the Peloponnese, where ancient olive trees whisper tales of valor and piety, lies Olympia, a city that stood as the spiritual heart of ancient Greece. Known as the birthplace of the Olympic Games, Olympia was more than just a site of athletic competition; it was a sacred sanctuary where gods and mortals converged. With its grand temples, treasuries, and athletic facilities, Olympia remains a symbol of human excellence and divine reverence.

The Temple of Zeus: The Pinnacle of Devotion

At the heart of Olympia stood the magnificent Temple of Zeus, one of the Seven Wonders of the Ancient World. This colossal temple, dedicated to the king of the gods, housed the famed Statue of Zeus, created by the master sculptor Phidias. The statue, made of ivory and gold, depicted Zeus seated on his throne, exuding a sense of awe and majesty.

The temple's grand columns and elaborate pediments, adorned with scenes from Greek mythology, showcased the artistic and architectural brilliance of the ancient Greeks. The Temple of Zeus was not only a center of worship but also a symbol of unity, as it drew pilgrims and athletes from all over the Greek world to pay homage to the deity.

The Olympic Games: A Festival of Excellence

Every four years, Olympia transformed into a bustling hub of activity and celebration as it hosted the Olympic Games, the most prestigious athletic event in ancient Greece. Athletes from city-states across the Greek world gathered to compete in a series of events, including foot races, wrestling, boxing, and the pentathlon. The games were held in honor of Zeus and were a testament to human physical prowess and competitive spirit.

The Olympic Games were more than just a sporting event; they were a unifying force that fostered peace and camaraderie among the often-warring Greek city-states. The sacred truce, or ekecheiria, ensured that conflicts were suspended, allowing athletes and spectators to travel safely to Olympia. Victors of the games were crowned with olive wreaths and immortalized in statues and poems, achieving eternal glory.

The Heraion: A Sanctuary of the Goddess

The Heraion, or Temple of Hera, was one of the oldest and most revered sanctuaries in Olympia. Dedicated to Hera, the wife of Zeus, this temple was a center of religious worship and ritual. The Heraion housed the cult statue of Hera and was the site of the Heraia, a series of foot races held in honor of the goddess, featuring female athletes.

The Heraion's architectural elegance and historical significance under-scored the importance of female participation in religious and athletic life. The temple's columns and altars witnessed countless offerings and prayers, reflecting the deep spiritual connection between the people and their deities.

The Stadium: Arena of Heroes

The stadium of Olympia, with its elongated, U-shaped design, was the primary venue for the athletic competitions of the Olympic Games. Built to accommodate thousands of spectators, the stadium provided a grand stage for athletes to demonstrate their skills and strength. The starting line, marked by stone slabs, and the judges' seats, known as the Hellanodikai, were integral parts of the stadium's layout.

The echoes of cheering crowds and the rhythmic pounding of feet on the track brought the stadium to life, creating an atmosphere of excitement and anticipation. The achievements of athletes in this sacred arena were celebrated not just for their physical excellence but also for their embodiment of the Greek ideal of arete, or virtue.

The Altis: The Sacred Grove

The Altis, a sacred grove within Olympia, was the spiritual heart of the sanctuary. This lush, wooded area was dotted with altars, statues, and treasuries dedicated to various gods and heroes. The Altis was a place of serenity and reflection, where pilgrims could offer sacrifices and seek divine favor.

The grove's peaceful ambiance was contrasted by the vibrant energy of the surrounding temples and athletic facilities, creating a harmonious blend of spirituality and physicality. The Altis was also home to the Philippeion, a circular building dedicated by Philip II of Macedon, which housed statues of his family, including his son, Alexander the Great.

The Treasuries: Monuments of Pride

The treasuries of Olympia, built by various Greek city-states, were small but ornate buildings that housed valuable offerings and votive gifts. These treasuries were symbols of civic pride and competitive spirit, as each city-state sought to outshine the others with their architectural and artistic contributions.

The treasuries showcased the wealth and piety of their respective city-states, filled with precious artifacts, statues, and inscriptions. They served as tangible reminders of the collective devotion and rivalry that characterized the Greek world.

The Gymnasium and Palaestra: Schools of Strength

The gymnasium and palaestra of Olympia were essential facilities for the training and preparation of athletes. The gymnasium, with its open courtyards and covered walkways, provided a space for physical exercises and athletic drills. The palaestra, a rectangular building with an internal courtyard, was specifically designed for wrestling and other combat sports.

These training facilities were places of discipline and camaraderie, where athletes honed their skills under the guidance of experienced trainers. The rigorous training regimens and competitive spirit fostered in these venues were critical to the success of the athletes in the Olympic Games.

The Decline and Rediscovery

The decline of Olympia began with the rise of the Roman Empire and the eventual ban on pagan festivals by Emperor Theodosius in the 4th century CE. The sanctuary fell into disrepair, and natural disasters, such as earthquakes and floods, further contributed to its decline. Despite its abandonment, the legacy of Olympia endured through the tales of ancient historians and the enduring symbol of the Olympic Games.

The rediscovery of Olympia in the 18th and 19th centuries by archaeologists, notably by the German archaeologist Ernst Curtius, brought the ancient sanctuary back to light. Excavations revealed the grandeur of the temples, stadium, and other structures, offering invaluable insights into the religious, cultural, and athletic life of ancient Greece.

Key Events

1. **c. 1000 BCE** - Early Settlement and Worship: Olympia becomes a sacred site dedicated to Zeus, attracting worshippers from across Greece.
2. **c. 776 BCE** - First Olympic Games: The first recorded Olympic Games are held, establishing Olympia as the most important religious and

athletic center in Greece.

3. **c. 600-400 BCE** - Peak of Olympia: Olympia flourishes as a cultural and religious center, with the construction of iconic structures like the Temple of Zeus, which housed the Statue of Zeus, one of the Seven Wonders of the Ancient World.

4. **c. 393 CE** - End of the Ancient Olympics: The Roman Emperor Theodosius I bans pagan festivals, leading to the end of the Olympic Games.

5. **c. 426 CE** - Destruction of Olympia: The sanctuary is destroyed by earthquakes and deliberate destruction by Theodosius II, marking the end of Olympia's significance as a sacred site.

Argos: The Timeless City of Heroes and Myths

The Ancient Heart of the Peloponnese

In the fertile plains of the Argolid, where the sun-drenched landscape meets the distant whispers of the Aegean Sea, lies Argos, one of the oldest and most storied cities of ancient Greece. Known as the city of heroes and legends, Argos was more than a mere settlement; it was a crucible of myth, history, and innovation. With its ancient ruins, legendary king lists, and vibrant cultural life, Argos stands as a testament to the enduring legacy of human endeavor and imagination.

The Heraion: The Sanctuary of the Goddess

At the heart of Argos's religious life was the Heraion, a grand sanctuary dedicated to Hera, the queen of the gods and the city's protector. Nestled on the slopes of Mount Euboea, the Heraion was a magnificent complex of temples, altars, and treasuries. Pilgrims from across Greece flocked to this sacred site to offer prayers, sacrifices, and votive gifts to Hera, seeking her favor and guidance.

The central temple, with its stately columns and rich decorations, housed a revered cult statue of Hera, reflecting the artistic and architectural brilliance of the Argive craftsmen. The sanctuary's annual festival, the Heraia, featured athletic competitions and processions, celebrating both the divine and communal spirit of Argos.

The Larisa Fortress: Guardian of the City

Perched high above the city on a steep hill, the Larisa Fortress stood as a formidable guardian of Argos. This ancient acropolis, named after the nymph Larisa, offered strategic advantage and protection against invaders. The fortress's massive walls, towers, and gates showcased the engineering prowess of the Argives and served as a symbol of their resilience and strength.

Within the fortress, the remains of Mycenaean palaces and Cyclopean walls harkened back to a time of legendary kings and epic tales. The Larisa was not only a military stronghold but also a center of political power and religious significance, housing temples and altars dedicated to various gods.

The Agora: Hub of Civic Life

The Agora of Argos was the bustling heart of the city, a vibrant marketplace and civic center where citizens gathered to trade, debate, and celebrate. Surrounded by stoas, public buildings, and temples, the Agora was a microcosm of Argive society, reflecting its economic vitality and cultural dynamism.

The Buleuterion, the council house, was where the city's leaders met to discuss and decide on matters of governance, while the Tholos served as a venue for public gatherings and religious ceremonies. The Agora was also a place of education and intellectual exchange, where philosophers, poets, and orators shared their ideas and works.

The Theater of Argos: Stage of Drama and Music

The grand theater of Argos, carved into the southern slope of Larisa, was one of the largest theaters in ancient Greece. With a seating capacity of over 20,000, the theater was a venue for dramatic performances, musical contests, and public assemblies. The open-air structure, with its impressive acoustics and panoramic views, provided a stunning backdrop for the cultural life of the city.

Here, the works of Aeschylus, Sophocles, and Euripides were brought to life, exploring themes of fate, justice, and human nature. The theater was a place where the citizens of Argos came together to experience the power of storytelling and the beauty of artistic expression.

The Mythic Legacy: Heroes and Legends

Argos is deeply woven into the fabric of Greek mythology, its name echoing through the tales of heroes and gods. The city was the home of Perseus, the slayer of Medusa and founder of Mycenae, and the birthplace of Heracles, the greatest of Greek heroes known for his twelve labors. The legends of the Danaids, the fifty daughters of Danaus who fled to Argos to escape forced marriages, added to the city's rich mythological tapestry.

The Argive Heraion and the stories of its priestesses, such as the tale of Io, the maiden transformed into a cow and pursued by Hera, further enriched the city's mythic heritage. Argos was a land where history and legend converged, creating a timeless narrative of heroism, divine intervention, and human resilience.

The Art and Innovation

Argos was renowned for its artistic achievements and technological innovations. The city was a center of bronze work, producing exquisite statues, weapons, and armor that were highly prized across the ancient world. The Argive artisans were also known for their pottery, with distinctive styles and motifs that reflected the city's cultural identity.

Innovations in architecture, such as the development of the Doric order, showcased the Argives' contributions to Greek art and design. The city's public buildings, temples, and theaters were adorned with intricate carvings, sculptures, and frescoes that celebrated both the divine and the human spirit.

The Rise and Decline

Argos's history is marked by periods of prosperity and decline, shaped by its strategic location and political alliances. The city played a significant role in the Peloponnesian War and the struggles for dominance in the Greek world. Despite the challenges of invasions, internal conflicts, and shifting power dynamics, Argos maintained its cultural and political significance.

In the Hellenistic and Roman periods, Argos continued to thrive as a center of learning and culture. The city's rich heritage and enduring legacy were preserved through its monuments, myths, and traditions, offering a glimpse into the grandeur of its past.

Key Events

1. **c. 2000 BCE** - Early Settlement: Argos is established in the Peloponnese, becoming one of the oldest continuously inhabited cities in Greece.
2. **c. 1600-1100 BCE** - Mycenaean Period: Argos flourishes as a significant center during the Mycenaean civilization, associated with legendary heroes such as Perseus.
3. **c. 1100-800 BCE** - Dark Ages: Argos survives the Greek Dark Ages and begins to reemerge as a powerful city-state.
4. **c. 700 BCE** - Rise of Argos: Under King Pheidon, Argos becomes one of the most powerful city-states in Greece, known for its military strength and innovations in hoplite warfare.
5. **c. 480 BCE** - Persian Wars: Argos remains neutral during the Persian Wars, avoiding direct conflict with the Persians.
6. **c. 431-404 BCE** - Peloponnesian War: Argos sides with Athens against Sparta, though it plays a less prominent role in the conflict.
7. **c. 146 BCE** - Roman Conquest: Argos is absorbed into the Roman Empire, continuing to exist as a significant urban center throughout antiquity.

Delphi: The Oracle of the World

The Navel of the Earth

Perched on the slopes of Mount Parnassus, where the craggy peaks meet the azure sky, lies Delphi, a city that served as the spiritual and prophetic heart of the ancient Greek world. Known as the omphalos, or navel, of the earth, Delphi was more than just a city; it was a sacred sanctuary where the divine and mortal realms converged. With its legendary oracle, grand temples, and awe-inspiring landscapes, Delphi remains a symbol of divine wisdom and human aspiration.

The Oracle of Apollo: Voice of the Gods

At the heart of Delphi stood the Temple of Apollo, the epicenter of the Delphic Oracle. Pilgrims from across the ancient world journeyed to this sacred site to seek the counsel of the Pythia, the high priestess of Apollo, who delivered cryptic prophecies believed to be inspired by the god himself. The Pythia's pronouncements, given in a trance induced by ethylene vapors, shaped the destinies of individuals and nations alike.

The temple's grand colonnades and intricate sculptures depicted scenes from mythology and celebrated the god's triumphs, reflecting the artistic and spiritual devotion of the Greeks. The sacred spring of Castalia, where pilgrims purified themselves before consulting the oracle, added to the sanctity of the site.

The Omphalos Stone: Center of the World

Delphi was believed to be the center of the world, marked by the omphalos stone, a conical stone that signified the meeting point of divine energy. According to myth, Zeus released two eagles from opposite ends of the earth, and they met at Delphi, establishing it as the earth's navel. The omphalos stone, housed within the temple, was a powerful symbol of Delphi's cosmic significance.

This stone was more than a geographical marker; it was a testament to the city's role as a universal center of spiritual and temporal guidance. The omphalos reminded visitors of Delphi's unique position as a bridge between heaven and earth.

The Sacred Way: Path to Enlightenment

The Sacred Way, a winding path that led to the Temple of Apollo, was lined with treasuries, statues, and monuments dedicated by various Greek city-states. Each offering was a testament to the city-state's piety, wealth, and artistic achievement. The treasuries, such as the exquisite Treasury of the Athenians, housed precious votive gifts and were adorned with intricate carvings that celebrated heroic deeds and divine favor.

Walking the Sacred Way, pilgrims encountered these symbols of devotion and civic pride, reflecting the collective reverence for Apollo and the shared cultural heritage of the Greek world. The path culminated at the temple, where the divine prophecies awaited.

The Theater of Delphi: A Stage of Reverence

Nestled above the Temple of Apollo, the theater of Delphi offered breathtaking views of the valley below and the distant Gulf of Corinth. This theater, with its semi-circular seating carved into the hillside, was a venue for dramatic performances, musical contests, and religious festivals held in honor of Apollo. The theater's design ensured that the audience could see and hear the performers clearly, enhancing the communal experience of worship and entertainment.

The annual Pythian Games, held at Delphi, featured athletic competitions, choral performances, and dramatic presentations, celebrating both physical prowess and artistic excellence. The theater was a place where the spiritual and cultural life of Delphi converged, creating a harmonious blend of devotion and celebration.

The Sanctuary of Athena Pronaia: Gateway to the Divine

At the entrance to Delphi stood the Sanctuary of Athena Pronaia, a complex of temples and altars dedicated to Athena, the goddess of wisdom and warfare. The tholos, a circular temple with elegant Doric columns, was the centerpiece of this sanctuary, embodying the harmony and balance of Greek architectural design.

The sanctuary served as a protective gateway to the main oracle site, offering pilgrims a place of reverence and preparation before they ascended to the Temple of Apollo. The dual sanctuaries of Apollo and Athena underscored Delphi's role as a center of both prophetic insight and martial strength.

The Castalian Spring: Waters of Purity

The Castalian Spring, nestled in a ravine at the base of Mount Parnassus, was a sacred source of water where pilgrims purified themselves before entering the sanctuary. The spring's crystal-clear waters were believed to possess divine properties, cleansing the body and spirit of those who bathed in them.

The spring was also associated with the muses, inspiring poets and artists who sought creative enlightenment. The sound of the water, flowing from the rocks, created a serene and contemplative atmosphere, enhancing the spiritual ambiance of Delphi.

The Sibyl Rock: Echoes of Prophecy

Near the Temple of Apollo stood the Sibyl Rock, a large boulder where the sibyl, an ancient prophetess, was said to have delivered her oracles before the establishment of the Delphic Oracle. The sibyl's utterances were believed to be inspired by Gaia, the earth goddess, and carried profound wisdom and insight.

The Sibyl Rock symbolized the deep historical roots of Delphi's prophetic tradition, connecting the ancient past with the more structured practices of the Delphic Oracle. It served as a reminder of the timeless quest for divine knowledge and guidance.

The Archaeological Treasures: Echoes of Grandeur

Today, the ruins of Delphi and the artifacts housed in the Delphi Archaeological Museum offer a glimpse into the city's glorious past. The Charioteer of Delphi, a bronze statue depicting a victorious charioteer, exemplifies the artistic mastery and celebratory spirit of the ancient Greeks. The twin kouroi statues, the Sphinx of Naxos, and the frieze of the Siphnian Treasury are among the many treasures that reveal the city's rich cultural and religious heritage.

Excavations have uncovered the remains of the Temple of Apollo, the treasuries, the theater, and the stadium, providing invaluable insights into the architectural and ceremonial grandeur of Delphi.

Key Events

1. **c. 1400 BCE** - Early Settlement and Worship: Delphi is established as a sacred site dedicated to the earth goddess Gaia, later associated with Apollo.
2. **c. 800 BCE** - Rise of the Oracle: The Oracle of Delphi becomes the most important religious and prophetic center in the Greek world, attracting visitors from all over the Mediterranean.

3. **c. 590 BCE** - First Sacred War: Delphi is liberated from Phocian control by a coalition of Greek city-states, reinforcing its independence and sacred status.

4. **c. 480 BCE** - Persian Wars: Delphi is spared from destruction by the Persians, which the Greeks attribute to divine intervention.

5. **c. 356-346 BCE** - Third Sacred War: Delphi becomes the focus of conflict between the Phocians and the Amphictyonic League, leading to further consolidation of its sacred status.

6. **c. 146 BCE** - Roman Influence: Delphi continues to thrive under Roman rule, though its influence begins to wane as Rome rises in power.

7. **c. 394 CE** - End of the Oracle: The Roman Emperor Theodosius I orders the closure of all pagan temples, marking the end of the Oracle's influence.

Thebes: The Heartbeat of Boeotia

The City of Heroes and Tragedies

Nestled in the fertile plains of Boeotia, where the mountains watch over the rolling fields and the air carries the whispers of ancient myths, lies Thebes, a city as rich in legend as it is in history. More than just a city, Thebes was a crucible of Greek civilization, a place where heroes were born, epic battles were fought, and tragedies unfolded on the grand stage of human existence. With its seven gates, storied past, and deep ties to both myth and reality, Thebes remains a symbol of the complex interplay between fate, power, and the enduring spirit of Greece.

The Seven Gates: Guardians of Myth and Memory

Thebes was famously known as the city of the seven gates, each one a passage into the city's heart and a symbol of its strength and resilience. These gates—Proetides, Electra, Neista, Crenae, Hypsista, Ogygia, and Homoloides—were more than just defensive structures; they were the thresholds through which the great dramas of Theban history and myth passed. The most famous of these was the Electra Gate, which played a key role in many of the city's legendary tales.

The gates of Thebes were also the setting for one of its most defining moments: the epic conflict of the Seven Against Thebes, where seven Argive leaders, each assigned to a gate, laid siege to the city in an attempt to dethrone the ruler Eteocles. The battle was not only a test of the city's fortifications but also a tragic story of fate and family, where brother fought against brother, and the gods themselves seemed to conspire in the unfolding of destiny. The seven gates of Thebes stood as silent witnesses to the city's triumphs and tragedies, marking the passage of time and the ebb and flow of power.

The House of Cadmus: The Founding Legend

Thebes was founded by Cadmus, a Phoenician prince who, according to legend, followed a sacred cow to the site where the city would rise. Cadmus's journey was not just a physical one; it was a quest that led him to slay a dragon and sow its teeth into the earth, from which sprang a race of fierce warriors known as the Spartoi. These warriors, after fighting among themselves, became the first citizens of Thebes, symbolizing the city's origins in struggle and strength.

The House of Cadmus, from which many of Thebes' legendary figures descended, was both blessed and cursed by the gods. Cadmus himself was a figure of wisdom and resilience, credited with introducing the Phoenician alphabet to Greece, which laid the foundation for Greek literacy and culture. However, his descendants were marked by tragedy, including his daughter Semele, mother of Dionysus, and his great-grandson Oedipus, whose story of patricide and incest would cast a long shadow over Thebes. The legacy of Cadmus was a blend of heroism and sorrow, reflecting the dual nature of Thebes itself—a city both powerful and vulnerable, glorious and tragic.

The Tale of Oedipus: The Tragedy of Kings

The story of Oedipus, the doomed king of Thebes, is one of the most powerful and enduring myths in Greek literature. Oedipus's tale is a tragedy of fate, where attempts to avoid destiny only lead to its fulfillment. Unwittingly killing his father, King Laius, and marrying his mother, Queen Jocasta, Oedipus's rise to the throne brought with it a curse that would plague Thebes.

The tragedy of Oedipus, immortalized in the plays of Sophocles, is not just a story of individual downfall; it is a reflection of the human condition, where knowledge and ignorance, power and helplessness, are intertwined. Thebes itself becomes a character in this drama, a city gripped by plague and despair, seeking salvation through the unraveling of terrible truths. The tale of Oedipus is a testament to the power of myth to capture the complexities of human life, and it forever ties the name of Thebes to the themes of fate, guilt, and redemption.

The Theban Cycle: A Tapestry of Heroism and Conflict

The history of Thebes is woven into the larger tapestry of Greek mythology through the Theban Cycle, a series of stories that chronicle the city's rise, fall, and resurrection. From the founding by Cadmus to the tragedies of Oedipus and the wars that followed, the Theban Cycle is a saga of heroism and conflict, where the deeds of gods and mortals shape the fate of the city.

One of the most famous episodes in this cycle is the battle of the Seven Against Thebes, where seven champions, led by Polynices, attempt to seize the city from his brother Eteocles. The conflict ends in mutual destruction, with both brothers dying by each other's hand, leaving Thebes to be ruled by Creon, who would later face his own tragic downfall in the story of Antigone.

The Theban Cycle also includes the tale of the Epigoni, the sons of the original seven, who return years later to successfully conquer Thebes, avenging their fathers. These stories, filled with prophecy, betrayal, and the interplay of divine and human will, form a rich narrative that captures the essence of Thebes as a city where heroism and tragedy are eternally linked.

The Boeotian League: Thebes as a Powerhouse of Greece

Beyond its mythic significance, Thebes was a powerful city-state in its own right, playing a crucial role in the political and military history of ancient Greece. The city was the leading force in the Boeotian League, a confederation of cities in central Greece that often found itself at odds with its more famous neighbors, Athens and Sparta. Thebes' military prowess was demonstrated in the Battle of Leuctra in 371 BCE, where its army, led by the brilliant general Epaminondas, shattered the Spartan hegemony and established Thebes as the preeminent power in Greece.

This victory was a turning point in Greek history, showcasing Thebes' ability to challenge and overcome even the mightiest of foes. Under Epaminondas, Thebes briefly became the dominant power in Greece, leading the city into a period of prosperity and influence. However, Thebes' dominance was short-lived, and the city eventually faced decline, particularly after its destruction by Alexander the Great in 335 BCE.

The Sanctuary of Apollo Ismenios: A Sacred Refuge

Thebes was not only a center of political power but also a place of deep religious significance. Among its many temples, the Sanctuary of Apollo Ismenios was particularly important, serving as a major religious site where oracles were sought, and sacrifices were made to the god Apollo. This sanctuary, situated on the banks of the Ismenus River, was a place where Thebans connected with the divine, seeking guidance and protection from their patron deity.

The sanctuary was also a symbol of the city's enduring connection to the spiritual world, reflecting the belief that Thebes was a place where the gods themselves intervened in the affairs of men. The Sanctuary of Apollo Ismenios, with its rituals and oracles, was a sacred refuge in a city often marked by strife and conflict, offering solace and a connection to the divine amidst the challenges of mortal life.

The Decline and Enduring Legacy of Thebes

Thebes' decline came in the wake of its conflicts with Macedonia, culminating in its destruction by Alexander the Great in 335 BCE. The city was razed to the ground, and its inhabitants were sold into slavery, marking the end of Thebes as a major power in Greece. However, the city was later rebuilt, and its legacy endured through its myths, its contributions to Greek culture, and its role in the broader history of Greece.

In modern times, the ruins of Thebes, along with its myths and stories, continue to captivate the imagination, serving as a reminder of the city's profound impact on Greek history and culture. Thebes' enduring legacy is evident in the rich tapestry of literature, drama, and art that continues to draw inspiration from its tales of heroism, tragedy, and the complex interplay of human and divine.

Key Events

1. **c. 1600 BCE** - Mycenaean Period: Thebes is established as a significant center during the Mycenaean civilization, with connections to legendary figures such as Cadmus and Oedipus.
2. **c. 1200 BCE** - Trojan War Era: Thebes is involved in the epic narratives of the Trojan War, though its prominence declines with the fall of the Mycenaean civilization.
3. **c. 700-600 BCE** - Archaic Period: Thebes reemerges as a powerful city-state in Boeotia, known for its military strength and rivalry with Athens.
4. **c. 479 BCE** - Persian Wars: Thebes initially sides with Persia during the Greco-Persian Wars, leading to a temporary decline in its influence after Persia's defeat.
5. **c. 371 BCE** - Battle of Leuctra: Thebes defeats Sparta in the Battle of Leuctra under the leadership of Epaminondas, establishing Theban hegemony over Greece.
6. **c. 362 BCE** - Battle of Mantinea: Theban power wanes after the death of Epaminondas at Mantinea, leading to the city's decline as a dominant power.
7. **c. 335 BCE** - Destruction by Alexander the Great: Thebes is destroyed by Alexander the Great as punishment for its rebellion, marking the end of its prominence in ancient Greece.

Samos: The Isle of Innovation and Serenity

The Aegean Gem of Science and Beauty

Off the coast of Asia Minor, nestled amidst the azure waters of the Aegean Sea, lies Samos, an island that shone as a beacon of innovation, culture, and natural beauty. Known for its fertile lands, strategic harbors, and illustrious inhabitants, Samos was more than a mere city; it was a vibrant hub of intellectual and artistic brilliance. With its serene landscapes, advanced engineering, and rich mythology, Samos remains a symbol of human creativity and the harmonious coexistence of nature and civilization.

The Heraion: Sanctuary of the Goddess

At the heart of Samos's religious life was the Heraion, a grand sanctuary dedicated to Hera, the queen of the gods. This colossal temple, one of the largest in the ancient Greek world, was a testament to the island's devotion and architectural prowess. The Heraion's massive columns and elaborate altars created a majestic space where pilgrims from across the Mediterranean came to honor the goddess.

The sanctuary's sacred road, lined with votive offerings and statues, led worshippers to the temple, reinforcing the spiritual journey towards divine communion. The annual festival of Hera, featuring athletic competitions, processions, and sacrifices, celebrated both the religious and communal spirit of Samos.

The Tunnel of Eupalinos: Engineering Marvel

One of the most remarkable achievements of Samos was the Tunnel of Eupalinos, an extraordinary feat of ancient engineering. This underground aqueduct, designed by the engineer Eupalinos of Megara, provided a steady supply of fresh water to the city, solving the island's water shortage problem. The tunnel, carved through solid rock, stretched over a kilometer and was constructed from both ends simultaneously, an incredible testament to the precision and ingenuity of ancient Greek engineers.

The Tunnel of Eupalinos not only showcased the technical expertise of the Samian engineers but also ensured the prosperity and growth of the city by providing a reliable water source. This marvel of engineering remains one of the greatest achievements of ancient infrastructure and a symbol of human ingenuity.

Pythagoras: The Philosopher and Mathematician

Samos was the birthplace of Pythagoras, the legendary philosopher and mathematician whose contributions to geometry, music theory, and philosophy have left an indelible mark on human knowledge. Pythagoras's teachings, particularly the Pythagorean theorem, revolutionized mathematics and influenced subsequent generations of thinkers.

His philosophical school, the Pythagorean Brotherhood, combined rigorous mathematical study with mystical and ethical teachings, exploring the harmony and order of the cosmos. Pythagoras's legacy as a seeker of truth and harmony reflected the intellectual spirit of Samos, an island that valued knowledge and innovation.

The Samian Fleet: Masters of the Seas

Samos was renowned for its powerful navy and maritime prowess. The island's strategic location and advanced shipbuilding techniques allowed it to develop a formidable fleet that dominated the Aegean Sea. The Samian triremes, swift and agile warships, were a key factor in the island's military and commercial success.

The maritime strength of Samos enabled it to establish colonies, engage in trade, and protect its interests against rival city-states. The island's sailors and merchants forged connections across the Mediterranean, bringing wealth and cultural exchanges that enriched Samian society.

The Artistic Heritage: Craftsmanship and Beauty

Samos was a center of artistic excellence, known for its exquisite pottery, sculpture, and jewelry. The island's craftsmen were celebrated for their skill and creativity, producing works that reflected both the natural beauty of the island and the divine inspiration of the gods. The Samian pottery, with its intricate designs and vibrant colors, was highly prized and traded throughout the ancient world.

The island was also home to renowned sculptors like Rhoecus and Theodorus, who contributed to the development of Greek art and architecture. Their works, including monumental statues and temple decorations, showcased the artistic talent and cultural sophistication of Samos.

The Pythagoreion: A Cultural and Historical Hub

The ancient city of Pythagoreion, named after Pythagoras, was the cultural and political center of Samos. This bustling harbor town, with its impressive public buildings, temples, and theaters, was a microcosm of Samian society. The agora, or marketplace, was a hub of commercial activity and social interaction, where merchants, philosophers, and citizens mingled and exchanged ideas.

The town's theater, carved into the hillside, hosted dramatic performances and musical contests, reflecting the island's vibrant cultural life. The Pythagoreion also featured elaborate baths, sanctuaries, and public squares, creating a harmonious blend of utility, beauty, and spirituality.

The Myths and Legends: Echoes of the Divine

Samos was steeped in mythology, its name echoing through the tales of gods and heroes. The island was said to be the birthplace of Hera, and its sacred sites were imbued with her divine presence. The legends of the Argonauts, who stopped at Samos during their quest for the Golden Fleece, and the tales of the hero Ancaeus, who ruled the island, added to its rich mythological tapestry.

These stories, passed down through generations, reflected the deep connection between the island's inhabitants and the divine, creating a sense of wonder and reverence that permeated Samian culture.

The Decline and Rediscovery

Samos's influence waned with the rise of larger empires and shifting political landscapes. The island faced invasions and occupations, yet its spirit of resilience and innovation persisted. In modern times, archaeological excavations have uncovered the remnants of Samos's glorious past, revealing the grandeur of its temples, the ingenuity of its engineering, and the beauty of its art.

The rediscovery of the Tunnel of Eupalinos, the Heraion, and other historical sites has provided invaluable insights into the island's rich heritage and contributions to ancient civilization.

Key Events

1. **c. 3000 BCE** – Early Settlement: Samos is inhabited during the early Bronze Age, becoming an important center in the Aegean.
2. **c. 700-500 BCE** – Archaic Period: Samos flourishes as a major naval and commercial power under the rule of tyrants like Polycrates, known for its impressive engineering feats like the Tunnel of Eupalinos.
3. **c. 530 BCE** – Era of Polycrates: Samos reaches its peak under the tyrant Polycrates, becoming a center of culture, art, and science, and home

to the philosopher Pythagoras.

4. **c. 494 BCE** - Persian Conquest: Samos falls to the Persians after the Battle of Lade, but continues to thrive as a semi-autonomous state.

5. **c. 479 BCE** - Liberation: Samos joins the Delian League after the defeat of the Persians, playing a significant role in Athenian maritime dominance.

6. **c. 322 BCE** - Hellenistic Period: Samos is controlled by various Hellenistic rulers, continuing to be an important cultural and commercial center.

7. **c. 84 BCE** - Roman Period: Samos becomes part of the Roman Empire, maintaining its status as a prosperous island.

Eretria: The Gateway of Heroes and Mariners

The Coastal Haven of Innovation and Adventure

Nestled on the western shores of the island of Euboea, Eretria stood as a vibrant maritime city, where the blue waves of the Aegean Sea met the bustling activity of a thriving port. Known for its strategic location, rich cultural heritage, and storied past, Eretria was more than just a city; it was a gateway to adventure, exploration, and innovation. With its grand temples, advanced infrastructure, and legendary battles, Eretria remains a symbol of the spirit of ancient Greece—a blend of heroism, maritime prowess, and intellectual pursuit.

The Port of Eretria: Harbor of the Aegean

The port of Eretria was the lifeblood of the city, a bustling harbor that connected it to the wider Mediterranean world. Ships laden with goods from Egypt, Phoenicia, and the Greek mainland docked here, making Eretria a hub of commerce and cultural exchange. The city's skilled shipbuilders and sailors were renowned for their expertise, crafting vessels that ventured far and wide, exploring new territories and establishing trade routes.

The port was also a point of departure for Eretrian colonists, who founded settlements across the Mediterranean, spreading Eretrian culture and influence. These colonies, including the notable city of Pithekoussai (modern Ischia), became thriving centers of trade and innovation, reflecting Eretria's spirit of exploration and entrepreneurship.

The House of the Mosaics: Art and Elegance

One of the most remarkable discoveries in Eretria is the House of the Mosaics, an ancient residence adorned with exquisite mosaic floors that depict intricate scenes from mythology and daily life. These mosaics, crafted with colorful stones and glass, showcase the artistic talent and aesthetic sensibilities of the Eretrians. The scenes include depictions of the god Dionysus, intricate geometric patterns, and lively portrayals of marine life, reflecting the city's connection to both the divine and the natural world.

The House of the Mosaics is not just a testament to the artistic achievements of Eretria but also a window into the daily lives and cultural values of its inhabitants. The elegance and detail of the mosaics highlight the city's appreciation for beauty, storytelling, and craftsmanship.

The Temple of Apollo Daphnephoros: A Sanctuary of Light

At the heart of Eretria's spiritual life was the Temple of Apollo Daphnephoros, dedicated to Apollo, the god of light, music, and prophecy. This grand sanctuary, situated on a hill overlooking the city, was a center of worship and a symbol of Eretria's religious devotion. The temple's columns and altars were adorned with offerings and inscriptions, reflecting the deep connection between the Eretrians and their patron deity.

The annual festival of Daphnephoria, held in honor of Apollo, featured processions, music, and athletic competitions, celebrating both the divine and communal spirit of Eretria. The temple was not only a place of worship but also a gathering point for the community, where people came together to honor their gods and each other.

The Theater of Eretria: Stage of Culture and Drama

Eretria's theater, carved into the natural slope of a hill, was a cultural hub where citizens gathered to witness dramatic performances, musical contests, and public assemblies. The theater, with its stone seats and grand stage, provided a venue for the works of famous playwrights such as Aeschylus, Sophocles, and Euripides. These performances explored themes of heroism, fate, and morality, resonating deeply with the audience.

The theater also served as a space for civic engagement, where citizens could debate and discuss issues affecting their city. This blend of cultural and political life reflected Eretria's commitment to both artistic expression and democratic principles.

The Heroic Legacy: Battles and Warriors

Eretria's history is marked by tales of heroism and conflict, particularly during the Persian Wars. In 490 BCE, the city played a crucial role in the resistance against the Persian invasion. Despite being besieged and ultimately captured by the Persians, the bravery of the Eretrians became legendary, symbolizing their unyielding spirit and determination.

The city's warriors, known for their courage and skill, were celebrated in both local and pan-Hellenic traditions. The legacy of Eretria's resistance against overwhelming odds continues to inspire admiration and respect, highlighting the city's role in the broader narrative of Greek heroism.

The Philosophical Pursuit: Schools of Thought

Eretria was also a center of intellectual activity, home to the Eretrian school of philosophy founded by Menedemus in the 4th century BCE. This school emphasized ethics, logic, and natural philosophy, contributing to the rich intellectual tapestry of ancient Greece. The philosophers of Eretria engaged in dialogues and debates that explored the nature of existence, morality, and knowledge.

The city's intellectual legacy is reflected in its contributions to Greek thought and the enduring influence of its philosophers. Eretria's commitment to learning and wisdom underscored its cultural and intellectual vitality.

The Gymnasium and Palaestra: Training the Body and Mind

The gymnasium and palaestra of Eretria were essential facilities for the training of young men in both physical and intellectual pursuits. The gymnasium, with its spacious courtyards and training fields, provided a space for athletic exercises, while the palaestra focused on wrestling and other combat sports. These institutions were places of discipline and camaraderie, where the youth of Eretria honed their bodies and minds.

The rigorous training regimens and competitive spirit fostered in these venues were critical to the development of Eretrian athletes and warriors. The gymnasium and palaestra also served as centers of social interaction and education, reflecting the holistic approach to personal development in Eretrian society.

The Decline and Rediscovery

Eretria's fortunes fluctuated over the centuries, with periods of prosperity and decline influenced by political alliances, wars, and natural disasters. The city faced destruction during the Persian Wars and later conflicts but managed to rebuild and maintain its cultural and economic significance.

In modern times, archaeological excavations have uncovered the remnants of Eretria's rich past, revealing its grand temples, theaters, and mosaics. These discoveries have provided invaluable insights into the city's historical, cultural, and artistic achievements, allowing us to appreciate the legacy of this remarkable ancient city.

Key Events

1. **c. 1100 BCE** - Early Settlement: Eretria is established on the island of Euboea, growing into a significant maritime power.
2. **c. 700-600 BCE** - Archaic Period: Eretria becomes a major center of trade and colonization, founding colonies throughout the Mediterranean.

3. **c. 490 BCE** - Persian Wars: Eretria is destroyed by the Persians in retaliation for its support of the Ionian Revolt, but is later rebuilt.

4. **c. 480 BCE** - Battle of Salamis: Eretria contributes ships to the Greek fleet, playing a role in the decisive victory against the Persians.

5. **c. 431-404 BCE** - Peloponnesian War: Eretria is involved in the conflict, switching allegiances between Athens and Sparta.

6. **c. 338 BCE** - Macedonian Conquest: Eretria falls under Macedonian control after the Battle of Chaeronea.

7. **c. 146 BCE** - Roman Period: Eretria becomes part of the Roman Empire, continuing as a regional center of trade and culture.

Thessaloniki: The Crossroads of Empires

The Cosmopolitan Heart of the Aegean

Nestled along the Thermaic Gulf, where the blue waters of the Aegean Sea kiss the shores of Macedonia, lies Thessaloniki, a city that pulsated with the rhythms of diverse cultures, bustling trade, and political intrigue. Founded by King Cassander of Macedon in 315 BCE and named after his wife, Thessalonike, sister of Alexander the Great, Thessaloniki was more than a city; it was a melting pot of civilizations, a hub of commerce, and a beacon of intellectual and artistic brilliance.

The Via Egnatia: The Artery of Trade and Culture

Thessaloniki's strategic location along the Via Egnatia, the ancient Roman road that connected the Adriatic Sea to Byzantium (modern Istanbul), made it a vital artery of trade and cultural exchange. Merchants, soldiers, and travelers from across the Roman Empire and beyond passed through its gates, bringing with them goods, ideas, and stories.

The bustling markets of Thessaloniki offered a dazzling array of products from distant lands—silks from the East, spices from Arabia, grains from the fertile plains, and wines from the Mediterranean vineyards. The city's cosmopolitan atmosphere was a testament to its role as a crossroads where East met West, fostering a dynamic blend of traditions and innovations.

The White Tower: Guardian of the Harbor

One of Thessaloniki's most iconic landmarks is the White Tower, a cylindrical fortification that has stood sentinel over the city's harbor for centuries. Originally built by the Ottomans in the 15th century, the tower has served

297

various roles, from a defensive bastion to a notorious prison.

The White Tower, with its imposing presence and panoramic views, symbolizes Thessaloniki's resilience and strategic importance. It has witnessed the ebb and flow of empires, standing as a guardian over the city's rich maritime heritage and vibrant port life.

The Rotunda: A Monument of Transformation

The Rotunda, initially constructed as a mausoleum or temple by the Roman Emperor Galerius in the early 4th century CE, exemplifies Thessaloniki's capacity for transformation and adaptation. This massive circular building, with its thick walls and soaring dome, has served multiple religious purposes over the centuries—from a Christian church to an Islamic mosque and back to a church.

The Rotunda's interior is adorned with magnificent mosaics, depicting angelic figures and floral patterns, reflecting the artistic and spiritual aspirations of its creators. This monument stands as a testament to Thessaloniki's layered history and the city's ability to embrace and integrate diverse cultural influences.

The Arch of Galerius: Triumph and Glory

Adjacent to the Rotunda stands the Arch of Galerius, a grand triumphal arch erected to commemorate the victories of Emperor Galerius over the Persians. The arch, decorated with intricate reliefs depicting scenes of battle, victory, and imperial power, served as a monumental gateway into the heart of the city.

Walking beneath the arch, one could feel the grandeur of Roman engineering and the pride of Thessaloniki's citizens in their imperial connections. The Arch of Galerius remains a powerful symbol of the city's historical significance and its role in the broader narrative of the Roman Empire.

The Byzantine Walls: Fortresses of Faith and Defense

Thessaloniki's Byzantine Walls, encircling the upper part of the city, are a testament to its strategic importance and turbulent history. Built in the late 4th century CE, these formidable fortifications protected the city from invasions and preserved its status as a key center of the Byzantine Empire.

The walls, interspersed with towers and gates, offered a panoramic view of the city and the sea, reflecting the dual role of Thessaloniki as a fortress of defense and a beacon of faith. Within these walls, the city's religious and cultural life flourished, with numerous churches, monasteries, and public buildings contributing to its vibrant urban landscape.

The Church of Hagios Demetrios: A Sanctuary of Miracles

The Church of Hagios Demetrios, dedicated to the city's patron saint, is one of Thessaloniki's most revered religious sites. Built over the tomb of Saint Demetrius, a Roman soldier martyred for his Christian faith, the church has been a pilgrimage destination for centuries.

The basilica's interior, with its stunning mosaics, frescoes, and intricate architectural details, creates a serene and sacred atmosphere. The crypt, where Saint Demetrius was believed to have been imprisoned and martyred, is a place of reflection and veneration. The church's enduring significance as a center of spiritual devotion underscores Thessaloniki's role as a sanctuary of miracles and faith.

The Agora: Hub of Civic Life

The ancient Agora of Thessaloniki was the bustling heart of the city's civic and commercial life. This expansive marketplace and public space hosted a variety of activities, from trade and legal proceedings to social gatherings and political discussions. The remains of the Agora, including the Roman forum, the Odeon, and the public baths, reveal the vibrant and multifaceted nature of Thessaloniki's urban life.

The Agora was a microcosm of Thessaloniki's dynamic society, reflecting its economic prosperity, cultural diversity, and civic engagement. It was a place where citizens and visitors alike could experience the city's rich tapestry of life and interaction.

The Intellectual and Artistic Hub

Thessaloniki was not only a center of commerce and politics but also a hub of intellectual and artistic achievement. The city's schools and academies attracted scholars, philosophers, and artists from across the Greek and Roman worlds. It was a place where ideas were exchanged, and knowledge was cultivated, contributing to the rich intellectual heritage of the ancient Mediterranean.

The city's artistic contributions were equally significant, with its churches, public buildings, and private homes adorned with exquisite mosaics, sculptures, and frescoes. Thessaloniki's commitment to art and learning underscored its role as a cultural beacon and a center of innovation.

The Decline and Renaissance

Thessaloniki experienced periods of decline and resurgence, influenced by invasions, political changes, and economic shifts. Despite these challenges, the city's resilience and strategic importance ensured its continued significance. The Ottoman period brought new cultural influences and architectural styles, adding to the city's diverse heritage.

In modern times, Thessaloniki has emerged as a vibrant and dynamic city, preserving its historical legacy while embracing contemporary developments. The city's rich past is celebrated through its well-preserved monuments, museums, and cultural institutions, offering a glimpse into its storied history and enduring spirit.

Key Events

1. **c. 315 BCE** - Founding by Cassander: Thessaloniki is founded by King Cassander of Macedon, named after his wife Thessalonike, the sister of Alexander the Great.

2. **c. 168 BCE** - Roman Conquest: Thessaloniki becomes part of the Roman Empire and quickly rises to prominence as a major hub on the Via Egnatia, a key Roman road connecting the Adriatic Sea to Byzantium.

3. **c. 50 CE** - Early Christianity: Thessaloniki becomes an important center for early Christianity, with Paul the Apostle writing letters to the local Christian community (the Epistles to the Thessalonians).

4. **c. 300-500 CE** - Byzantine Period: Thessaloniki becomes the second most important city in the Byzantine Empire, known for its wealth, strategic location, and impressive architecture, including the Rotunda and the Hagios Demetrios.

VI

Italy

Rome: The Eternal City

The Heartbeat of an Empire

Straddling the seven hills along the banks of the Tiber River, Rome stood as the pulsating heart of an empire that stretched across three continents. Known as the Eternal City, Rome was more than just a metropolis; it was the epicenter of political power, cultural innovation, and architectural grandeur. With its sprawling forums, monumental structures, and teeming streets, Rome at its height around 100 BCE was a city of a million souls, embodying the triumphs and tribulations of the ancient world.

The Forum: The Nerve Center of the Republic

At the core of Rome's vibrant public life was the Roman Forum, a sprawling plaza that served as the hub of political, commercial, and social activity. The Forum was a microcosm of Roman society, where senators debated, merchants traded, and citizens gathered to hear the latest news and proclamations. Surrounded by grand temples, basilicas, and public buildings, the Forum was the beating heart of the Republic.

The Senate House, or Curia, resonated with the voices of Rome's most powerful men, who shaped the destiny of the Republic within its walls. Nearby, the Rostra, a large platform adorned with the prows of captured ships, served as the stage for orators to address the populace. The Temple of Saturn, the Basilica Julia, and the Arch of Septimius Severus stood as testaments to Rome's architectural and civic achievements.

The Colosseum: The Arena of Spectacles

Just a short walk from the Forum, the Colosseum, though not completed until 80 CE, was envisioned during the height of the Republic and stands as a symbol of Roman engineering and entertainment. This colossal amphitheater, capable of seating over 50,000 spectators, hosted gladiatorial games, animal hunts, and mock naval battles, captivating the public with its grand displays of spectacle and valor.

The Colosseum's intricate network of vaults, arches, and subterranean passages showcased Roman architectural ingenuity. The roar of the crowd, the clash of weapons, and the cries of the combatants filled the air, creating an atmosphere of excitement and drama that defined the Roman love for grand spectacles.

The Aqueducts: Lifelines of the City

Rome's unparalleled system of aqueducts was a marvel of ancient engineering, supplying the city with a steady flow of fresh water from distant sources. These monumental structures, with their graceful arches spanning valleys and hills, brought water to public baths, fountains, and private homes, ensuring the health and well-being of Rome's burgeoning population.

The Aqua Appia, Aqua Anio Vetus, and Aqua Marcia were among the earliest and most significant aqueducts, reflecting the city's commitment to public infrastructure and urban planning. The continuous flow of water into the city was a testament to the ingenuity and foresight of Roman engineers, who created a network that sustained the city's growth and vitality.

The Via Appia: The Queen of Roads

The Via Appia, known as the "Queen of Roads," was one of the most important and strategically significant highways of the Roman Republic. Stretching from Rome to the port city of Brundisium, this paved road facilitated trade, military movement, and communication across the empire. The Via Appia was a lifeline that connected Rome to its provinces, enabling the swift movement of armies, goods, and information.

Lined with tombs, villas, and waystations, the Via Appia was a bustling thoroughfare that showcased the reach and efficiency of Roman infrastructure. The road's durability and design, with its carefully laid stones and drainage systems, reflected the engineering prowess and practical genius of the Romans.

The Baths of Caracalla: Sanctuaries of Leisure

The concept of grand public baths was well-established during the height of the Republic, setting the stage for later constructions like the Baths of Caracalla, which became a symbol of Roman luxury and social life. These expansive bath complexes, with their soaring arches, mosaic floors, and elaborate decorations, provided a place for relaxation, exercise, and socialization.

The baths featured hot and cold pools, steam rooms, exercise courts, and libraries, creating a multifunctional space that catered to the needs of Rome's diverse populace. The baths were more than just a place for cleansing; they were social and cultural centers where citizens of all classes could gather, converse, and unwind.

The Pantheon: A Temple to All Gods

The Pantheon, originally constructed by Marcus Agrippa and later rebuilt by Emperor Hadrian, is a masterpiece of Roman architecture and a symbol of the city's religious diversity and architectural innovation. The Pantheon's massive dome, with its central oculus allowing sunlight to flood the interior, remains one of the most impressive engineering feats of the ancient world.

Dedicated to all the gods of Rome, the Pantheon's interior space, with its harmonious proportions and marble-clad walls, created an atmosphere of divine presence and human achievement. The building's enduring beauty and structural brilliance reflect Rome's ability to blend religious reverence with architectural excellence.

The Insulae: Urban Living

In the bustling neighborhoods of Rome, the insulae, or apartment buildings, housed the majority of the city's population. These multi-story structures, often cramped and poorly constructed, reflected the challenges of urban living in a rapidly growing metropolis. Despite their flaws, the insulae were vibrant communities where people lived, worked, and interacted daily.

The contrast between the insulae and the grand villas of the wealthy highlighted the social stratification of Roman society. However, the proximity of diverse social classes within the city created a dynamic and interconnected urban environment that fueled the economic and cultural vitality of Rome.

The Roman Forum: Political Powerhouse

The Roman Forum was the epicenter of political life, where the Senate convened and monumental decisions were made. The Comitium, an open-air public meeting space, was where citizens gathered to vote and engage in political discourse. The Temple of Concord, dedicated to harmony between the patricians and plebeians, symbolized the city's political aspirations and challenges.

The presence of triumphal arches, such as the Arch of Titus, commemorating military victories, underscored Rome's imperial power and its ability to integrate conquered peoples into its civic and cultural life. The Forum was a living testament to Rome's political complexity and its evolving identity as a republic transitioning to an empire.

The Palatine Hill: The Seat of Power

The Palatine Hill, one of the seven hills of Rome, was the traditional seat of power and the legendary birthplace of Romulus, the city's founder. By the late Republic, the Palatine had become the preferred residence of Rome's elite, including influential figures like Cicero and Julius Caesar. The hill's palatial residences, gardens, and temples reflected the wealth and influence of Rome's ruling class.

The Domus Aurea, Nero's opulent palace, later built on the slopes of the Palatine, epitomized the grandeur and excess of imperial architecture. The Palatine Hill's blend of myth, history, and luxury made it a symbol of Rome's enduring legacy and its connection to the city's ancient roots.

Key Events

1. **c. 753 BCE** - Founding of Rome: According to legend, Rome is founded by Romulus and Remus on the Palatine Hill.
2. **c. 509 BCE** - Establishment of the Roman Republic: Rome transitions from a monarchy to a republic, with the establishment of the Senate and consuls.
3. **c. 390 BCE** - Sack of Rome by the Gauls: Rome is sacked by the Gauls, leading to significant military and political reforms.
4. **c. 264-146 BCE** - Punic Wars: Rome engages in a series of wars against Carthage, emerging as the dominant power in the western Mediterranean.
5. **c. 44 BCE** - Assassination of Julius Caesar: The assassination leads to the end of the Roman Republic and the rise of the Roman Empire.
6. **c. 27 BCE** - Augustus Becomes Emperor: The Roman Empire is established under Augustus, marking the beginning of the Pax Romana.
7. **c. 64 CE** - Great Fire of Rome: A major fire devastates much of the city, leading to significant rebuilding efforts by Emperor Nero.
8. **c. 312 CE** - Constantine's Conversion to Christianity: Rome begins its transformation into a Christian empire.

9. **c. 410 CE** - Sack of Rome by the Visigoths: Rome is sacked by the Visigoths under Alaric, marking the decline of the Western Roman Empire.

10. **c. 476 CE** - Fall of the Western Roman Empire: The last Roman emperor, Romulus Augustulus, is deposed, marking the traditional end of ancient Rome.

Tarquinia: The Painted Tombs of Etruria

The City of the Dead and the Cradle of the Etruscans

Perched on a plateau overlooking the fertile plains of central Italy, where the Tyrrhenian Sea sparkles in the distance and the hills are dotted with ancient olive groves, lies Tarquinia, a city that was once the beating heart of the Etruscan civilization. Known to the ancient world as Tarchuna, Tarquinia was more than just a city; it was a cultural and religious center, a place where the living and the dead were intricately connected. With its vibrant painted tombs, rich artistic heritage, and deep ties to the mysteries of life and death, Tarquinia remains a symbol of the enigmatic and enduring legacy of the Etruscans—a civilization that influenced Rome and left its mark on the very fabric of Italian history.

The Painted Tombs: Windows into the Afterlife

The most iconic feature of Tarquinia is its necropolis, a vast city of the dead where the tombs of Etruscan nobles are adorned with some of the most exquisite wall paintings in the ancient world. These painted tombs, each a masterpiece in its own right, provide a vivid glimpse into the beliefs, customs, and daily life of the Etruscans. Unlike the stark and somber tombs of other ancient cultures, the tombs of Tarquinia are filled with color, movement, and life.

The walls of these tombs are alive with scenes of banquets, dances, and hunts, depicting a world where the joys of life continue in the afterlife. The Tomb of the Leopards, with its joyful depictions of feasting and music, and the Tomb of the Augurs, with its mysterious religious rites, are among the most famous, showcasing the Etruscans' belief in the continuity of life after death. The vibrant frescoes, with their rich colors and dynamic compositions, offer a window into a world where the line between the living and the dead was fluid, and where death was seen not as an end, but as a transition to another form of existence. The painted tombs of Tarquinia are more than just burial sites; they are portals to the Etruscan soul, preserving the essence of a civilization that celebrated life in all its forms.

The Etruscan Aristocracy: Lords of the Italian Hills

Tarquinia was one of the most powerful and influential cities of the Etruscan League, a confederation of city-states that dominated central Italy before the rise of Rome. The city's aristocracy, known for their wealth, power, and sophisticated tastes, were the lords of the Italian hills, overseeing vast estates and commanding respect across the region. These noble families built lavish tombs, commissioned intricate works of art, and played a crucial role in the religious and political life of the Etruscan civilization.

The wealth and influence of Tarquinia's aristocracy were evident in the city's grand temples, public buildings, and the fine craftsmanship of its artifacts. The Etruscan elites were patrons of the arts, and their support led to the flourishing of a unique artistic style that combined influences from Greece, the Near East, and native Italic traditions. The aristocracy of Tarquinia were not just rulers; they were custodians of a rich cultural heritage, preserving and transmitting the values and beliefs of their ancestors through the generations. Their legacy is still visible in the art, architecture, and religious practices that have survived the millennia, offering a glimpse into the world of the Etruscan nobility.

The Temple of Ara della Regina: A Sanctuary of the Gods

One of the most significant religious sites in Tarquinia was the Temple of Ara della Regina, a grand sanctuary dedicated to the Etruscan gods. This temple, perched on a hill overlooking the city, was the largest Etruscan temple ever discovered, reflecting the city's importance as a religious center. The temple was adorned with intricate terracotta sculptures, including the famous winged horses that once graced its roof, and was a place where the Etruscans performed rituals, offered sacrifices, and sought the favor of the gods.

The Temple of Ara della Regina was not just a religious site; it was a symbol of the city's connection to the divine and its role as a spiritual hub for the Etruscan people. The temple's architecture, with its imposing columns and richly decorated pediments, was a testament to the skill and creativity of Etruscan builders and artists. The sanctuary was a place where the sacred and the secular intersected, where the city's leaders sought to align their rule with the will of the gods, ensuring the prosperity and protection of Tarquinia. The Temple of Ara della Regina was a beacon of faith and power, a place where the Etruscans connected with their gods and affirmed their place in the cosmic order.

The Tarquin Kings: The Etruscan Legacy in Rome

Tarquinia's influence extended far beyond its own borders, reaching into the heart of Rome itself. The city is famously associated with the Tarquin dynasty, a line of Etruscan kings who ruled Rome in the 6th century BCE before the establishment of the Roman Republic. The most famous of these was Tarquin the Proud, the last king of Rome, whose expulsion led to the founding of the Republic and the end of Etruscan dominance over the city.

The legacy of the Tarquin kings is a complex one, marked by both their contributions to the development of Rome's infrastructure and culture, and the tyranny that eventually led to their downfall. Under their rule, Rome saw the construction of major public works, such as the Cloaca Maxima (Rome's great sewer) and the Temple of Jupiter on the Capitoline Hill, which were influenced by Etruscan engineering and religious practices. The Tarquin kings also brought Etruscan art, religion, and governance to Rome, leaving an indelible mark on the city's early development. The story of the Tarquins is a reminder of the deep connections between Rome and its Etruscan neighbors, and of the ways in which Tarquinia helped shape the destiny of one of history's greatest civilizations.

The Fall and Enduring Legacy of Tarquinia

Tarquinia's decline began with the rise of Rome, as the expanding Roman Republic gradually absorbed the Etruscan city-states into its growing empire. By the 4th century BCE, Tarquinia had lost much of its political power, and the city eventually became a Roman colony. Despite its decline, the legacy of Tarquinia endured, particularly through its artistic and cultural contributions, which continued to influence Roman art, religion, and architecture.

In modern times, the ruins of Tarquinia, with its painted tombs, ancient temples, and remnants of a once-great city, have become a UNESCO World Heritage site, attracting scholars and visitors who seek to uncover the secrets of the Etruscans. The city's enduring legacy is evident in its art, its connection to Rome, and its role as a cultural and religious center that helped shape the early history of Italy. Tarquinia remains a symbol of the enigmatic and sophisticated civilization that once flourished in the Italian peninsula, a reminder of the rich and complex history that lies beneath the surface of modern Italy.

Key Events

1. **c. 800 BCE** - Founding and Early Development: Tarquinia (Tarchuna) is established as one of the major cities of the Etruscan civilization, known for its rich culture and art.
2. **c. 7th-6th centuries BCE** - Etruscan Kings: Tarquinia becomes a powerful city-state, possibly the origin of the Tarquin kings who later ruled Rome.
3. **c. 600-500 BCE** - Height of Etruscan Power: Tarquinia thrives as a major political, religious, and cultural center in Etruria, known for its elaborate tombs and wall paintings.
4. **c. 509 BCE** - Fall of the Tarquins in Rome: The last Etruscan king, Tarquin the Proud, is overthrown in Rome, marking the beginning of the Roman Republic and the decline of Etruscan influence.

5. **c. 396 BCE** - Roman Conquest of Veii: The Roman conquest of Veii, a neighboring Etruscan city, signals the beginning of Roman expansion into Etruria, leading to increased pressure on Tarquinia.

6. **c. 300 BCE** - Decline under Roman Rule: Tarquinia falls under Roman control, gradually losing its autonomy and significance as Roman influence spreads throughout Italy.

Capua: The Gateway of Gladiators and Grandeur

The Jewel of Campania and the Heart of Roman Indulgence

In the fertile plains of southern Italy, where the rolling hills of Campania meet the vast expanse of the Mediterranean, lies Capua, a city renowned for its wealth, culture, and the brutal spectacles that captivated the ancient world. More than just a city, Capua was a vibrant crossroads of luxury and power, a place where the pleasures of life met the harsh realities of the Roman Empire. With its grand amphitheater, lavish villas, and strategic importance, Capua remains a symbol of the duality of Roman life—a city of indulgence and spectacle, where the joys of the elite intertwined with the struggles of the enslaved.

The Amphitheater of Capua: The Forge of Gladiators

The most iconic structure in Capua was its grand amphitheater, second in size only to the Colosseum in Rome. This colossal arena was the beating heart of the city, where thousands gathered to witness the fierce battles of gladiators, exotic animal hunts, and other spectacles that defined Roman entertainment. The Amphitheater of Capua was not just a venue for bloodsport; it was a place where the power of the Roman state was displayed in all its glory, where life and death hung in the balance with each clash of swords.

Capua's amphitheater was also famously known as the birthplace of Spartacus, the gladiator who would go on to lead one of the most significant slave revolts in Roman history. Trained in the gladiatorial school (ludus) of Capua, Spartacus and his fellow gladiators revolted against their brutal masters, sparking a rebellion that threatened the very heart of the Roman Republic. The amphitheater, once a place of spectacle and entertainment, became a symbol of resistance and the human desire for freedom. The legacy of the gladiators of Capua, forged in the heat of battle, lives on as a testament to the complex and often brutal nature of Roman society.

The Via Appia: The Lifeline of Capua

Capua's strategic location on the Via Appia, one of the most important roads in the Roman Empire, made it a vital hub of trade, military logistics, and cultural exchange. The Via Appia, known as the "Queen of Roads," connected Rome to the southern reaches of Italy, and Capua was a key stopping point along this ancient highway. The city's position allowed it to thrive as a center of commerce, where goods from across the Mediterranean flowed through its markets, enriching its citizens and enhancing its influence.

The Via Appia also made Capua a crucial military base, serving as a staging ground for Roman legions on their way to campaigns in the south. The city's wealth and strategic importance often made it a target during times of conflict, as various powers sought to control this key gateway to the Italian peninsula. The Via Appia was more than just a road; it was the lifeline of Capua, sustaining its prosperity and ensuring its place as a pivotal city in the Roman world.

The Villas of Capua: A Paradise of Luxury

Capua was famous throughout the Roman Empire for its opulent villas, which were the epitome of luxury and refinement. The wealthy elites of Rome and beyond built their estates in Capua, drawn by the region's fertile land, mild climate, and the city's vibrant cultural scene. These villas were not just homes; they were symbols of status and power, designed to showcase the wealth and taste of their owners.

The villas of Capua were adorned with exquisite mosaics, frescoes, and gardens that reflected the finest traditions of Roman art and architecture. They were places of leisure and indulgence, where the elite could retreat from the pressures of public life and enjoy the pleasures of the countryside.

The baths, dining rooms, and private theaters of these villas were scenes of lavish banquets, intellectual gatherings, and artistic performances, making Capua a center of cultural life as well as a retreat for the powerful. The villas of Capua were a paradise of luxury, a testament to the heights of Roman civilization and the pursuit of pleasure in all its forms.

The Temple of Mater Matuta: A Sanctuary of the Dawn

Capua was also a city of deep religious significance, home to the Temple of Mater Matuta, the goddess of the dawn and childbirth. This temple, one of the most important religious sites in the city, was a place where the people of Capua sought the blessings of the goddess for new beginnings and the protection of their families. The temple was a sanctuary of hope and renewal, where the light of the dawn was seen as a symbol of life's potential and the promise of the future.

The worship of Mater Matuta in Capua reflected the city's connection to the cycles of nature and the importance of fertility and growth in both the land and the community. The temple was not just a place of worship; it was a gathering point for the city's people, where rituals and festivals reinforced the bonds of society and the shared values of the community. The Temple of Mater Matuta was a beacon of faith and continuity in a city often defined by its indulgence and spectacle.

The Fall and Legacy of Capua

Capua's fortunes began to decline as the Roman Empire faced internal strife and external threats. The city's strategic importance made it a target during the Social War and later during the civil wars that plagued the late Republic. By the time of the Empire, Capua had lost much of its former glory, though it remained an important regional center.

The fall of Capua was hastened by the shifting tides of history, but its legacy endured through its contributions to Roman culture, its role in the life of the Empire, and its association with the story of Spartacus. The ruins of Capua, including its amphitheater and the remnants of its grand villas, still bear witness to a city that once stood at the crossroads of power and pleasure, a place where the grandeur of Rome met the struggles of its people.

In modern times, the site of ancient Capua continues to be a place of historical interest, drawing visitors who seek to understand the complexities of Roman life and the enduring impact of this once-great city. The legacy of Capua is a reminder of the heights of Roman civilization and the intricate web of power, culture, and humanity that defined the ancient world.

Key Events

1. **c. 600 BCE** - Founding and Early Settlement: Capua is established by the Etruscans, becoming a significant city in Campania.
2. **c. 424 BCE** - Conquest by the Samnites: Capua is captured by the Samnites, who make it one of the most prosperous cities in southern Italy.
3. **c. 343-341 BCE** - First Samnite War: Capua appeals to Rome for protection against the Samnites, leading to its alliance with Rome and its status as a Roman ally.
4. **c. 73 BCE** - Spartacus' Revolt: Capua becomes the starting point of the Spartacus-led slave revolt, as the gladiators break out of the city's school and incite a rebellion against Rome.
5. **c. 216 BCE** - Second Punic War: After the Battle of Cannae, Capua defects to Hannibal, becoming a base for the Carthaginian forces in Italy. The city is later recaptured and punished by Rome.
6. **c. 91-88 BCE** - Social War: Capua is involved in the Social War (War of the Allies) against Rome, seeking Roman citizenship and rights for its people.
7. **c. 1st century CE** - Roman Prosperity: Capua thrives as a major city under Roman rule, known for its wealth, gladiatorial games, and luxury.

Pompeii: The City Frozen in Fire

The Eternal Echo of a Vanished World

Nestled beneath the shadow of Mount Vesuvius, where the fertile plains of Campania meet the shimmering waters of the Bay of Naples, lies Pompeii—a city whose story is etched in ash and stone. More than just a city, Pompeii is a haunting tableau of daily life in the Roman Empire, frozen in time by the cataclysmic eruption of 79 CE. With its vibrant streets, grand villas, and poignant remnants of its final moments, Pompeii remains a symbol of the fragility of human existence, a city where the ordinary and the extraordinary collided in a single, catastrophic event. It is a place where the past speaks in whispers, preserved in the silence of volcanic ash.

The Streets of Pompeii: Life Before the Ashes Fell

The streets of Pompeii were the arteries of a bustling Roman town, where the sounds of commerce, laughter, and conversation filled the air. These streets, paved with volcanic stone, were lined with shops, taverns, and workshops, each a testament to the vitality of urban life. The forum, the heart of the city, was a hive of activity, where citizens gathered to debate, trade, and worship in the shadow of grand temples and public buildings.

Walking through Pompeii's streets today is like stepping into a time capsule, where the traces of daily life are etched into the very fabric of the city. The grooves worn into the stone by the passage of countless carts, the graffiti scrawled on walls, and the remains of half-eaten loaves of bread in abandoned bakeries all speak to a city that was vibrant and alive right up until the moment it was engulfed by ash. The streets of Pompeii are more than just pathways; they are the veins of a city that still pulses with the echoes of its lost inhabitants, a place where the mundane details of life are preserved in the most extraordinary way.

The Villas of Pompeii: Grandeur in the Face of Tragedy

Pompeii was a city of both the wealthy and the working class, and nowhere is the former more evident than in its grand villas. These luxurious homes, adorned with intricate frescoes, mosaics, and gardens, were the residences of Pompeii's elite, who lived in opulence amidst the beauty of Roman art and architecture. The Villa of the Mysteries, with its stunning frescoes depicting mysterious Dionysian rituals, and the House of the Faun, home to the famous Alexander Mosaic, are among the most remarkable examples of these grandiose estates.

These villas were more than just homes; they were statements of power and prestige, designed to impress guests and showcase the owner's wealth and cultural sophistication. The frescoes that adorn their walls are not merely decorations; they are windows into the minds and tastes of their inhabitants, reflecting the religious, mythological, and daily themes that were important to Roman society. The gardens, filled with statues and fountains, provided a serene retreat from the bustling city outside, a place where the elite could relax and entertain amidst nature's beauty. Yet, for all their grandeur, these villas are also poignant reminders of the fragility of human life, as they stand empty, their owners long since buried under the ash that preserves their homes.

The Forum and Public Baths: The Heartbeat of a Roman City

The forum of Pompeii was the city's political, religious, and social center, a bustling square where the life of the city converged. Surrounded by important buildings such as the basilica, the temple of Jupiter, and the macellum (market), the forum was where decisions were made, justice was administered, and citizens gathered to worship and socialize. The public baths, another key feature of Roman urban life, were places of relaxation and hygiene, where the people of Pompeii could cleanse themselves, both physically and socially, in the communal waters.

These public spaces were more than just functional; they were the heartbeat of the city, where the rhythms of daily life were played out in full view. The forum was where the city's pulse could be felt most strongly, with its open-air meetings, religious festivals, and market days filling the space with noise and activity. The public baths, with their complex heating systems and beautifully decorated rooms, were places where people from all walks of life could come together, reinforcing the sense of community that was central to Roman urban living. The forum and baths of Pompeii are more than just ruins; they are the remnants of a vibrant civic life that was suddenly and tragically interrupted.

The Temples of Pompeii: Sanctuaries of the Gods

Religion played a central role in the life of Pompeii, and its temples were the sacred spaces where the divine was honored and appeased. The temple of Apollo, one of the city's oldest, stood as a testament to the enduring worship of the god of prophecy and healing. The temple of Jupiter, dominating the forum, was a focal point of state religion, where the city's leaders sought the favor of the king of the gods. The temple of Isis, an Egyptian goddess whose cult had spread throughout the Roman Empire, reflected the cosmopolitan nature of Pompeii's religious life.

These temples were not just places of worship; they were symbols of the city's connection to the divine and its integration into the broader religious and cultural world of the Roman Empire. The rituals performed within their walls, the offerings laid on their altars, and the festivals held in their honor were all expressions of a belief system that sought to maintain harmony between the gods and the community. The temples of Pompeii are more than just ruins; they are the echoes of prayers and invocations, the silent witnesses to a faith that was as integral to the city's identity as its streets and buildings.

The Plaster Casts: The Ghosts of Pompeii

Perhaps the most haunting aspect of Pompeii's legacy is the plaster casts of its victims, created by filling the voids left in the ash by decomposed bodies with plaster. These casts, which capture the final moments of the city's inhabitants, offer a deeply personal and visceral connection to the tragedy that befell Pompeii. The figures of men, women, and children, caught in their final acts of life—cowering, running, or embracing—are frozen in time, a stark reminder of the suddenness and terror of the eruption.

These casts are more than just representations of death; they are the preserved emotions and stories of individuals who lived, loved, and ultimately perished in Pompeii. Each cast tells a story, whether it is of a family seeking refuge, a person shielding themselves from the falling ash, or a pet curled up in its final sleep. The plaster casts of Pompeii are the city's ghosts, the tangible remains of lives interrupted, and they speak to us across the millennia with a power and immediacy that no written record could convey.

The Legacy of Pompeii: A City That Lives On

The destruction of Pompeii was not the end of its story; rather, it marked the beginning of a new chapter in which the city would become a symbol of both human vulnerability and the enduring power of memory. Rediscovered in the 18th century, Pompeii has since become one of the world's most important archaeological sites, offering an unparalleled glimpse into the daily life of the Roman Empire. The city's ruins, preserved by the very catastrophe that destroyed it, have provided invaluable insights into Roman art, architecture, and society, making Pompeii a key to understanding the ancient world.

Today, Pompeii continues to captivate and educate, drawing visitors and scholars from around the globe who come to walk its streets, explore its buildings, and reflect on the lives that were lived there. The legacy of Pompeii is not just one of tragedy; it is also one of resilience and the enduring human desire to remember, learn, and connect with the past. Pompeii lives on, not only in the ruins that stand as a testament to its history but also in the stories and lessons it continues to impart to the modern world.

Key Events

1. **c. 7th-6th centuries BCE** - Early Settlement: Pompeii is founded by the Oscans, an Italic people. It becomes a small agricultural settlement in the region of Campania.
2. **c. 525-474 BCE** - Etruscan Influence: Pompeii comes under the influence of the Etruscans, who expand the city and fortify it.
3. **c. 474 BCE** - Samnite Conquest: Pompeii is conquered by the Samnites, an Italic tribe. Under Samnite control, the city grows in size and importance.
4. **c. 310 BCE** - Roman Alliance: Pompeii becomes an ally of Rome after the Second Samnite War. Although not yet a Roman colony, it falls under Roman influence.
5. **c. 80 BCE** - Roman Colony: After the Social War (91-88 BCE), Pompeii is formally established as a Roman colony by Sulla. It is settled by veterans of the Roman army and undergoes significant urban development.
6. **c. 1st century BCE** - Flourishing Period: Pompeii thrives as a prosperous Roman city, with the construction of grand public buildings, theaters, baths, temples, and villas. It becomes a popular resort for

wealthy Romans.

7. **62 CE** - Earthquake: A major earthquake strikes Pompeii, causing widespread damage. Reconstruction efforts are underway when the city meets its ultimate fate.

8. **24-25 August 79 CE** - Eruption of Mount Vesuvius: Pompeii is buried under volcanic ash and pumice during the catastrophic eruption of Mount Vesuvius. The city, along with nearby Herculaneum and other towns, is completely destroyed. The eruption preserves buildings, artifacts, and even the bodies of the inhabitants, providing a unique snapshot of Roman life.

VII

Iran

Susa: The Jewel of the East

The Eternal City of Empires

Set amidst the fertile plains of the Khuzestan province in modern-day Iran, where the Karkheh and Dez Rivers converge, lies Susa, a city that gleamed with the brilliance of successive empires and civilizations. Known as the jewel of the East, Susa was more than a mere city; it was a crucible of cultures, a center of political power, and a beacon of architectural and artistic grandeur. With its grand palaces, bustling markets, and storied past, Susa remains a symbol of the enduring legacy of human achievement and cultural fusion.

The Palace of Darius: A Testament to Achaemenid Splendor

At the heart of Susa stood the grand palace of Darius the Great, a monumental complex that epitomized the opulence and architectural prowess of the Achaemenid Empire. Built around 521 BCE, the palace was adorned with intricate bas-reliefs, colossal columns, and luxurious gardens, reflecting the empire's wealth and artistic achievements.

The Apadana, or audience hall, was the centerpiece of the palace, where Darius received emissaries from across the known world. Its grand staircase, decorated with carvings of tribute-bearing delegations, showcased the empire's vast reach and the diversity of its subjects. The palace was not only a residence but also a symbol of imperial power and cultural sophistication.

The Ziggurat of Chogha Zanbil: A Sacred Mountain

Near Susa, the ancient ziggurat of Chogha Zanbil stood as a testament to the religious and architectural legacy of the Elamite civilization. This massive terraced structure, built around 1250 BCE, was dedicated to the god Inshushinak and served as a focal point of religious worship and pilgrimage.

The ziggurat's towering height and its intricate brickwork, decorated with glazed tiles and inscribed with cuneiform texts, reflected the Elamites' devotion and engineering skill. The site was surrounded by temples, palaces, and tombs, creating a sacred landscape that embodied the spiritual and cultural identity of the Elamites.

The Market of Susa: A Melting Pot of Commerce

Susa's bustling markets were a microcosm of the city's vibrant and cosmopolitan nature. Merchants from across the Persian Empire and beyond converged in Susa, bringing goods such as spices from India, gold from Lydia, textiles from Egypt, and pottery from Greece. The market was a place of vibrant exchange, where traders haggled, craftsmen showcased their wares, and ideas flowed freely.

The city's strategic location on the Royal Road, the ancient highway that connected the Achaemenid capitals, further cemented its status as a hub of commerce and cultural exchange. The market of Susa was not just a center of economic activity but also a space where diverse cultures and traditions met and mingled.

The Royal Road: The Artery of an Empire

The Royal Road, stretching over 2,500 kilometers from Sardis to Susa, was a marvel of ancient engineering and logistics. This well-maintained network facilitated the swift movement of troops, officials, and goods across the vast Persian Empire. Relay stations along the route provided fresh horses and provisions, ensuring that messages and travelers could cover the distance in record time.

The road was more than just a transportation route; it was the lifeline of the empire, connecting its far-flung provinces and enabling the centralized administration that characterized Achaemenid rule. Susa, as a terminus of the Royal Road, was a vital nexus of communication and control.

The Hanging Gardens of Susa: A Paradise on Earth

The palatial grounds of Susa were renowned for their hanging gardens, a series of terraced landscapes filled with exotic plants, flowing water, and shaded walkways. These gardens were a testament to the Persian love for nature and horticultural excellence. They provided a serene retreat for the royal family and their guests, offering a space for relaxation and contemplation.

The gardens were meticulously designed to create a sense of harmony and tranquility, reflecting the Persian ideal of paradise. The combination of lush greenery, intricate water features, and architectural elements created a sensory experience that was both luxurious and spiritually uplifting.

The Inscriptions of Darius: Voices from the Past

The palace of Darius and other monuments in Susa were adorned with inscriptions that proclaimed the achievements and divine favor of the Achaemenid kings. These inscriptions, carved in Old Persian, Elamite, and Babylonian, provided a rich historical record of the empire's conquests, administrative practices, and religious beliefs.

The famous inscription on the Darius Canal, which connected the Nile to the Red Sea, celebrated the engineering prowess and visionary leadership of Darius. These texts were not only propaganda tools but also invaluable sources of historical and cultural knowledge, offering insights into the values and worldview of the Achaemenid rulers.

The Fall and Resilience

Susa experienced periods of decline and resurgence, shaped by the shifting tides of history. The city fell to Alexander the Great in 331 BCE, who marveled at its splendor and integrated it into his vast empire. Later, Susa continued to thrive under the Seleucid, Parthian, and Sassanian dynasties, each contributing to the city's architectural and cultural landscape.

Despite the devastations of invasions and the ravages of time, Susa's legacy endured. Archaeological excavations in the 19th and 20th centuries uncovered the ruins of its grand palaces, temples, and ziggurats, revealing the city's historical significance and artistic achievements.

Key Events

1. **c. 4200 BCE** - Early Settlement: Susa is established as one of the oldest cities in the world, located in the region of Elam (modern-day Iran).
2. **c. 2000-1500 BCE** - Elamite Civilization: Susa becomes the capital of the Elamite civilization, known for its rich culture and art.
3. **c. 647 BCE** - Assyrian Conquest: Susa is sacked by the Assyrian king Ashurbanipal, but it is later rebuilt.

4. **c. 539 BCE** - Persian Conquest: Susa becomes one of the key administrative capitals of the Achaemenid Persian Empire under Cyrus the Great.

5. **c. 522-486 BCE** - Darius I's Rule: Susa serves as one of the royal residences of Darius I, who builds the grand Apadana palace.

6. **c. 331 BCE** - Conquest by Alexander the Great: Susa is captured by Alexander during his conquest of the Persian Empire, and it remains an important city under the Seleucids.

7. **c. 224 CE** - Sassanian Period: Susa continues to be an important city in the Sassanian Empire, although it eventually declines after the Arab conquest in the 7th century.

Rhages: The Veiled City of the Silk Road

The Crossroads of Empires and Cultures

Hidden within the rugged mountains of northern Iran, where the highlands meet the expansive plains, lies Rhages—an ancient city that once pulsed with the vibrant energy of trade, conquest, and culture. Known in Persian as Rey or Rayy, this city was more than just a stop along the Silk Road; it was a vital nexus where East met West, where merchants, warriors, and pilgrims from across the known world converged in a rich tapestry of human experience. With its ancient fortifications, bustling bazaars, and deep spiritual heritage, Rhages remains a symbol of the resilience and dynamism of a city that thrived at the heart of empires, only to be veiled in the mists of time.

The Fortifications of Rhages: Guardians of an Ancient Crossroad

The city of Rhages was ringed by formidable walls, a necessity for a settlement that sat at the crossroads of some of the most powerful empires in history. These fortifications, built and rebuilt by successive rulers, were designed to protect the city from the constant ebb and flow of armies that passed through this strategic region. The walls of Rhages, with their towering gates and sturdy towers, were not just defensive structures; they were symbols of the city's enduring strength and importance in the face of countless sieges and battles.

Rhages was a coveted prize for empires—from the Medes and the Achaemenids to the Parthians and the Sassanids—each of whom left their mark on the city's architecture and culture. The city's strategic location made it a key military and administrative center, where decisions that shaped the fate of empires were made. The fortifications of Rhages stood as guardians of the city's legacy, watching over the bustling streets and

339

vibrant markets that lay within, where the world's goods, ideas, and peoples came together in a unique blend of tradition and innovation.

The Bazaar of Rhages: A Melting Pot of Trade and Culture

The bazaar of Rhages was the beating heart of the city, a labyrinthine marketplace where the scents of exotic spices, the gleam of precious metals, and the chatter of countless languages filled the air. As a major stop along the Silk Road, Rhages was a hub of commerce, where traders from China, India, Central Asia, and the Mediterranean exchanged goods and stories. The bazaar was more than just a place of trade; it was a melting pot of cultures, where merchants from distant lands brought not only their wares but also their traditions, beliefs, and innovations.

Silk, spices, jewels, and textiles flowed through the bazaar of Rhages, alongside ideas, art, and religion. The city's artisans were renowned for their craftsmanship, producing fine pottery, glassware, and textiles that were sought after across the ancient world. The bazaar was also a place of learning and exchange, where scholars and poets, inspired by the diversity around them, composed works that reflected the city's cosmopolitan spirit. The bazaar of Rhages was a microcosm of the Silk Road itself—a place where the world came together, where commerce and culture intertwined to create something greater than the sum of its parts.

The Towers of Silence: A City of Living and Dead

Rhages was not only a center of trade and politics but also a place of deep spiritual significance. The city was home to several Zoroastrian fire temples, where priests tended to the sacred flames that were central to their faith. These temples were not just places of worship; they were symbols of the city's ancient spiritual heritage, connecting Rhages to the religious traditions that had shaped the region for centuries.

One of the most striking features of Rhages was its Towers of Silence, or Dakhmas, which were used in Zoroastrian funerary practices. These towers, perched on the hills overlooking the city, were where the dead were laid out to be consumed by vultures, a practice that reflected the Zoroastrian belief in the purity of the earth, water, and fire. The Towers of Silence were more than just burial sites; they were a reminder of the city's connection to the ancient rituals and beliefs that had guided its people for generations. The presence of these towers, alongside the bustling life of the city below, highlighted the duality of Rhages as a place of both the living and the dead, a city where the spiritual and the material worlds coexisted in harmony.

The Ravages of Time: Rhages' Fall and Rediscovery

Rhages' prominence made it a target for numerous invaders throughout its long history. The city faced devastating invasions, most notably by the Mongols in the 13th century, which led to its decline and eventual abandonment. Once a thriving center of trade, culture, and spirituality, Rhages was reduced to ruins, its streets and bazaars falling silent as the sands of time slowly covered its once-great walls.

However, the legacy of Rhages was not entirely lost. The ruins of the city, buried beneath the modern-day city of Rey, near Tehran, have been the focus of archaeological efforts that have uncovered its rich history. Ancient pottery, coins, and remnants of its grand architecture offer a glimpse into the city's past, revealing a place that was once a beacon of civilization in the heart of Persia. Rhages may have been veiled by time, but its memory endures in the layers of history that still speak of its former glory.

Key Events

1. **c. 3000 BCE** - Early Settlement: Rhages (Rayy) is established as one of the oldest cities in the region of Media, known for its strategic location along trade routes.
2. **c. 8th-7th centuries BCE** - Median Empire: Rhages becomes a significant city in the Median Empire, serving as a key political and commercial center.

3. **c. 550 BCE** - Conquest by Cyrus the Great: Rhages is incorporated into the Achaemenid Empire after Cyrus the Great's conquest of Media, continuing to thrive as a provincial capital.

4. **c. 330 BCE** - Alexander the Great: Rhages is captured by Alexander during his conquest of the Persian Empire, later becoming part of the Seleucid Empire.

5. **c. 3rd century BCE** - Parthian and Sassanian Periods: Rhages remains an important city under Parthian and Sassanian rule, known for its economic and cultural significance.

Persepolis: The Splendor of the Persian Empire

The Ceremonial Capital of Majesty

Rising from the rocky plains of southwestern Iran, at the foot of the Kuh-e Rahmat (Mountain of Mercy), lies Persepolis, a city that shimmered with the grandeur of the Achaemenid Empire. Known as Parsa to the Persians and Persepolis to the Greeks, this ceremonial capital was more than a city; it was a monumental testament to the glory, power, and artistry of the ancient Persian civilization. With its grand palaces, intricate reliefs, and towering columns, Persepolis remains a symbol of imperial splendor and cultural fusion.

The Apadana: The Audience Hall of Kings

At the heart of Persepolis stood the Apadana, a majestic audience hall where the kings of Persia received dignitaries and subjects from across their vast empire. Built by Darius the Great and completed by his son Xerxes, the Apadana was supported by 72 colossal columns, each soaring 20 meters high, topped with intricate capitals featuring double-headed bulls and lions.

The walls and staircases of the Apadana were adorned with bas-reliefs depicting the procession of tribute-bearers from various nations, bringing gifts to the Persian king. These detailed carvings showcased the diversity and unity of the empire, celebrating the king's role as a ruler of a multicultural realm. The Apadana was not just a space of political power but a stage for the empire's grandeur and inclusivity.

The Tachara: The Private Palace of Darius

The Tachara, or the Palace of Darius, was a more intimate and luxurious residence, reflecting the personal taste and refinement of the Achaemenid rulers. Built on a raised platform, the palace featured finely carved stonework, elaborate doorways, and polished floors that glittered in the sunlight.

The reliefs on the walls of the Tachara depicted scenes of the king in royal attire, accompanied by courtiers and guards. These images conveyed a sense of regal serenity and divine favor, emphasizing the king's role as both a political leader and a spiritual figure. The Tachara's elegant design and artistic details highlighted the sophistication and aesthetic sensibilities of the Persian court.

The Hall of a Hundred Columns: A Fortress of Administration

One of the most impressive structures in Persepolis was the Hall of a Hundred Columns, an expansive hall used for royal receptions and administrative functions. This massive building, with its forest of columns and imposing gateways, symbolized the administrative might and organizational prowess of the Achaemenid Empire.

The hall's immense size and symmetrical layout created a sense of order and authority, reflecting the efficient bureaucracy that governed the empire. The reliefs on the walls depicted scenes of the king on his throne, surrounded by attendants and officials, illustrating the hierarchical yet orderly nature of Persian governance.

The Treasury: Wealth of Nations

The Treasury of Persepolis was a vast complex where the wealth of the empire was stored, including precious metals, gemstones, and luxury goods from across the known world. The treasures housed here were not merely symbols of material wealth but also represented the economic and cultural connections that spanned the empire.

Archaeological excavations have uncovered inscriptions and tablets that detailed the administrative records and inventories of the treasury, providing insights into the economic management and extensive trade networks of the Achaemenids. The wealth of Persepolis was a testament to the prosperity and stability that the empire brought to its vast territories.

The Gate of All Nations: A Portal of Unity

The Gate of All Nations, built by Xerxes, was a grand entrance to the ceremonial complex of Persepolis. Flanked by massive statues of winged bulls with human heads, the gate symbolized the king's dominion over a diverse and far-reaching empire. The inscription on the gate proclaimed Xerxes' authority and welcomed visitors from all corners of the empire, emphasizing the inclusivity and cosmopolitan nature of the Persian state.

Passing through the Gate of All Nations, visitors would feel the awe-inspiring scale and splendor of Persepolis, a city that embodied the unity and diversity of the Achaemenid realm. The gate was both a literal and symbolic threshold, marking the transition from the outer world to the sacred space of imperial power and ceremony.

The Art and Symbolism: A Canvas of Empire

The art of Persepolis was rich with symbolism and intricate detail, reflecting the religious and cultural values of the Achaemenid Persians. The bas-reliefs and carvings depicted a harmonious blend of human figures, animals, and mythical creatures, each with specific meanings and associations. The lion attacking a bull, for example, was a common motif symbolizing the eternal struggle between opposing forces.

The use of vibrant colors, precious materials, and skilled craftsmanship in the decoration of buildings and objects highlighted the importance of beauty and artistry in Persian culture. The art of Persepolis was not just decorative but conveyed messages of power, spirituality, and harmony, reinforcing the ideological foundations of the empire.

The Persepolis Inscriptions: Voices from the Past

Inscriptions in Old Persian, Elamite, and Babylonian, etched into the stone walls and columns of Persepolis, offered a glimpse into the thoughts and proclamations of the Achaemenid kings. These inscriptions celebrated the achievements, divine favor, and moral principles of the rulers, serving as enduring records of their reigns.

The famous inscription by Darius the Great on the foundation of the Apadana, for example, expressed gratitude to Ahura Mazda, the supreme god, for the king's success and prosperity. These texts provided not only historical information but also insights into the religious beliefs and ethical values that underpinned the Achaemenid governance.

The Legacy and Destruction

The splendor of Persepolis came to an abrupt end in 330 BCE when Alexander the Great captured and subsequently set fire to the city, allegedly as an act of revenge for the Persian invasion of Greece. Despite its destruction, the ruins of Persepolis remained a powerful symbol of the grandeur and achievements of the Achaemenid Empire.

Archaeological excavations in the 20th century uncovered the remains of Persepolis, revealing its architectural brilliance and cultural significance. The ruins, now a UNESCO World Heritage site, continue to inspire awe and admiration, offering a window into the grandeur of one of the greatest empires of the ancient world.

Key Events

1. **c. 518 BCE** - Founding by Darius I: Darius I begins the construction of Persepolis as the ceremonial capital of the Achaemenid Empire.
2. **c. 486-465 BCE** - Reign of Xerxes I: Persepolis is expanded under

Xerxes I, including the construction of the Gate of All Nations and the Hall of 100 Columns.

3. **c. 330 BCE** - Destruction by Alexander the Great: Persepolis is looted and burned by Alexander the Great during his conquest of Persia, symbolizing the fall of the Achaemenid Empire.

4. **c. 330 BCE and beyond** - Decline: Persepolis is abandoned and falls into ruin, although it remains a powerful symbol of Persian heritage.

Pasargadae: The Birthplace of an Empire

The Garden of Kings and the Dawn of Persia

In the wide-open plains of southern Iran, where the Zagros Mountains loom in the distance and the air is filled with the scent of wildflowers, lies Pasargadae, the ancient city that marked the beginning of one of history's greatest empires. Founded by Cyrus the Great in the 6th century BCE, Pasargadae was more than just a city; it was the birthplace of the Achaemenid Empire, a place where the seeds of Persian greatness were sown and nurtured in a landscape of unparalleled beauty. With its grand palaces, serene gardens, and the simple yet profound tomb of its founder, Pasargadae remains a symbol of the ideal of kingship, the harmony between nature and power, and the enduring legacy of Cyrus the Great.

The Tomb of Cyrus: A Monument to Humility and Greatness

At the heart of Pasargadae stands the tomb of Cyrus the Great, a modest yet deeply moving monument that reflects both the humility and the greatness of its occupant. Unlike the towering ziggurats or opulent mausoleums of other ancient rulers, the tomb of Cyrus is a simple, stepped structure, resembling a house more than a royal tomb. Constructed from limestone, its clean lines and unadorned façade evoke a sense of timeless dignity and quiet strength.

Cyrus's tomb was more than just his final resting place; it was a symbol of his philosophy of kingship—one that emphasized justice, tolerance, and the well-being of his subjects. The inscription that once adorned the tomb, said to have read, "O man, I am Cyrus, who founded the Persian Empire and was king of Asia. Grudge me not, therefore, this monument," speaks to the lasting impact of his reign and the deep respect in which he was held by his people. The tomb of Cyrus remains a place of pilgrimage, where visitors can reflect on the legacy of a man who changed the course of history with his vision of a unified and benevolent empire.

The Royal Gardens: The Paradise of Pasargadae

Pasargadae was not just a city of stone and mortar; it was a city of gardens, designed to be a paradise on earth. The royal gardens of Pasargadae, known as "Pairidaeza" (from which the word "paradise" is derived), were a masterpiece of landscape architecture, carefully planned to reflect the harmony between nature and the divine order. These gardens were laid out in a geometric pattern, with pathways, water channels, and lush vegetation creating a serene and orderly environment that symbolized the ideal of kingship.

The gardens of Pasargadae were filled with fruit trees, flowering plants, and aromatic herbs, all carefully chosen to create a sensory experience that was both pleasing and symbolic. Water, a precious resource in the arid Persian landscape, flowed through the gardens in carefully constructed channels and pools, representing life, purity, and the king's ability to bring prosperity to his land. The royal gardens were more than just a place of leisure; they were a microcosm of the empire, a living representation of the Achaemenid vision of a world in harmony under a just and powerful ruler.

The Palace of Pasargadae: A Vision of Power and Grace

The palace complex of Pasargadae was a blend of Persian, Median, and Mesopotamian architectural styles, reflecting the diverse cultural influences that shaped the Achaemenid Empire. The audience hall, or Apadana, was a grand space where Cyrus received ambassadors, dignitaries, and subjects, showcasing the power and inclusiveness of his rule. The hall was supported by massive stone columns, each adorned with intricate carvings that depicted scenes of royal power, divine favor, and the harmonious coexistence of different peoples within the empire.

The walls of the palace were adorned with reliefs that celebrated the king's achievements and the empire's prosperity, while the architecture itself was designed to convey both the majesty and the accessibility of the Achaemenid rulers. The palace was not just a seat of power; it was a symbol of the empire's cosmopolitan nature, where different cultures, traditions, and ideas came together to create something greater than the sum of its parts. The palace of Pasargadae was a vision of power tempered by grace, a place where the ideals of the Achaemenid Empire were brought to life in stone and space.

The Gate of All Nations: A Symbol of Unity and Diversity

One of the most striking features of Pasargadae was the Gate of All Nations, an entrance that symbolized the inclusive and multicultural nature of the Achaemenid Empire. This gate was designed to welcome people from all corners of the empire and beyond, reflecting Cyrus's policy of tolerance and respect for different cultures and religions. The gate was adorned with carvings of mythical creatures, such as winged bulls and lions, which symbolized the power and protection of the king.

The Gate of All Nations was more than just an architectural feature; it was a statement of the Achaemenid vision of a world where different peoples could coexist under the rule of a just and benevolent king. It embodied the idea that the empire was not just a collection of conquered territories, but a unified whole where diversity was celebrated and different cultures contributed to the richness of the imperial tapestry. The Gate of All Nations stood as a testament to the Achaemenid commitment to unity in diversity, a principle that would become a hallmark of the empire's rule.

The Legacy of Cyrus the Great: The Founding of an Empire

Pasargadae was the first capital of the Achaemenid Empire, the birthplace of a new era in history, where Cyrus the Great laid the foundations for an empire that would stretch from the Aegean Sea to the Indus River. Cyrus's reign was marked by his innovative approach to governance, where he respected the customs and religions of the peoples he conquered, ensuring their loyalty and the stability of his empire. This approach set the tone for the Achaemenid rulers who followed, making the empire one of the most successful and enduring in history.

Cyrus's legacy was not just in the vast territories he conquered, but in the principles of governance he established—principles that emphasized justice, tolerance, and respect for human dignity. These ideals were reflected in the architecture, art, and culture of Pasargadae, making the city a symbol of the Achaemenid vision of a just and harmonious world. The legacy of Cyrus the Great lives on in the ruins of Pasargadae, a city that continues to inspire with its message of unity, peace, and the power of enlightened leadership.

Key Events

c. 550 BCE - Founding by Cyrus the Great: Pasargadae is established by Cyrus the Great as the first capital of the Achaemenid Empire, symbolizing the beginning of Persian imperial power.

c. 530 BCE - Death and Burial of Cyrus: Cyrus the Great is buried in a grand tomb at Pasargadae, which becomes a symbol of Persian royal authority and a sacred site.

c. 500 BCE - Development under Darius I: Although the capital is moved to Persepolis under Darius I, Pasargadae continues to be a significant ceremonial center.

c. 330 BCE - Conquest by Alexander the Great: Pasargadae is captured by Alexander the Great during his conquest of the Persian Empire, who reportedly pays his respects at Cyrus's tomb.

c. 4th-3rd centuries BCE - Hellenistic Influence: Pasargadae retains some importance during the Hellenistic period, though its prominence declines as Persepolis and later other cities rise in importance.

c. 224 CE - Sassanian Period: Pasargadae becomes a historical site revered by the Sassanian kings, though it is no longer a major urban center.

Ecbatana: The Enchanted Fortress of the Medes

The Royal Haven of the Highlands

Nestled in the verdant valleys of the Zagros Mountains, where the air is crisp and the landscape dotted with blooming wildflowers, lies Ecbatana, a city that stood as a beacon of splendor and strategic might in the ancient world. Known as the royal summer capital of the Medes and later the Achaemenid Persians, Ecbatana was more than a city; it was an enchanted fortress of kings, a center of opulence, and a hub of cultural convergence. With its majestic palaces, impregnable walls, and vibrant marketplaces, Ecbatana remains a symbol of regal elegance and the harmonious blend of cultures.

The Seven Walls: A Fortress of Colors

Ecbatana was renowned for its unique and striking fortifications—seven concentric walls, each painted a different color, ascending to the royal citadel at the center. According to Herodotus, these walls were a marvel of ancient engineering and artistry, with the innermost wall plated in gold and silver, reflecting the city's wealth and the king's divine status.

These walls, designed for both defense and display, symbolized the city's layered protection and the progression towards the sacred heart of the kingdom. The vibrant hues of the walls—white, black, scarlet, blue, orange, silver, and gold—created a visual spectacle that could be seen from miles away, reinforcing Ecbatana's reputation as a city of unparalleled beauty and power.

355

The Royal Palace: A Jewel of Splendor

At the heart of Ecbatana stood the royal palace, an opulent complex that served as the residence of the Median and later Achaemenid kings. This palace, described as being adorned with precious metals, gemstones, and luxurious fabrics, was a testament to the empire's prosperity and the king's supreme authority.

The grand halls of the palace, with their soaring columns and intricately decorated ceilings, hosted lavish banquets, diplomatic meetings, and royal ceremonies. The throne room, where the king received emissaries and subjects, was a space of grandeur and majesty, reflecting the divine right and absolute power of the monarch.

The Treasury: Vault of Wealth

Ecbatana's treasury was famed throughout the ancient world for its vast riches, accumulated through tribute, trade, and conquest. This immense storehouse contained gold, silver, precious stones, and luxury goods from across the empire and beyond. The wealth of the treasury not only funded the lavish lifestyle of the royal court but also financed military campaigns, public works, and religious offerings.

The treasury was heavily guarded and strategically located within the fortified heart of the city, symbolizing the economic strength and stability of the kingdom. It was a tangible representation of Ecbatana's status as a center of wealth and power.

The Gardens of Ecbatana: Oasis of Serenity

Surrounding the palace were the famed gardens of Ecbatana, lush with exotic plants, flowing water, and shaded pathways. These gardens were designed to provide a serene retreat from the rigors of royal duties and the heat of the summer capital. The carefully tended flora, sparkling fountains, and aromatic blossoms created an atmosphere of tranquility and beauty.

These gardens were not only places of leisure but also reflected the Persian love for nature and horticultural excellence. The harmony and order of the gardens symbolized the king's ability to cultivate both the land and his realm, creating a paradise on earth.

The Cultural Convergence: A Melting Pot of Traditions

Ecbatana was a city where diverse cultures and traditions converged, creating a rich tapestry of art, language, and customs. As the administrative and cultural center of the Median Empire, and later an important city in the Achaemenid and Seleucid empires, Ecbatana attracted people from various regions, including Babylonians, Assyrians, Greeks, and Persians.

This cultural melting pot was reflected in the city's architecture, art, and daily life. The fusion of styles and influences created a unique and dynamic urban environment, where different traditions coexisted and enriched one another. Ecbatana was a living testament to the empire's inclusivity and its ability to integrate diverse peoples.

The Great Market: Bazaar of Wonders

The bustling markets of Ecbatana were a hub of commercial activity, where merchants traded goods from across the ancient world. Spices from India, silk from China, gold from Lydia, and crafts from Greece filled the stalls, creating a vibrant and dynamic atmosphere.

The market was a place of exchange not only of goods but also of ideas and knowledge. Travelers and traders brought stories, inventions, and cultural practices, contributing to the city's cosmopolitan character. The market of Ecbatana was a microcosm of the wider world, reflecting the city's role as a center of commerce and cultural exchange.

The Seat of Power: From Medes to Achaemenids

Ecbatana was originally the capital of the Median Empire, founded by Deioces in the 8th century BCE. It served as the political and ceremonial center of the Medes, reflecting their power and sophistication. After the conquest by Cyrus the Great, Ecbatana became one of the key cities of the Achaemenid Empire, serving as a summer residence for the Persian kings.

The city's strategic location and impressive infrastructure made it an important administrative center throughout its history. Ecbatana's ability to adapt and thrive under different empires underscored its resilience and enduring significance.

The Decline and Legacy

The decline of Ecbatana began with the fall of the Achaemenid Empire and continued through the subsequent Seleucid and Parthian periods. However, the city's legacy endured through its ruins and the stories of its grandeur recorded by ancient historians.

Archaeological excavations in modern times have uncovered the remnants of Ecbatana's fortifications, palaces, and marketplaces, providing valuable insights into its historical and cultural significance. The city's unique blend of architectural styles, its strategic importance, and its role as a center of power and culture continue to captivate historians and archaeologists.

Key Events

1. **c. 700 BCE** - Founding by the Medes: Ecbatana (modern-day Hamadan, Iran) is established as the capital of the Median Empire, known for its impressive fortifications.
2. **c. 550 BCE** - Conquest by Cyrus the Great: Ecbatana is captured by Cyrus, becoming one of the key cities of the Achaemenid Empire.
3. **c. 330 BCE** - Alexander the Great: Ecbatana becomes a major city

under Alexander the Great and his successors, the Seleucids.

4. **c. 224 CE** – Sassanian Period: Ecbatana remains an important city in the Sassanian Empire, although it loses some of its earlier prominence.

Ctesiphon: The Splendor of the Tigris

The Jewel of Mesopotamia

Rising majestically along the banks of the Tigris River, Ctesiphon stood as a beacon of architectural brilliance and cultural fusion in ancient Mesopotamia. Known as the capital of the Parthian and later the Sassanian Empire, Ctesiphon was more than a city; it was a symbol of imperial power, a hub of intellectual and artistic achievements, and a crossroads of civilizations. With its grand palaces, bustling bazaars, and storied past, Ctesiphon remains a testament to the enduring legacy of human creativity and political ambition.

The Taq Kasra: The Arch of Triumph

At the heart of Ctesiphon stood the Taq Kasra, also known as the Arch of Ctesiphon, an architectural marvel that symbolized the grandeur and engineering prowess of the Sassanian Empire. This immense vaulted hall, constructed from brick and mortar, boasted the largest single-span arch in the ancient world. The arch, with its intricate brickwork and imposing height, was part of the imperial palace complex and served as a ceremonial hall for the Sassanian kings.

The Taq Kasra's majestic silhouette against the Mesopotamian sky represented the zenith of Sassanian architectural innovation and imperial authority. It was a place where grand receptions, royal audiences, and state ceremonies were held, embodying the power and splendor of the empire.

The Royal Palaces: A Tapestry of Opulence

Ctesiphon's royal palaces were renowned for their opulence and architectural sophistication. These palaces, adorned with intricate mosaics, frescoes, and stucco decorations, reflected the artistic achievements and luxurious lifestyle of the Sassanian court. The throne rooms, with their soaring columns and ornate decorations, were spaces of grandeur where the king received ambassadors and dignitaries from across the known world.

The gardens surrounding the palaces, lush with exotic plants, fountains, and shaded pavilions, provided a serene retreat for the royal family and their guests. These gardens were meticulously designed to create a sense of harmony and beauty, reflecting the Persian ideal of paradise on earth.

The Great Bazaar: Heartbeat of Commerce

Ctesiphon's great bazaar was a bustling marketplace that served as the commercial heart of the city. Merchants from across the Persian Empire and beyond converged in Ctesiphon to trade goods such as silks from China, spices from India, precious metals from Arabia, and textiles from Rome. The bazaar was a vibrant hub of economic activity and cultural exchange, where traders haggled, artisans showcased their wares, and scholars discussed ideas.

The diversity of goods and the cosmopolitan nature of the bazaar underscored Ctesiphon's role as a key trading center on the Silk Road. The market was not only a place of commerce but also a melting pot of cultures, where people of different backgrounds interacted and exchanged knowledge.

The Academy of Gundeshapur: A Beacon of Knowledge

Nearby Ctesiphon, the Academy of Gundeshapur was a renowned center of learning and intellectual activity. Founded in the 3rd century CE, this academy attracted scholars, scientists, and physicians from across the Persian Empire and beyond. It was a place where Greek, Persian, Indian, and Christian scholars came together to study and share knowledge in fields such as medicine, astronomy, philosophy, and mathematics.

The academy's library, filled with manuscripts and texts from various cultures, was a treasure trove of knowledge. The Academy of Gundeshapur was a testament to the Sassanian Empire's commitment to learning and cultural exchange, and it played a crucial role in preserving and advancing human knowledge.

The Ctesiphon Inscriptions: Voices of the Past

The inscriptions found in Ctesiphon, written in Middle Persian, Parthian, and other languages, offer valuable insights into the history, culture, and administration of the city. These texts, carved into stone and metal, recorded royal decrees, religious edicts, and historical events. They provided a glimpse into the governance and daily life of the Sassanian Empire, reflecting its complexity and sophistication.

One of the most famous inscriptions is the Res Gestae Divi Saporis, which commemorates the victories and achievements of Shapur I, including his capture of the Roman Emperor Valerian. These inscriptions are not only historical records but also symbols of the empire's power and legacy.

The Siege and Resilience

Ctesiphon's strategic location and wealth made it a target for numerous sieges and invasions, including by the Romans, Arabs, and other rival forces. Despite these challenges, the city demonstrated remarkable resilience and adaptability. Each conquest brought new influences and changes, contributing to the city's rich and diverse cultural heritage.

The fall of Ctesiphon to the Arab forces in 637 CE marked the end of the Sassanian Empire, but the city's legacy endured. The ruins of Ctesiphon, particularly the Taq Kasra, stand as enduring symbols of its historical significance and architectural brilliance.

Key Events

1. **c. 120 BCE** - Founding by the Parthians: Ctesiphon is established as a major city on the Tigris River by the Parthians, serving as a winter capital.

2. **c. 226 CE** - Sassanian Period: Ctesiphon becomes the capital of the Sassanian Empire, known for its grand palaces and the iconic Taq Kasra arch.

3. **c. 363 CE** - Roman-Sassanian Conflicts: Ctesiphon is frequently contested in wars between the Romans and the Sassanians, changing hands several times.

VIII

South Asia

Mohenjo-Daro: The Enigma of the Indus Valley

The Ancient City of Mastery and Mystery

Amidst the vast plains of the Indus River, where the fertile land meets the clear skies, lies Mohenjo-Daro, a city that thrived with unparalleled sophistication around 2500 BCE. Known as one of the principal settlements of the Indus Valley Civilization, Mohenjo-Daro was more than just a city; it was a testament to early urban planning, advanced engineering, and a society that valued cleanliness and order. With its well-planned streets, intricate drainage systems, and enigmatic artifacts, Mohenjo-Daro remains a symbol of ancient ingenuity and the mysteries of early human civilization.

The Great Bath: A Ceremonial Oasis

At the heart of Mohenjo-Daro lies the Great Bath, a massive, rectangular tank built from meticulously arranged bricks and coated with bitumen to ensure water-tightness. This impressive structure, measuring about 12 meters by 7 meters and over 2 meters deep, is believed to have served a ceremonial purpose, perhaps for ritual purification or community gatherings.

Surrounding the Great Bath are colonnaded galleries and small rooms, possibly used for changing or storing sacred items. The precision and care taken in constructing the Great Bath highlight the advanced engineering skills and the significance of water in the spiritual and social life of the city's inhabitants.

The Granary: Storehouse of Abundance

Adjacent to the Great Bath, the Granary of Mohenjo-Daro stands as a monumental testament to the city's agricultural wealth and sophisticated storage methods. This large, brick-built structure featured air ducts and platforms that allowed for the efficient storage and preservation of grain.

The granary's strategic location and design ensured a stable food supply for the city's population, reflecting the importance of agricultural planning and resource management.

The presence of the granary indicates the central role of agriculture in the city's economy and the advanced administrative capabilities of its society. The meticulous planning and construction of such a facility underscore the city's commitment to sustainability and prosperity.

The Citadel: The Fortress of Authority

The elevated citadel of Mohenjo-Daro, surrounded by impressive fortifications, housed some of the city's most significant structures, including the Great Bath and the Granary. This raised platform, built from mud-brick, provided a commanding view of the city and served as the administrative and possibly religious center.

The citadel's strategic elevation and fortified walls suggest that it was designed to protect important public buildings and possibly the ruling elite. The separation of the citadel from the lower city reflects a hierarchical social structure and the importance placed on governance and communal activities.

The Urban Grid: A Blueprint of Precision

Mohenjo-Daro is renowned for its grid-based urban planning, with streets laid out in a precise, orderly fashion. The city was divided into rectangular blocks, with wide main streets intersected by narrower lanes, creating a well-organized and navigable urban environment. This level of planning indicates a high degree of social organization and an understanding of urban design principles that were advanced for its time.

The residential buildings, made from standardized fired bricks, were equipped with courtyards, private wells, and sophisticated drainage systems. The uniformity and functionality of the architecture reflect the community's emphasis on hygiene, comfort, and sustainability.

The Drainage System: Engineering Marvel

One of the most remarkable features of Mohenjo-Daro is its advanced drainage system, which underscores the city's commitment to public health and sanitation. Covered drains, built from carefully fitted bricks, ran along the streets, connected to individual houses through smaller channels. These drains carried wastewater out of the city, preventing flooding and maintaining cleanliness.

The presence of this extensive drainage network, including manholes for maintenance, illustrates the ingenuity and engineering expertise of the Indus Valley people. This system not only improved the quality of life for the residents but also demonstrated their ability to solve complex urban challenges.

The Artifacts: Echoes of Daily Life

The artifacts discovered in Mohenjo-Daro, from intricate pottery and seals to statuettes and tools, provide a glimpse into the daily life and culture of its inhabitants. The famous "Dancing Girl" statuette, made of bronze, captures the grace and dynamism of human movement, reflecting the artistic skills and cultural expressions of the time.

Seals bearing animal motifs and script-like symbols suggest a system of trade and possibly a form of writing, although the Indus script remains undeciphered. These artifacts hint at a society that valued art, commerce, and communication, and they continue to intrigue scholars and historians.

The Great Mystery: The Unanswered Questions

Despite its advanced infrastructure and rich cultural heritage, much about Mohenjo-Daro remains shrouded in mystery. The lack of decipherable written records leaves many aspects of the city's social, political, and religious life open to speculation. The reasons for the city's decline and eventual abandonment are still debated, with theories ranging from natural disasters to shifts in trade routes or ecological changes.

The enigmatic nature of Mohenjo-Daro fuels ongoing research and exploration, as archaeologists and historians strive to uncover the secrets of this ancient metropolis. Each discovery adds a piece to the puzzle, offering new insights into the life and times of the Indus Valley civilization.

Key Events

1. **c. 2500 BCE** - Founding and Flourishing: Mohenjo-Daro is established as one of the largest and most advanced cities of the Indus Valley Civilization, featuring sophisticated urban planning, drainage systems, and architecture.
2. **c. 2300-1900 BCE** - Peak Period: Mohenjo-Daro reaches its zenith, becoming a major urban center with a population likely in the tens of thousands, and a hub for trade and craft production.
3. **c. 1900-1700 BCE** - Decline: The city begins to decline due to factors that are still debated, such as climate change, shifting river patterns, or invasions.
4. **c. 1700 BCE** - Abandonment: Mohenjo-Daro is gradually abandoned, possibly due to the drying up of the Sarasvati River and other environmental factors.

Harappa: The Silent Sentinel of the Indus Valley

The Ancient City of Order and Innovation

Amidst the vast and fertile plains of the Punjab region, where the Ravi River once flowed mightily, lies Harappa, a city that stood as a beacon of organization, innovation, and mysterious grandeur around 2600 BCE. As one of the key centers of the Indus Valley Civilization, Harappa was more than just a city; it was a marvel of urban planning, a hub of trade and craftsmanship, and a silent witness to one of the earliest known complex societies in human history. With its meticulously designed streets, advanced infrastructure, and enigmatic legacy, Harappa remains a symbol of ancient ingenuity and the forgotten echoes of a civilization that once thrived in harmony with nature.

The Granaries: Storehouses of Sustenance

Harappa's granaries, large and strategically placed near the riverbanks, were the lifeblood of the city's economy. These massive brick-built structures, designed with ventilation shafts and raised platforms, stored surplus grain, ensuring food security for the population and facilitating trade with neighboring regions.

The granaries were more than mere storage facilities; they were a testament to Harappa's advanced agricultural practices and its ability to manage resources effectively. The careful planning and construction of these granaries reflected the city's emphasis on stability, sustainability, and communal welfare, ensuring that the population could thrive even in times of scarcity.

The Citadel: The Heart of Power and Protection

Rising above the surrounding city, the citadel of Harappa was a fortified stronghold that served as the administrative and religious center of the settlement. Constructed from massive mud bricks, the citadel housed public buildings, granaries, and possibly temples or administrative offices, indicating its importance in the social and political life of Harappa.

The elevated position of the citadel, protected by thick walls and strategic positioning, suggests that it was designed to withstand both environmental challenges and potential threats. The citadel's dominance over the cityscape symbolized the authority and order that governed Harappan society, a reflection of the community's commitment to protection, governance, and religious rituals.

The Streets of Harappa: A Grid of Precision

Harappa is renowned for its grid-based urban layout, a masterpiece of ancient city planning that reveals a society deeply invested in order and efficiency. The city's streets were laid out in a precise grid pattern, with wide avenues intersecting at right angles, creating well-defined blocks for residential and public buildings.

The uniformity of the streets, combined with the standardized construction of houses from baked bricks, indicates a high level of social organization and a collective approach to urban development. The planning of Harappa's streets allowed for effective transportation, communication, and drainage, demonstrating a sophisticated understanding of urban infrastructure that was ahead of its time.

The Drainage System: A Blueprint of Cleanliness

One of Harappa's most impressive features was its advanced drainage system, a testament to the civilization's concern for public health and hygiene. Every house in Harappa was connected to a network of covered drains that ran along the streets, efficiently channeling wastewater out of the city.

The presence of this well-maintained drainage system, complete with inspection holes and gradient slopes, highlights the Harappans' ingenuity and their commitment to creating a clean and habitable urban environment. This system not only improved the quality of life for the inhabitants but also showcased the city's forward-thinking approach to urban planning.

The Craftsmanship: A Legacy of Art and Industry

Harappa was a center of craftsmanship, where artisans produced a wide array of goods, from finely crafted pottery and jewelry to tools and toys. The city's artisans were skilled in working with materials such as copper, bronze, shell, and terracotta, creating items that were both functional and aesthetically pleasing.

The discovery of standardized weights and measures in Harappa suggests a highly organized economy, with regulated trade practices and quality control. The intricately designed seals, featuring animals and symbols, were likely used in trade and administration, indicating a complex and far-reaching commercial network. These artifacts provide a glimpse into the daily life, economy, and artistic achievements of the Harappan people.

The Harappan Script: The Silent Enigma

One of the greatest mysteries of Harappa is its undeciphered script, a series of symbols inscribed on seals, pottery, and tablets. Despite extensive research, the meaning of these symbols remains elusive, shrouding much of Harappan society's intellectual and administrative practices in mystery.

The Harappan script hints at a literate society with a complex system of communication, likely used for trade, administration, and religious purposes. The enigmatic nature of the script adds to the allure of Harappa, leaving us to wonder about the thoughts, beliefs, and stories that once flowed through the minds of its people.

The Wells: Lifelines of the City

Harappa was dotted with wells, strategically placed throughout the city to provide a steady supply of fresh water to its inhabitants. These wells, constructed from bricks, were an essential part of daily life, ensuring that the population had access to clean water for drinking, cooking, and bathing.

The abundance of wells in Harappa reflects the civilization's advanced understanding of water management and its commitment to maintaining public health and hygiene. The careful construction and maintenance of these wells highlight the city's practical ingenuity and the importance placed on sustainable living.

The Decline and Rediscovery

Harappa's decline remains one of the enduring mysteries of the ancient world. Theories range from climate change and shifting river patterns to invasions and internal strife. Whatever the cause, the city was eventually abandoned, its once-thriving streets falling silent as the sands of time reclaimed the land.

Rediscovered in the 19th century, Harappa has since been the subject of extensive archaeological research, revealing a civilization of remarkable complexity and sophistication. The city's ruins, now a UNESCO World Heritage site, continue to captivate historians, archaeologists, and visitors, offering a window into a world that once flourished in harmony with nature.

Key Events

1. **c. 3300 BCE** - Early Settlement: Harappa is established as one of the early urban centers of the Indus Valley Civilization.
2. **c. 2600-1900 BCE** - Mature Harappan Phase: Harappa becomes a major city of the Indus Valley Civilization, known for its grid-like street patterns, sophisticated drainage systems, and standardized weights and measures.

3. **c. 1900-1700 BCE** - Decline: Harappa begins to decline, with evidence of urban disintegration and reduced trade activity.
4. **c. 1700 BCE** - Abandonment: The city is largely abandoned, with remnants of the population possibly migrating to other regions.

Lothal: The Harbor of Innovation and Maritime Dreams

The Port City of the Indus

Amidst the arid plains of the modern-day state of Gujarat, where the Sabarmati River once merged with the Arabian Sea, lies Lothal, a city that thrived as a hub of trade and innovation around 2000 BCE. As one of the key maritime centers of the Indus Valley Civilization, Lothal was more than just a city; it was a bustling port, a cradle of technological advancement, and a beacon of early urban planning. With its ingenious dockyard, thriving marketplace, and pioneering spirit, Lothal remains a symbol of ancient maritime prowess and the enduring quest for connectivity and prosperity.

The Dockyard: A Masterpiece of Engineering

The crown jewel of Lothal was its meticulously constructed dockyard, one of the earliest known in the world. This massive, rectangular basin, built from precisely cut bricks and equipped with a sophisticated sluice gate system, was ingeniously designed to accommodate the ebb and flow of the tides, allowing ships to safely dock and unload their cargo.

The dockyard's design reflects a deep understanding of tidal patterns, hydraulics, and maritime engineering, highlighting Lothal's importance as a major trading port. The presence of this dockyard underscores the city's role as a vital link in the trade networks that connected the Indus Valley Civilization with distant lands, from Mesopotamia to the Persian Gulf. It was here that goods such as beads, gems, textiles, and metals were exchanged, fueling the economy and cultural exchanges of the ancient world.

The Bead Factory: Workshop of Wonders

Lothal was renowned for its bead-making industry, which produced intricate and finely crafted beads that were highly prized across the ancient world. The city's artisans, working in well-organized workshops, used a variety of materials, including carnelian, agate, shell, and terracotta, to create beads of various shapes, sizes, and colors.

These beads were not only a major export item but also a testament to the artistic skill and technological innovation of Lothal's craftsmen. The discovery of tools, furnaces, and unfinished beads in the city's workshops reveals the meticulous processes involved in bead production, from shaping and drilling to polishing and stringing. The beads of Lothal adorned the necks and wrists of people far beyond the Indus Valley, serving as symbols of beauty, status, and cultural connection.

The Marketplace: A Hub of Commerce

The bustling marketplace of Lothal was the economic heart of the city, where merchants, traders, and artisans gathered to exchange goods, ideas, and stories. This vibrant bazaar was a melting pot of cultures, where traders from the Indus Valley mingled with those from Mesopotamia, Persia, and beyond.

The goods traded in Lothal's market included precious stones, metals, textiles, pottery, and spices, reflecting the city's diverse and far-reaching trade connections. The orderly layout of the market, with its wide streets and standardized shops, reflects the city's commitment to efficient commerce and the importance of trade in sustaining its economy. The marketplace was not only a center of economic activity but also a space of social interaction and cultural exchange, where the world met in the heart of the Indus.

The Advanced Drainage System: A Blueprint of Sanitation

Lothal, like other cities in the Indus Valley Civilization, was renowned for its advanced urban planning, particularly its sophisticated drainage system. The city's streets were equipped with covered drains, carefully laid out to prevent flooding and maintain cleanliness.

Each house in Lothal was connected to the drainage network, ensuring that wastewater was efficiently removed from the city. The system's design, with its gradients and inspection holes, demonstrates a deep understanding of engineering and public health. This commitment to sanitation and urban order contributed to the high quality of life in Lothal, reflecting the city's innovative spirit and concern for the well-being of its inhabitants.

The Warehouse: Storehouse of Wealth

Adjacent to the dockyard was Lothal's massive warehouse, a structure designed to store and protect valuable goods awaiting shipment or trade. Built from fired bricks and equipped with ventilation systems, the warehouse was a secure and efficient space that played a crucial role in the city's economy.

The warehouse's strategic location near the dockyard facilitated the swift and secure movement of goods between ships and storage, minimizing the risk of spoilage or theft. The presence of this warehouse underscores Lothal's role as a key logistics hub, where goods from across the region were accumulated, stored, and distributed, fueling the city's prosperity.

The Seal Workshop: Tokens of Trade and Identity

Lothal was a center of seal production, where artisans crafted intricately engraved seals that were used to mark goods, authenticate documents, and symbolize ownership. These seals, typically made from steatite, featured a variety of motifs, including animals, mythical creatures, and geometric patterns, often accompanied by inscriptions in the undeciphered Indus script.

The seals of Lothal were more than just practical tools; they were works of art that reflected the cultural and commercial sophistication of the city. The widespread discovery of these seals in distant lands attests to Lothal's extensive trade connections and the importance of these tokens in the ancient world's economic and social networks.

The Decline and Legacy

Like other cities of the Indus Valley Civilization, Lothal eventually experienced a decline, possibly due to changes in river patterns, climatic shifts, or disruptions in trade routes. Despite its abandonment, the legacy of Lothal endures through the archaeological discoveries that have shed light on its remarkable achievements.

Today, the ruins of Lothal, with its dockyard, warehouses, and workshops, offer a glimpse into a city that was a hub of innovation and maritime ambition. The site continues to captivate historians and archaeologists, revealing the ingenuity and far-reaching influence of the Indus Valley Civilization.

Key Events

1. **c. 2400 BCE** - Founding of Lothal: Lothal is established as a major port city of the Indus Valley Civilization, strategically located near the Sabarmati River and the Gulf of Khambhat.
2. **c. 2400-1900 BCE** - Peak Period: Lothal becomes a significant center for maritime trade, with a well-planned dockyard, warehouses, and a thriving bead-making industry.
3. **c. 1900-1700 BCE** - Decline: Lothal begins to decline, possibly due to changes in river patterns and reduced trade.
4. **c. 1600 BCE** - Abandonment: The city is gradually abandoned, though it continues to be remembered for its innovations in urban planning and maritime activities.

Pataliputra: The Seat of Power and Enlightenment

The Jewel of the Ganges

Nestled at the confluence of the Ganges and Son Rivers, in the heart of the fertile plains of northern India, lies Pataliputra, a city that once glittered as the capital of ancient empires. Known as the political and cultural epicenter of the Maurya and Gupta dynasties, Pataliputra was more than just a city; it was a thriving metropolis, a hub of intellectual brilliance, and a bastion of imperial authority. With its grand palaces, bustling streets, and flourishing institutions, Pataliputra remains a symbol of ancient India's might, wisdom, and enduring legacy.

The Wooden Walls: A Fortress of the Ganges

Pataliputra was renowned for its formidable defenses, particularly its massive wooden walls and deep moats, which stretched for miles around the city. These fortifications, described in the writings of ancient travelers like Megasthenes, were designed to protect the city from invasions and ensure its status as an impregnable capital.

The walls, made from teak and other robust timber, were reinforced with guard towers and battlements, providing a powerful deterrent to would-be invaders. The surrounding moats, filled with water from the Ganges, added an additional layer of protection, making Pataliputra a true fortress city. The scale and strength of these defenses reflected the city's importance as the administrative and military center of one of the world's greatest empires.

The Mauryan Palace: A Monument of Majesty

At the heart of Pataliputra stood the magnificent Mauryan Palace, an architectural marvel that served as the residence of the Mauryan emperors, including the legendary Ashoka. The palace, constructed from wood and later embellished with stone, was adorned with intricate carvings, gilded pillars, and sprawling courtyards.

The grandeur of the palace was a testament to the wealth and power of the Mauryan Empire, reflecting the emperor's divine right to rule. The palace's halls and chambers hosted diplomatic meetings, royal ceremonies, and intellectual gatherings, serving as the nerve center of the empire's vast administration. The splendor of the Mauryan Palace was a symbol of the empire's golden age, where art, governance, and culture flourished under imperial patronage.

The Ashokan Pillars: Edicts of Enlightenment

Pataliputra was home to several of the famous Ashokan pillars, towering stone monuments inscribed with edicts that conveyed Emperor Ashoka's messages of Dharma (righteousness), tolerance, and non-violence. These pillars, capped with elaborate carvings of lions, bulls, and lotuses, were scattered across the city, serving as reminders of Ashoka's commitment to justice and the spread of Buddhism.

The inscriptions on these pillars, written in Brahmi script, communicated the emperor's moral and ethical principles to his subjects, promoting unity and compassion throughout the empire. The Ashokan pillars of Pataliputra were not only architectural masterpieces but also powerful symbols of the emperor's enlightened rule and his efforts to create a just and harmonious society.

The Great University: A Beacon of Learning

Pataliputra was a center of intellectual and cultural activity, home to one of the greatest universities of the ancient world. Scholars, philosophers, and students from across India and beyond gathered in Pataliputra to study subjects ranging from philosophy and mathematics to medicine and astronomy. The city's universities and libraries were repositories of knowledge, where ancient texts were preserved, studied, and disseminated.

The intellectual environment of Pataliputra fostered the development of significant philosophical schools, including Buddhism and Jainism, which found patronage and support in the city. The teachings of great thinkers like Chanakya (Kautilya), who authored the Arthashastra, and the spread of Buddhist philosophy under Ashoka, made Pataliputra a beacon of learning and spiritual enlightenment.

The Thriving Marketplaces: Hubs of Trade and Culture

Pataliputra's bustling marketplaces were the lifeblood of its economy, where traders, artisans, and merchants exchanged goods from across the Indian subcontinent and beyond. The city's strategic location along the Ganges River facilitated trade with regions as far as Central Asia, Southeast Asia, and the Mediterranean.

The markets of Pataliputra offered a dazzling array of goods, including silk, spices, gemstones, ivory, and fine textiles. These bustling bazaars were also centers of cultural exchange, where ideas, languages, and traditions mingled, reflecting the city's cosmopolitan character. The prosperity of Pataliputra's markets underscored the city's role as a major economic hub and a melting pot of cultures.

The Gardens of Pataliputra: Oases of Serenity

Pataliputra was renowned for its beautiful gardens and parks, carefully designed to provide a serene retreat from the bustling city life. These gardens, filled with flowering plants, fruit trees, and flowing water, offered a space for relaxation, meditation, and recreation.

The gardens of Pataliputra were not only places of leisure but also symbols of the city's harmony with nature and its commitment to creating a balanced and aesthetically pleasing environment. The lush greenery and tranquil ambiance of these gardens reflected the city's sophisticated urban planning and its emphasis on well-being.

The Decline and Rediscovery

Pataliputra's fortunes waxed and waned over the centuries, with the city experiencing periods of decline following invasions, political upheavals, and shifting trade routes. Despite these challenges, the city's legacy endured, with its name and influence echoing through the annals of Indian history.

In modern times, archaeological excavations have unearthed the remnants of Pataliputra's grand past, revealing its palaces, fortifications, and other structures. These discoveries have provided valuable insights into the city's architecture, urban planning, and the daily lives of its inhabitants. The ruins of Pataliputra continue to captivate historians and archaeologists, offering a window into one of the most important cities of ancient India.

Key Events

1. **c. 490 BCE** - Founding of Pataliputra: Pataliputra (modern-day Patna) is founded by Ajatashatru as a small fort near the Ganges River.
2. **c. 321 BCE** - Capital of the Maurya Empire: Under Chandragupta Maurya, Pataliputra becomes the capital of the Mauryan Empire, one of the largest empires in ancient India.

3. **c. 273-232 BCE** - Reign of Ashoka: Pataliputra flourishes under Emperor Ashoka, becoming a center of Buddhist learning and administration. Ashoka's reign marks the height of Pataliputra's influence and power.

4. **c. 185 BCE** - Decline after the Mauryan Empire: Following the fall of the Mauryan Empire, Pataliputra experiences a period of decline, though it remains an important city.

5. **c. 320-550 CE** - Gupta Empire: Pataliputra serves as a major center of learning and culture during the Gupta Empire, known as the "Golden Age of India."

Magadha: The Cradle of Empires

The Land of Power and Spiritual Awakening

In the fertile plains of the Ganges River, where the sacred waters nourish the land and ancient paths weave through dense forests and open fields, lies Magadha, a kingdom that blossomed into one of the most powerful and influential regions in ancient India around 600 BCE. More than just a city or a kingdom, Magadha was the cradle of empires, a nexus of political power, spiritual enlightenment, and intellectual flourishing. With its fortified capitals, grand monasteries, and vibrant markets, Magadha remains a symbol of India's enduring legacy of empire-building, cultural synthesis, and philosophical inquiry.

Rajagriha: The Seat of Kings

Rajagriha, the capital of Magadha during its early rise, was a city nestled in a valley surrounded by five hills, each crowned with fortifications. The natural defenses of the hills, combined with man-made stone walls and gates, made Rajagriha a formidable stronghold and the seat of the Magadhan kings. This city, with its strategic location and robust defenses, was the political and military heart of Magadha, where the kings planned their conquests and administered their growing realm.

Rajagriha was not just a military bastion but also a center of culture and spirituality. The city's palaces, built from stone and wood, were grand and imposing, reflecting the wealth and power of the Magadhan rulers. The courts of these palaces were where the fate of kingdoms was decided, alliances forged, and new ideas debated. Rajagriha's hills also housed ancient monasteries and meditation caves, where sages and monks sought enlightenment, adding a spiritual dimension to the city's grandeur.

The Rise of Pataliputra: A Metropolis of Ambition

As Magadha expanded its influence under the Maurya and later the Gupta dynasties, the capital shifted from Rajagriha to Pataliputra, which grew into a sprawling metropolis and one of the largest cities of the ancient world. Pataliputra, located strategically along the Ganges River, became the nerve center of the Magadhan Empire, a city that buzzed with the energy of trade, politics, and intellectual activity.

Pataliputra's streets were lined with grand buildings, from the imperial palace to vast administrative offices, reflecting the city's role as the capital of an empire that stretched across the Indian subcontinent. The city was also known for its beautiful gardens, well-planned streets, and efficient drainage systems, embodying the sophisticated urban planning that characterized Magadhan civilization. The thriving markets of Pataliputra, filled with goods from distant lands, underscored the city's importance as a hub of commerce and cultural exchange.

The Buddhist Legacy: A Birthplace of Enlightenment

Magadha is forever linked with the rise of Buddhism, as it was here, under the reign of King Bimbisara and his successors, that Siddhartha Gautama, the Buddha, found patronage and support. The kingdom's deep connection to Buddhism is epitomized by Bodh Gaya, the site where the Buddha attained enlightenment under the Bodhi tree. This sacred place, located within the boundaries of Magadha, became one of the most important pilgrimage sites in the world.

Magadha's kings, particularly Ashoka the Great, embraced Buddhism and spread its teachings far and wide. Under Ashoka's rule, stupas, monasteries, and inscriptions were erected across the empire, making Magadha the heartland of Buddhist thought and practice. The kingdom's role in the early development and spread of Buddhism highlights its significance not just as a political power but also as a spiritual and cultural epicenter.

The Nalanda University: A Beacon of Knowledge

Nalanda, a renowned center of learning in Magadha, was one of the earliest universities in the world, attracting scholars and students from across Asia. Founded in the 5th century CE, Nalanda was a place where Buddhist philosophy, mathematics, astronomy, medicine, and other subjects were studied and taught. The university's vast library, known as the Dharmaganja, housed thousands of manuscripts and texts, making it a treasure trove of knowledge.

Nalanda was more than just an educational institution; it was a symbol of Magadha's intellectual prowess and its commitment to the pursuit of knowledge. The university's influence extended far beyond India, shaping the intellectual and spiritual life of much of Asia for centuries. Nalanda's existence is a testament to Magadha's role as a cradle of learning and a beacon of wisdom.

The Strategic Power: Forge of Empires

Magadha's rise to power was fueled by its strategic location, fertile lands, and strong military traditions. The kingdom's control over key trade routes and river systems allowed it to dominate the economic and political landscape of northern India. The use of war elephants, innovative military tactics, and the ability to forge strong alliances helped Magadha expand its territory and influence.

Magadha's kings, from Bimbisara and Ajatashatru to Chandragupta Maurya and Ashoka, were master strategists who turned their kingdom into the nucleus of the first pan-Indian empires. The Mauryan Empire, founded by Chandragupta and expanded by Ashoka, became one of the largest and most powerful empires in the ancient world, with Magadha at its heart.

The Decline and Endurance

Magadha's fortunes fluctuated over the centuries, with periods of great prosperity followed by invasions, internal strife, and the eventual fragmentation of its empire. Despite these challenges, the legacy of Magadha endured, influencing the political, cultural, and religious development of the Indian subcontinent for millennia.

In modern times, the ruins of ancient Magadhan cities like Rajagriha and Pataliputra, as well as the enduring spiritual significance of sites like Bodh Gaya, continue to attract scholars, pilgrims, and visitors. These remnants of Magadha's past serve as reminders of a kingdom that once shaped the course of history and left an indelible mark on the world.

Key Events

1. **c. 600 BCE** - Rise of Magadha: Magadha emerges as a powerful kingdom in the eastern Gangetic plain, with its capital initially at Rajagriha and later at Pataliputra.
2. **c. 490-321 BCE** - Expansion under the Haryanka and Nanda Dynasties: Magadha expands its territory and influence, becoming one of the most powerful states in ancient India.
3. **c. 321-185 BCE** - Mauryan Empire: Magadha becomes the heart of the Mauryan Empire under Chandragupta Maurya, with Pataliputra as its capital.
4. **c. 185 BCE-320 CE** - Post-Mauryan Period: Magadha continues to be a significant region, though its dominance wanes as other regional powers rise.
5. **c. 320-550 CE** - Gupta Empire: Magadha regains prominence under the Gupta Empire, becoming a center of learning, culture, and religious activity.

Taxila: The Crossroads of Wisdom and Conquest

The Gateway to the East

Perched on the fertile plains of the Pothohar Plateau, where the ancient trade routes of Central Asia and the Indian subcontinent converged, lies Taxila—a city that stood as a beacon of learning, culture, and strategic importance around 600 BCE. More than just a city, Taxila was a vibrant hub of intellectual exchange, a cradle of Buddhism, and a pivotal nexus in the ancient world's web of commerce and conquest. With its renowned universities, bustling markets, and rich cultural tapestry, Taxila remains a symbol of the enduring legacy of knowledge, diversity, and the dynamic interplay of empires.

The University of Taxila: The Fountain of Knowledge

Taxila was home to one of the most prestigious centers of learning in the ancient world, attracting scholars, students, and seekers of wisdom from across Asia and beyond. The University of Taxila, an informal yet influential institution, was not housed in a single building but spread across monasteries, temples, and private homes, creating a citywide campus where knowledge flowed freely.

Here, subjects as diverse as mathematics, astronomy, medicine, philosophy, and military strategy were taught by renowned teachers like the legendary Chanakya (Kautilya), author of the Arthashastra, and Panini, the great grammarian whose work laid the foundations of Sanskrit grammar. The intellectual atmosphere of Taxila fostered debate, innovation, and the synthesis of ideas, making it a melting pot of cultures and disciplines. The university was a beacon of wisdom, where the brightest minds of the ancient world came to study and share their knowledge, shaping the course of history and thought.

The Dharmarajika Stupa: A Beacon of Faith

Taxila was not only a center of secular learning but also a crucial site in the spread of Buddhism. The Dharmarajika Stupa, built by the Mauryan emperor Ashoka, was one of the earliest and most important Buddhist monuments in the region. This massive stupa, surrounded by smaller stupas and monastic ruins, served as a place of pilgrimage and meditation, attracting devotees from near and far.

The stupa's construction was a testament to Ashoka's commitment to spreading the teachings of the Buddha and fostering a culture of peace and compassion. The Dharmarajika Stupa stood as a symbol of spiritual enlightenment, where pilgrims gathered to pay homage, seek solace, and find inspiration in the Buddha's teachings. The presence of this stupa, along with other religious structures, reflected Taxila's role as a spiritual crossroads where different faiths and philosophies coexisted and flourished.

The Sirkap: The Walled City of Multicultural Splendor

The ancient city of Sirkap, one of the key archaeological sites in Taxila, offers a glimpse into the city's rich multicultural heritage. Founded by the Indo-Greek king Demetrius in the 2nd century BCE, Sirkap was laid out in a grid pattern, reflecting Hellenistic urban planning principles. The city's architecture blended Greek, Persian, and Indian styles, creating a unique fusion that symbolized the diverse influences that shaped Taxila.

Sirkap was a bustling metropolis, with wide streets lined with houses, temples, and public buildings. The Double-Headed Eagle Stupa, a striking example of this cultural synthesis, combined Greek architectural elements with Buddhist symbolism, showcasing the harmonious coexistence of different cultures and religions in Taxila. The city's vibrant markets, filled with goods from across the ancient world, further emphasized Taxila's role as a commercial hub where East met West.

The Strategic Importance: A Prize of Empires

Taxila's strategic location made it a coveted prize for empires seeking to control the trade routes that connected Central Asia, China, and the Indian subcontinent. The city was successively ruled by the Achaemenid Persians, the Greeks under Alexander the Great, the Mauryans, the Indo-Greeks, the Scythians, the Parthians, and the Kushans, each leaving their mark on the city's culture, architecture, and governance.

Taxila's ability to absorb and integrate these diverse influences made it a cosmopolitan center of power and learning. The city's fortifications, built to protect against invaders, reflected its importance as a military stronghold, while its thriving economy underscored its role as a vital link in the ancient world's trade networks. Taxila was a city where cultures clashed and coalesced, where conquerors became patrons, and where the exchange of goods was matched by the exchange of ideas.

The Markets of Taxila: A Melting Pot of Commerce

The markets of Taxila were renowned for their diversity and vibrancy, offering a wide array of goods that reflected the city's connections to distant lands. Traders from across the ancient world—Central Asia, Persia, India, and the Mediterranean—converged in Taxila, bringing with them silk from China, spices from India, precious stones from Afghanistan, and gold from Rome.

These bustling bazaars were not only centers of economic activity but also spaces of cultural exchange, where merchants, travelers, and locals interacted, exchanged stories, and forged relationships. The variety of goods and the presence of traders from different regions underscored Taxila's importance as a commercial hub, where the wealth of empires passed through and where the city's cosmopolitan character was on full display.

397

The Decline and Rediscovery

Taxila's fortunes declined as trade routes shifted and empires rose and fell. By the 5th century CE, the city was largely abandoned, its once-thriving streets falling silent as the sands of time covered its grandeur. However, the legacy of Taxila endured, with its ruins preserving the echoes of its illustrious past.

In the 19th and 20th centuries, archaeological excavations led by British and Indian scholars uncovered the remains of Taxila's ancient cities—Bhir Mound, Sirkap, and Sirsukh—revealing its rich history and cultural significance. The artifacts discovered, including sculptures, coins, pottery, and inscriptions, provided invaluable insights into the life and times of this ancient metropolis. Today, Taxila is a UNESCO World Heritage site, attracting scholars, pilgrims, and tourists who come to explore its ruins and reflect on its enduring legacy.

Key Events

1. **c. 1000 BCE** - Early Settlement: Taxila (Takshashila) is established as an important city in the northwestern part of the Indian subcontinent, strategically located on the trade routes between India, Central Asia, and the West.
2. **c. 600-500 BCE** - Center of Learning: Taxila becomes a renowned center of learning, attracting students from across the ancient world to study subjects such as philosophy, medicine, and mathematics.
3. **c. 326 BCE** - Conquest by Alexander the Great: Taxila is peacefully surrendered to Alexander during his invasion of India, marking its integration into the Hellenistic world.
4. **c. 305 BCE** - Mauryan Control: Taxila becomes part of the Mauryan Empire under Chandragupta Maurya, continuing to thrive as a center of learning and trade.
5. **c. 185 BCE-55 CE** - Indo-Greek and Kushan Rule: Taxila flourishes under Indo-Greek and later Kushan rule, maintaining its status as a

major cultural and educational hub.

6. **c. 5th century CE** – Decline: Taxila begins to decline, possibly due to invasions by the Huns and the shifting of trade routes.

Sravasti: The City of Enlightenment and Serenity

The Sacred Grove of the Buddha's Teachings

In the lush plains of northern India, where the sacred Ganges River flows and the air is filled with the fragrance of ancient banyan trees, lies Sravasti—a city that once echoed with the profound teachings of the Buddha. More than just a city, Sravasti was a spiritual haven, a place where seekers of truth gathered to hear the words of the Enlightened One, where the ordinary and the divine converged in a timeless dance of wisdom and compassion. With its serene monasteries, sacred groves, and vibrant community of monks and lay followers, Sravasti remains a symbol of the eternal quest for inner peace and enlightenment, a beacon of serenity in a world often shadowed by turmoil.

Jetavana Grove: The Sanctuary of the Buddha

At the heart of Sravasti was the Jetavana Grove, one of the most revered sites in the Buddhist world. Donated by the wealthy merchant Anathapindika, this grove became the Buddha's primary residence during the rainy season retreats, where he spent many years teaching his disciples and guiding them on the path to enlightenment. Jetavana was not just a physical place; it was a sanctuary of the mind, where the Buddha's teachings took root and flourished, offering refuge to all who sought liberation from suffering.

The grove was dotted with simple yet elegant monasteries, meditation halls, and sacred stupas, each radiating the tranquility that the Buddha's presence imparted. It was here that the Buddha delivered some of his most important discourses, including the famous "Discourse on Loving-Kindness" (Metta Sutta) and the "Discourse on the Four Noble Truths," which laid the foundation for the entire Buddhist path. Jetavana Grove was more than a retreat; it was a living embodiment of the Middle Way, a place where monks and laypeople alike could find solace and wisdom in the Buddha's teachings.

The Miracle of the Twin Marvels: A Display of Enlightened Power

Sravasti is also remembered as the site of one of the most extraordinary events in Buddhist tradition—the Miracle of the Twin Marvels (Yamaka Patihariya). According to legend, the Buddha, challenged by skeptics and rival teachers, performed a miraculous display at Jetavana, simultaneously emitting flames from the upper part of his body and streams of water from the lower part. This miraculous event was a powerful demonstration of his mastery over the elements and his deep understanding of the nature of reality.

The Miracle of the Twin Marvels was not just a display of supernatural power; it was a profound teaching in itself, illustrating the Buddha's ability to transcend ordinary perceptions and embody the limitless potential of the awakened mind. This event drew countless followers to Sravasti, solidifying its reputation as a center of spiritual power and enlightenment. The miracle became a pivotal moment in the spread of Buddhism, inspiring devotion and awe among the faithful and reinforcing Sravasti's status as a sacred city.

The Monasteries of Sravasti: Cradles of Compassion and Wisdom

Sravasti was home to numerous monasteries, each a cradle of learning, meditation, and community life. These monasteries, built by wealthy patrons and dedicated followers, were centers of Buddhist practice, where monks lived according to the Vinaya (monastic discipline) and engaged in deep study and contemplation. The monasteries of Sravasti were more than just places of residence; they were vibrant communities where the Buddha's teachings were lived and practiced every day.

Each monastery had its own unique character, with its gardens, meditation halls, and shrines providing the perfect environment for spiritual growth. The monks of Sravasti were known for their dedication to the path of liberation, their compassion for all beings, and their commitment to spreading the Dharma far and wide. The monasteries also served as places of refuge for laypeople, offering guidance, healing, and support to those who sought solace in the Buddha's teachings. The monasteries of Sravasti were the beating heart of the city's spiritual life, where the seeds of enlightenment were sown and nurtured.

The Lay Community: A City United in Faith

The lay community of Sravasti played a crucial role in the city's spiritual life, supporting the monastic community and participating in the Buddha's teachings. Merchants, artisans, farmers, and nobles all came together in a spirit of generosity (dana), providing food, clothing, and shelter to the monks and contributing to the construction and maintenance of the city's monasteries and sacred sites. The people of Sravasti were united in their devotion to the Buddha and his teachings, creating a harmonious and supportive environment where the Dharma could flourish.

The relationship between the monks and the laypeople was one of mutual respect and interdependence, with each group playing a vital role in the other's spiritual journey. The laypeople of Sravasti found inspiration in the Buddha's teachings and sought to apply his wisdom to their daily lives, cultivating virtues such as loving-kindness, compassion, and mindfulness. In return, the monks provided guidance, taught the Dharma, and served as living examples of the path to liberation. The lay community of Sravasti was not just a passive audience; they were active participants in the city's spiritual life, contributing to the spread and preservation of the Buddha's teachings.

The Decline and Enduring Legacy of Sravasti

Over time, Sravasti, like many ancient cities, faced decline due to political changes, invasions, and the shifting sands of history. By the end of the first millennium CE, the city had largely fallen into obscurity, its once-thriving monasteries and sacred groves gradually overtaken by the jungle. However, the memory of Sravasti lived on in the hearts and minds of Buddhists around the world, preserved in the teachings, scriptures, and traditions that had been nurtured there.

In modern times, the ruins of Sravasti have been rediscovered, and the site has become a place of pilgrimage for Buddhists from around the globe. The remnants of its ancient monasteries, stupas, and the Jetavana Grove still inspire those who visit, offering a tangible connection to the time when the Buddha himself walked these sacred grounds. The legacy of Sravasti endures in the teachings of the Buddha, which continue to guide and inspire millions of people on the path to enlightenment.

Key Events

1. **c. 600 BCE** - Founding and Early Development: Sravasti is established as the capital of the Kosala Kingdom in ancient India, becoming a significant political and commercial center.
2. **c. 5th century BCE** - Gautama Buddha's Teachings: Sravasti becomes a major center of Buddhism during the time of Gautama Buddha. It is said that Buddha spent 25 rainy seasons in Sravasti, preaching at the Jetavana Monastery.
3. **c. 400 BCE** - Expansion of Buddhism: Sravasti flourishes as a hub for Buddhist learning, attracting monks and scholars from across the region. Many important discourses of the Buddha are said to have been delivered here.
4. **c. 3rd century BCE** - Mauryan Influence: Under the Mauryan Empire, especially during Ashoka's reign, Sravasti continues to be a major center of Buddhism, with several stupas and monasteries being constructed.
5. **c. 5th century CE** - Gupta Period: Sravasti remains a significant religious center during the Gupta period, though it begins to decline as other cities rise in prominence.

IX

East Asia

Anyang: The Oracle of the Middle Kingdom

The Cradle of Chinese Civilization and the Whispering Bones of the Shang

Amid the vast plains of the Yellow River Valley, where the fertile earth nourished the roots of one of the world's oldest continuous civilizations, lies Anyang—a city that was once the beating heart of ancient China. Known as Yin during its height, Anyang was more than just a city; it was the sacred capital of the Shang Dynasty, a place where the early foundations of Chinese culture, statecraft, and spirituality were laid. With its royal palaces, ritual bronzes, and enigmatic oracle bones, Anyang remains a symbol of the deep connection between the mortal and the divine, a city where the ancestors spoke and the future was written in the cracks of tortoise shells.

The Oracle Bones: Voices from the Past

The most extraordinary discovery from Anyang is the vast collection of oracle bones—inscribed pieces of ox scapulae and turtle plastrons used in divination rituals by the Shang kings. These bones, cracked by heat and interpreted by royal diviners, were the medium through which the Shang rulers communicated with their ancestors and the gods, seeking guidance on everything from harvests and weather to warfare and royal succession.

The inscriptions on these oracle bones are the earliest known form of Chinese writing, providing a direct link to the thoughts, concerns, and beliefs of the Shang rulers. The bones were not just tools for divination; they were sacred texts, recording the questions posed by the kings and the answers revealed by the cracks. These inscriptions offer a unique window into the world of the Shang, revealing a society deeply concerned with the will of the heavens and the fortunes of the state. The oracle bones of Anyang are more than just artifacts; they are the voices of the past, whispering the hopes and fears of a civilization that laid the foundations for millennia of

Chinese culture.

The Tomb of Fu Hao: The Warrior Queen's Legacy

One of the most remarkable figures to emerge from the history of Anyang is Fu Hao, a consort of King Wu Ding and a powerful general in her own right. Her tomb, discovered in the 20th century, is one of the most significant archaeological finds in China, revealing the life and legacy of a woman who played a pivotal role in the Shang Dynasty's military and religious affairs.

Fu Hao's tomb was filled with treasures—bronze weapons, jade ornaments, and elaborate ritual vessels—attesting to her status and influence. Among the most notable finds were inscriptions on the oracle bones that mentioned her military campaigns, where she led troops into battle and brought victory to the Shang. The tomb also contained evidence of human and animal sacrifices, reflecting the Shang's complex religious practices and the belief in the afterlife. Fu Hao's legacy is one of strength and leadership, a testament to the power and influence that women could wield in the ancient world. Her tomb is a reminder of the complexity and richness of Shang society, where warriors, rulers, and spiritual leaders were often one and the same.

The Ritual Bronzes: The Sacred Vessels of Kings

Anyang is renowned for its exquisite ritual bronzes—elaborately decorated vessels used in ceremonies to honor the ancestors and the gods. These bronzes, often cast in intricate designs featuring mythical creatures, were not just functional objects; they were symbols of power, authority, and the divine right to rule. The Shang kings used these vessels in rituals that reinforced their connection to the heavens and legitimized their rule over the Middle Kingdom.

The process of casting these bronzes was itself a sacred act, involving complex techniques that required great skill and knowledge. The designs on the bronzes were laden with symbolism, reflecting the Shang's cosmology and their understanding of the world's order. These vessels were used in offerings of food and drink to the spirits, ensuring the continued favor of the ancestors and the prosperity of the state. The ritual bronzes of Anyang are masterpieces of ancient craftsmanship, embodying the spiritual and political ideals of the Shang Dynasty and offering a tangible link to the rituals that shaped the lives of its people.

The Royal Palace and Temple Complex: The Seat of Power

The heart of Anyang was its royal palace and temple complex, the epicenter of political, military, and religious life in the Shang capital. This vast complex was where the king lived, ruled, and conducted the rituals that ensured the stability and prosperity of the kingdom. The palace was not just a residence; it was a symbol of the king's divine authority, a place where the earthly and the heavenly realms intersected.

The temple within the complex was dedicated to the ancestors and the gods, where the king performed sacrifices and offerings that reinforced his role as the mediator between the people and the divine. The architecture of the palace and temples, with their wooden structures and rammed-earth foundations, reflected the Shang's mastery of construction techniques and their deep connection to the natural world. The royal complex was the nerve center of the Shang state, where decisions that shaped the fate of the kingdom were made and where the rituals that sustained the cosmic order were performed.

The Fall and Legacy of Anyang

The Shang Dynasty eventually fell to the Zhou, but the legacy of Anyang lived on, both in the physical remains of its buildings and artifacts and in the cultural and spiritual traditions that continued to influence Chinese civilization for centuries. The fall of Anyang marked the end of one of the earliest and most significant dynasties in Chinese history, but it also laid the groundwork for the cultural and political developments that would follow.

In modern times, the ruins of Anyang, particularly the site of Yinxu, have become a UNESCO World Heritage site, attracting scholars and visitors who seek to understand the origins of Chinese civilization. The discoveries made at Anyang have reshaped our understanding of early China, revealing the complexity and sophistication of a society that was deeply connected to both the natural and spiritual worlds. The legacy of Anyang is one of innovation, spirituality, and the enduring power of the written word, a city that remains central to the story of China's ancient past.

Key Events

1. **c. 1300 BCE** - Founding as the Shang Capital: Anyang (Yin) is established as the capital of the Shang Dynasty, becoming the political, cultural, and religious center of ancient China.
2. **c. 1300-1046 BCE** - Shang Dynasty Flourishes: Anyang thrives as the center of the Shang civilization, known for its advanced bronze casting, oracle bone inscriptions, and large-scale construction projects.
3. **c. 1200 BCE** - Height of Power: The city reaches its peak under King Wu Ding, with significant military conquests and cultural achievements.
4. **c. 1046 BCE** - Fall of the Shang Dynasty: The Shang Dynasty is overthrown by the Zhou, leading to the decline of Anyang as a major political center.
5. **c. 1046 BCE onwards** - Abandonment: After the fall of the Shang, Anyang (Yin) is largely abandoned, though it remains a significant cultural and archaeological site.

Luoyang: The Heart of the Celestial Empire

The City of Nine Provinces

Situated at the confluence of the Luo and Yellow Rivers, where the fertile plains of the Central Plain meet the rolling hills, lies Luoyang, a city that pulsated with life and power around 200 BCE. More than just a city, Luoyang was the spiritual and cultural heart of ancient China, a place where emperors ruled, scholars thrived, and religions flourished. As the capital of multiple dynasties, Luoyang was the seat of the Mandate of Heaven, a hub of cultural synthesis, and a beacon of Chinese civilization. With its majestic palaces, serene temples, and bustling markets, Luoyang remains a symbol of ancient China's enduring legacy and the cradle of its timeless traditions.

The Eternal City of the Han: A Capital Reborn

Luoyang was one of China's oldest and most venerated cities, its history stretching back to the early dynasties. By the Han dynasty, Luoyang had become a major capital, reborn under Emperor Gaozu and his successors as a city of unparalleled grandeur. The city's layout followed a meticulous grid pattern, with broad avenues lined by grand administrative buildings, residential quarters, and bustling markets.

The imperial palace, nestled within the walled city, was a symbol of the emperor's divine right to rule, embodying the harmony and order that were central to Han governance. The Weiyang Palace, although officially in Chang'an, had its echoes in Luoyang, where the Han emperors would hold court, preside over ceremonies, and administer the vast empire. The city's architectural splendor reflected the Han dynasty's vision of a centralized and harmonious state, where the emperor served as the intermediary between Heaven and Earth.

The White Horse Temple: The Cradle of Chinese Buddhism

Luoyang holds a special place in the history of Buddhism in China. It was here, during the Eastern Han dynasty, that the White Horse Temple, the first Buddhist temple in China, was established. According to legend, Emperor Ming of Han dreamt of a golden figure, which his advisors identified as the Buddha. In response, the emperor sent envoys to India to bring back Buddhist scriptures and relics.

Upon their return, the White Horse Temple was built to house these sacred texts and to serve as a center for the translation and dissemination of Buddhist teachings. The temple, named after the white horse that carried the scriptures, became a vital hub for the spread of Buddhism in China. The temple's serene courtyards, filled with the fragrance of incense and the sound of chanting monks, became a place of spiritual awakening and cultural exchange, marking the beginning of Buddhism's profound influence on Chinese civilization.

The Longmen Grottoes: A Symphony in Stone

Just outside Luoyang, along the banks of the Yi River, lie the Longmen Grottoes, one of the finest examples of Chinese Buddhist art. These grottoes, carved into the limestone cliffs, house thousands of Buddha statues, bodhisattvas, and intricate reliefs, reflecting the artistic and religious fervor of the Northern Wei and Tang dynasties.

The centerpiece of the Longmen Grottoes is the colossal statue of Vairocana Buddha, seated in serene majesty, symbolizing the cosmic Buddha's enlightenment. The grottoes are a testament to the devotion, artistry, and craftsmanship of the period, with each carving telling a story of spiritual transcendence and imperial patronage. The Longmen Grottoes not only reflect the deep religious faith of the Chinese people but also stand as a monument to the synthesis of art, culture, and spirituality in ancient Luoyang.

The Sui and Tang Legacy: A Cultural Renaissance

Under the Sui and Tang dynasties, Luoyang reached new heights as a cultural and political center. The city was rebuilt and expanded, becoming one of the largest and most cosmopolitan cities in the world. The grandeur of Luoyang during this period was unmatched, with the city boasting wide avenues, grand palaces, and an intricate network of canals and gardens.

Luoyang became a melting pot of cultures, where scholars, poets, artists, and merchants from across Asia converged. The Tang dynasty's emphasis on cultural flourishing saw the city become a center for literature, music, and art, with the works of poets like Bai Juyi and Li Bai capturing the essence of the era. The city's libraries were filled with texts on Confucianism, Buddhism, and Daoism, reflecting the intellectual vibrancy of the period. Luoyang's role as the eastern capital during the Tang dynasty cemented its place as a center of learning, culture, and power in China's golden age.

The Grand Canal: A Lifeline of Trade and Prosperity

Luoyang's strategic location along the Grand Canal, one of the world's greatest engineering feats, made it a crucial hub for trade and transportation. The canal connected the city to the Yangtze River in the south and the Yellow River in the north, facilitating the movement of goods, people, and ideas across the vast empire.

The markets of Luoyang were bustling with activity, offering goods from all corners of the empire, from silk and tea to ceramics and spices. The canal not only fueled the city's economy but also its cultural exchange, bringing together diverse peoples and traditions. The Grand Canal was more than just a waterway; it was a lifeline that sustained the prosperity and cultural vibrancy of Luoyang, making it a vital artery of the Chinese empire.

The Confucian Academies: Pillars of Education and Governance

Luoyang was also a center of Confucian learning, with numerous academies dedicated to the study of Confucian texts and the training of scholars and officials. The city's academies were pillars of education and governance, where students were rigorously trained in the principles of Confucianism, which emphasized moral integrity, social harmony, and respect for hierarchy.

These academies played a crucial role in shaping the bureaucratic elite of China, producing officials who would go on to serve in the imperial court and administer the empire. The emphasis on education and meritocracy in Luoyang's academies reflected the city's role as a center of intellectual and moral authority, where the ideals of Confucianism were cultivated and propagated.

The Decline and Enduring Legacy

Luoyang's fortunes waned with the decline of the Tang dynasty and the subsequent periods of instability and invasion. The city, once the center of an empire, faced destruction and abandonment. However, its legacy endured, with its influence on Chinese culture, art, and governance continuing to resonate through the centuries.

In modern times, the ruins of Luoyang, along with its surviving temples, grottoes, and artifacts, offer a glimpse into the city's glorious past. The city's role in shaping Chinese civilization is remembered and celebrated, making Luoyang a symbol of China's enduring legacy and its place in the annals of history.

Key Events

1. **c. 1600 BCE** - Early Settlement: Luoyang is established in the Yellow River valley, becoming one of the oldest continuously inhabited cities in China.

2. **c. 770 BCE** - Eastern Zhou Dynasty: Luoyang becomes the capital of the Eastern Zhou Dynasty, solidifying its status as a major political and cultural center.

3. **c. 25 CE** - Eastern Han Dynasty: Luoyang is chosen as the capital of the Eastern Han Dynasty, becoming a center of art, culture, and Buddhism.

4. **c. 220-280 CE** - Three Kingdoms Period: Luoyang remains a contested city during the period of disunity following the fall of the Han Dynasty.

5. **c. 493-534 CE** - Northern Wei Dynasty: Luoyang is the capital of the Northern Wei Dynasty, known for the construction of the Longmen Grottoes, a major site of Buddhist art.

Chang'an: The Eternal City of the Middle Kingdom

The Pulsing Heart of the Silk Road

Nestled at the meeting point of the Wei River and the Qinling Mountains, in the heart of the ancient Middle Kingdom, lies Chang'an, a city that stood as the nerve center of the vast Han Empire around 200 BCE. More than just a city, Chang'an was the lifeblood of Chinese civilization, a beacon of imperial power, cultural brilliance, and cosmopolitan exchange. With its grand palaces, wide avenues, and teeming markets, Chang'an remains a symbol of China's ancient glory and its enduring influence across Asia and beyond.

The City Walls: Guardians of the Empire

Chang'an was renowned for its immense and formidable city walls, stretching over 25 kilometers in length and towering above the landscape. These massive fortifications, built from rammed earth and later reinforced with bricks, were a marvel of ancient engineering, designed to protect the city from invaders and assert the might of the Han dynasty.

The walls were punctuated by imposing gates, each leading to different parts of the city and beyond. These gates, such as the Ancestral Gate and the Peace Gate, were not only entry points but also symbols of the emperor's control over his realm. The watchtowers and barracks that lined the walls underscored the strategic importance of Chang'an as the political and military heart of the Han Empire. Within these walls, emperors ruled, armies mobilized, and the destiny of the empire was shaped.

The Weiyang Palace: A Monument to Majesty

At the heart of Chang'an stood the Weiyang Palace, the largest palace complex in the ancient world and the residence of the Han emperors. This sprawling palace, with its vast halls, elegant pavilions, and serene gardens, was the epicenter of imperial authority. The Hall of Diligent Government, where the emperor conducted state affairs, was the nerve center of the Han administration, where laws were decreed, and policies formulated.

The Weiyang Palace was more than just a royal residence; it was a symbol of the emperor's divine mandate and the grandeur of the Han dynasty. The palace's grandeur, with its richly decorated interiors and carefully manicured landscapes, reflected the sophistication and wealth of the empire. It was within these walls that the emperor hosted foreign dignitaries, conducted ceremonies, and ruled over a vast and diverse realm.

The Silk Road: A Corridor of Cultures

Chang'an was the eastern terminus of the Silk Road, the ancient trade network that connected China with Central Asia, the Middle East, and Europe. The city's bustling markets were filled with merchants and traders from distant lands, bringing with them silks, spices, precious stones, and ideas. The Silk Road was more than a trade route; it was a corridor of cultural exchange, where philosophies, religions, and technologies flowed along with goods.

In the markets of Chang'an, one could find Roman glassware, Persian carpets, Indian spices, and Central Asian horses. The diversity of goods and people in the city's bazaars reflected Chang'an's cosmopolitan character and its role as a global hub. The wealth generated by this trade fueled the city's prosperity and contributed to its cultural vibrancy, making Chang'an a melting pot of cultures and a beacon of cross-cultural interaction.

The Imperial Academy: A Beacon of Learning

Chang'an was not only a center of political power but also a hub of intellectual and cultural life. The city was home to the Imperial Academy, where scholars, officials, and students gathered to study Confucian classics, philosophy, literature, and the arts. The academy was the training ground for the empire's bureaucrats, who were selected through rigorous examinations based on their knowledge of Confucian texts and principles.

The Imperial Academy was more than just a school; it was a symbol of the Han dynasty's commitment to education, moral governance, and the cultivation of virtuous leaders. The academy's influence extended far beyond the classroom, shaping the intellectual and cultural life of the empire. The scholars of Chang'an contributed to the flourishing of Chinese literature, history, and philosophy, leaving a lasting legacy that would shape Chinese civilization for centuries.

The Buddhist Temples: Sanctuaries of Enlightenment

As Buddhism spread along the Silk Road and into China, Chang'an became a significant center for Buddhist thought and practice. The city's Buddhist temples, such as the White Horse Temple, were not only places of worship but also centers of learning and cultural exchange. Monks from India, Central Asia, and China gathered in Chang'an to translate Buddhist scriptures, debate philosophical ideas, and spread the teachings of the Buddha.

These temples were sanctuaries of enlightenment, where the spiritual and intellectual life of the city intersected. The presence of Buddhist art, sculpture, and architecture in Chang'an reflected the religion's growing influence in China and its integration into Chinese culture. The city's role as a center of Buddhist learning and practice made it a beacon of spiritual and intellectual exchange in the ancient world.

The Han Dynasty: Builders of Empire

Chang'an's rise to prominence was closely tied to the Han dynasty, one of China's most illustrious and enduring imperial dynasties. Under the Han, Chang'an grew from a regional capital into the heart of an empire that stretched across East Asia, Central Asia, and beyond. The Han emperors, particularly Emperor Wu, expanded the empire's borders, developed its infrastructure, and established Chang'an as the political, economic, and cultural center of the known world.

The city's grand architecture, sophisticated urban planning, and vibrant cultural life were all products of the Han dynasty's vision and ambition. Chang'an became a symbol of the Han dynasty's achievements, a city that embodied the empire's power, prosperity, and cultural richness. The legacy of the Han dynasty, with its contributions to governance, culture, and science, continues to resonate in Chinese history and civilization.

The Decline and Legacy

Chang'an's fortunes waned with the decline of the Han dynasty, as the city faced invasions, rebellions, and political instability. Despite these challenges, Chang'an remained a vital cultural and economic center, continuing to influence the development of Chinese civilization long after the fall of the Han. The city's layout and architecture would later inspire the design of other great Chinese capitals, including the Tang dynasty's Chang'an and Ming dynasty's Beijing.

In modern times, the ruins of ancient Chang'an, with its palaces, temples, and city walls, offer a glimpse into the grandeur of a city that once stood at the heart of the ancient world. The legacy of Chang'an, as a symbol of imperial power, cultural exchange, and intellectual achievement, endures in the collective memory of China and the world.

Key Events

1. **c. 202 BCE** - Founding as the Han Capital: Chang'an (modern-day Xi'an) is established as the capital of the Han Dynasty by Emperor Gaozu, becoming the political and cultural heart of China.
2. **c. 140-87 BCE** - Reign of Emperor Wu: Chang'an reaches its height as the capital of the Han Empire, becoming the eastern terminus of the Silk Road and a center of trade and culture.
3. **c. 582 CE** - Sui Dynasty: Chang'an is rebuilt and expanded by the Sui Dynasty, becoming a model city for future Chinese capitals.

Nanjing: The Gateway of the South

The Southern Sentinel of Empires

Cradled by the winding curves of the Yangtze River, surrounded by lush hills and verdant plains, lies Nanjing, a city that has long stood as a sentinel of power and culture in southern China. Around 500 BCE, during the tumultuous era of the Spring and Autumn period, Nanjing was more than just a city; it was a gateway between the heart of the ancient Chinese world and the fertile lands of the south. With its strategic location, fortified walls, and rich cultural heritage, Nanjing became a symbol of resilience, innovation, and the enduring spirit of the southern kingdoms.

The Stone City: A Fortress of Resilience

Nanjing, known in ancient times as Yecheng and later as Jinling, was forti-fied by the State of Wu during the Spring and Autumn period, transforming it into a formidable military stronghold. The city's defenses, built with solid stone walls, perched on high ridges overlooking the Yangtze, made Nanjing nearly impregnable. These walls were not merely barriers; they were symbols of strength, protecting the city from northern invaders and asserting its importance as the southern bastion of Chinese civilization.

The strategic location of Nanjing, at the crossroads of vital trade routes and near the mouth of the Yangtze River, made it a key military and economic hub. The Stone City, as it came to be known, became a staging ground for armies, a refuge for kings, and a beacon of southern pride. The city's resilience in the face of external threats underscored its role as a protector of the rich southern territories, a city that would rise again and again from the ashes of conflict.

424

The Birthplace of Wu Culture: A Cradle of Innovation

During the Spring and Autumn period, Nanjing was part of the powerful State of Wu, one of the dominant southern states that challenged the northern hegemony. Wu culture, with its emphasis on martial prowess, naval innovation, and distinct artistic traditions, flourished in and around Nanjing. The city became a center of innovation, particularly in military technology, as the Wu were pioneers in the development of advanced weaponry, shipbuilding techniques, and naval tactics.

The artisans and craftsmen of Nanjing were known for their skill in creating intricate bronze vessels, weapons, and ceremonial items, which were both functional and symbols of status. The city's vibrant cultural scene was marked by the blending of northern and southern traditions, creating a unique Wu identity that would influence Chinese art, music, and literature for centuries. Nanjing's role as a cradle of Wu culture highlighted its importance as a center of innovation and creativity in ancient China.

The Waterways of Nanjing: Lifelines of Prosperity

Nanjing's proximity to the Yangtze River and its network of natural and man-made waterways made the city a vital link in the ancient trade networks that crisscrossed China. The river served as a lifeline, carrying goods, people, and ideas between the northern heartlands and the southern regions. Nanjing's bustling docks and markets were filled with the sounds of traders haggling over silk, grain, ceramics, and other goods that flowed through the city's arteries.

The city's waterways were more than just channels of commerce; they were also the veins of cultural exchange. As goods moved through Nanjing, so too did knowledge, technology, and cultural practices, enriching the city's intellectual and artistic life. The river, with its constant ebb and flow, mirrored the city's dynamic nature, constantly renewing itself while remaining a steadfast center of southern Chinese civilization.

The Gardens and Temples: Sanctuaries of Harmony

Even in its early days, Nanjing was known for its natural beauty and its harmonious blend of urban life with the surrounding landscape. The city's gardens, temples, and shrines were places of contemplation and worship, where the natural world was revered and celebrated. These sanctuaries, nestled amidst hills and along riverbanks, provided refuge from the turmoil of the era, offering spaces for spiritual reflection and artistic expression.

The temples of Nanjing, dedicated to various deities and ancestors, were integral to the city's cultural and religious life. These sites, often surrounded by meticulously landscaped gardens, reflected the southern Chinese aesthetic that valued harmony between human constructions and the natural environment. The tranquil settings of these gardens and temples provided inspiration for poets, artists, and philosophers, who found in Nanjing a wellspring of creativity and spiritual insight.

The Rise of the Southern Capitals: Nanjing's Enduring Legacy

While Nanjing's prominence in the Spring and Autumn period laid the foundations for its future greatness, it was in later centuries that the city would truly come into its own as a capital of southern China. As dynasties rose and fell, Nanjing would be chosen time and again as a capital, from the Eastern Wu during the Three Kingdoms period to the Southern Dynasties, and later the Ming dynasty.

Each era brought new layers of culture, architecture, and history to the city, making Nanjing a living tapestry of Chinese civilization. The city's enduring legacy as a capital of the south, a center of learning, and a symbol of resilience can be traced back to its early days as the Stone City, where the seeds of its greatness were sown.

The Decline and Rebirth

Nanjing, like many ancient cities, experienced periods of decline, as wars, invasions, and political upheavals took their toll. However, the city's strategic importance and cultural significance ensured that it would never fade entirely. Each time Nanjing was ravaged by conflict, it rose again, renewed and transformed, drawing strength from its deep roots in Chinese history and culture.

In modern times, the ancient city of Nanjing, with its historic temples, walls, and ruins, continues to draw visitors who come to explore its rich past. The city's role as a gateway between north and south, a protector of southern China, and a cradle of innovation and culture endures, making Nanjing a living testament to the resilience and creativity of the Chinese people.

Key Events

1. **c. 229 CE** - Sun Quan's Capital: Nanjing (then known as Jianye) becomes the capital of the Eastern Wu during the Three Kingdoms period, marking its rise as a significant southern city.
2. **c. 317–420 CE** - Eastern Jin Dynasty: Nanjing serves as the capital of the Eastern Jin Dynasty and later the Southern Dynasties, becoming a center of culture and learning.

Oc Eo: The Maritime Crossroads of the Mekong

The Lost Port of the Southeast Asian Silk Road

Where the lush deltas of the Mekong River spread into the vast network of waterways and rice paddies of southern Vietnam, lies the ancient city of Oc Eo—a vibrant port that once served as a vital link between the East and West. More than just a city, Oc Eo was a thriving maritime hub at the heart of the Funan Kingdom, a place where cultures, goods, and ideas converged from across the Indian Ocean to the South China Sea. With its bustling harbors, intricate canals, and rich blend of influences, Oc Eo remains a symbol of the cosmopolitan spirit of early Southeast Asia—a city where the currents of trade and culture flowed freely, connecting distant worlds.

The Canals of Oc Eo: A Network of Life and Commerce

The lifeblood of Oc Eo was its extensive network of canals and waterways, which crisscrossed the city and connected it to the Mekong River and beyond. These canals were more than just transportation routes; they were the arteries of commerce and communication, enabling the flow of goods, people, and ideas between Oc Eo and distant lands. The city's strategic location along these waterways made it a crucial port in the maritime Silk Road, linking it to India, China, and the wider world.

The canals of Oc Eo were lined with bustling markets where traders from across Asia and beyond exchanged wares—spices from the Indonesian archipelago, silks from China, beads and gold from India, and exotic goods from as far away as the Roman Empire. The city's docks were filled with boats of all shapes and sizes, their sails billowing in the tropical breeze, as merchants negotiated deals and loaded their cargoes for the next leg of their journeys. The canals were the veins through which the lifeblood of Oc

Eo flowed, sustaining its economy and fostering a vibrant, multicultural community that was as diverse as the goods it traded.

The Temples of Oc Eo: Sanctuaries of a Syncretic Faith

Oc Eo was not only a center of trade but also a melting pot of religious and cultural traditions. The city's temples, scattered throughout its urban landscape, reflected a unique blend of Hindu, Buddhist, and indigenous beliefs, brought together by the diverse peoples who lived and traded in the city. These temples, often constructed from brick and adorned with intricate carvings, were places of worship and spiritual refuge for the city's inhabitants, offering a connection to the divine amidst the hustle and bustle of urban life.

The temples of Oc Eo were dedicated to a pantheon of deities, including Vishnu, Shiva, and Buddha, as well as local spirits and ancestors, reflecting the syncretic nature of Funanese religion. The city's religious practices were deeply influenced by the Indian subcontinent, with its art and architecture bearing the hallmarks of Gupta and Pallava styles. However, these influences were adapted to local traditions, creating a distinct spiritual landscape that was both familiar and unique. The temples of Oc Eo were sanctuaries of faith, where the city's diverse population could find solace and express their devotion in a shared, yet multifaceted, religious tradition.

The Gold and Beads of Oc Eo: Treasures of Trade and Artistry

Oc Eo was renowned for its wealth and the exquisite craftsmanship of its artisans, who produced fine gold jewelry, intricate beads, and luxurious textiles that were highly prized across Asia. The city's goldsmiths, working with gold brought by traders from India and Southeast Asia, created delicate ornaments—earrings, bracelets, and necklaces—adorned with precious stones and intricate designs that reflected both local and foreign influences.

Bead-making was another specialty of Oc Eo's artisans, who crafted glass and stone beads in a dazzling array of colors and shapes. These beads, often used in jewelry or as trade goods, were highly sought after by merchants from India, China, and beyond. The craftsmanship of Oc Eo's artisans was not just a reflection of the city's wealth; it was a testament to the cultural exchange that defined the city, where techniques, styles, and materials from across the world were blended into something uniquely Oc Eo. The gold and beads of Oc Eo were more than just commodities; they were symbols of the city's place at the crossroads of ancient trade networks, where the art of the craftsman met the demands of global commerce.

The Roman Connection: A Distant Empire's Reach

One of the most intriguing aspects of Oc Eo is the discovery of Roman artifacts, including coins and glassware, within its archaeological sites. These finds suggest that Oc Eo was connected, albeit indirectly, to the far-flung Roman Empire, indicating the vast reach of the trade networks that converged on the city. The presence of Roman goods in Oc Eo highlights the city's role as a key node in the ancient global economy, where goods from the Mediterranean could find their way to the shores of Southeast Asia.

The Roman artifacts found in Oc Eo are a testament to the city's cosmopolitan nature and its position as a gateway between the East and West. These goods, likely brought by merchants traveling along the maritime Silk Road, would have been rare and valuable commodities, prized for their exotic origins and fine craftsmanship. The Roman connection adds a layer of complexity to Oc Eo's history, revealing a city that was not only a local center of power but also a participant in a global network of exchange that spanned continents and civilizations.

The Fall and Legacy of Oc Eo

Like many ancient cities, Oc Eo eventually faced decline, likely due to shifts in trade routes, environmental changes, and the rise of competing powers in the region. By the end of the first millennium CE, the city had largely faded from prominence, its once-bustling canals and markets falling silent. However, the legacy of Oc Eo endures, both in the archaeological remains that have been uncovered and in the influence it had on the development of Southeast Asian culture and trade.

In modern times, the ruins of Oc Eo have become a focus of scholarly interest, with archaeologists piecing together the story of this once-great city from the artifacts and structures that remain. The discoveries made at Oc Eo have shed light on the early history of Southeast Asia, revealing a sophisticated and cosmopolitan society that played a crucial role in the ancient world's trade networks. The legacy of Oc Eo is a reminder of the interconnectedness of ancient civilizations and the enduring impact of cultural exchange.

Key Events

1. **c. 1st century CE** - Founding of Oc Eo: Oc Eo is established as a major port city in the Mekong Delta, serving as a key hub of the Funan Kingdom, a powerful maritime empire in Southeast Asia.
2. **c. 1st-7th centuries CE** - Flourishing as a Trade Hub: Oc Eo thrives as a bustling port, facilitating trade between the Indian subcontinent, China, and other parts of Southeast Asia. The city is known for its advanced canal systems, workshops, and a cosmopolitan population.

X

Central America

Teotihuacan: The City of the Gods

The Mysterious Metropolis of the Valley of Mexico

Rising from the high plateau of central Mexico, where the land stretches towards the heavens and the ancient mountains stand like silent sentinels, lies Teotihuacan, a city that was already a flourishing metropolis around 100 BCE. More than just a city, Teotihuacan was a grand urban experiment, a religious and political center that inspired awe and reverence across Mesoamerica. With its monumental pyramids, vast avenues, and vibrant murals, Teotihuacan remains an enigma—both a testament to human ingenuity and a place shrouded in mystery, known to the Aztecs as the City of the Gods.

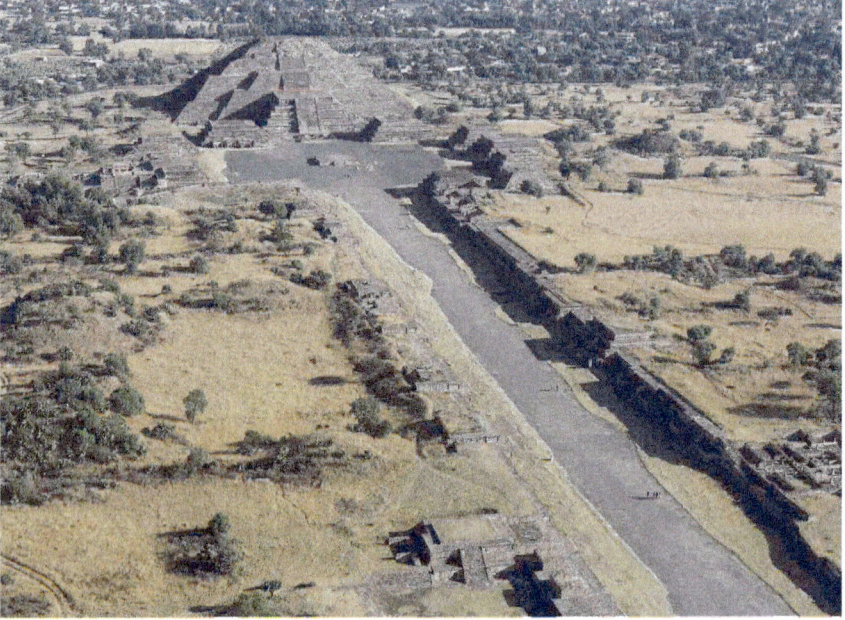

The Avenue of the Dead: A Processional Path of Power

The heart of Teotihuacan was the Avenue of the Dead, a broad, linear boulevard that stretched for miles through the city, connecting its most significant monuments. This grand avenue was more than just a thoroughfare; it was a ceremonial pathway, where priests, rulers, and citizens participated in rituals and processions that underscored the city's religious and political power.

Lined with temples, plazas, and residences, the Avenue of the Dead was a microcosm of Teotihuacan's social and spiritual life. It led from the Pyramid of the Moon in the north to the Ciudadela in the south, guiding the faithful through a landscape infused with cosmic symbolism. The avenue's design reflected the city's deep connection to the cosmos, with each structure and space aligned to celestial bodies and events, creating a physical manifestation of the heavens on earth.

The Pyramid of the Sun: A Monument to the Cosmos

Dominating the landscape of Teotihuacan, the Pyramid of the Sun is one of the largest pyramidal structures in the world, a massive stone monument that rises over 200 feet into the sky. Built with millions of tons of volcanic rock, this pyramid was a testament to the city's engineering prowess and its deep spiritual connection to the cosmos.

The Pyramid of the Sun was more than just an architectural marvel; it was a sacred mountain, a place where the earthly and the divine intersected. The pyramid's alignment with the sun and its connection to the underworld through a tunnel beneath its base suggest that it was a site of powerful rituals, where offerings were made to the gods to ensure the fertility of the land and the prosperity of the people. Climbing the steep steps of the Pyramid of the Sun, one could feel the weight of history and the presence of the divine, standing at the very axis of the Teotihuacan universe.

The Pyramid of the Moon: The Heart of Rituals

At the northern end of the Avenue of the Dead stands the Pyramid of the Moon, slightly smaller but no less significant than its solar counterpart. The Pyramid of the Moon was the focal point of Teotihuacan's ritual life, a place where ceremonies dedicated to the gods of water, fertility, and the underworld were conducted.

The pyramid was built in stages, each layer representing a new phase in the city's development and its evolving religious practices. The plaza in front of the pyramid, surrounded by smaller pyramids and temples, served as a stage for public rituals and sacrifices, witnessed by thousands of Teotihuacanos. The Pyramid of the Moon's connection to the nearby Cerro Gordo mountain reinforced its symbolic role as the axis mundi, linking the city's inhabitants to the natural world and the gods who governed it.

The Ciudadela and the Temple of the Feathered Serpent: A Seat of Power

In the southern part of Teotihuacan lies the Ciudadela, a massive complex that served as the administrative and ceremonial heart of the city. Within its walls stands the Temple of the Feathered Serpent (Quetzalcoatl), one of the most iconic and intricately decorated structures in the city. The temple's façade is adorned with hundreds of stone carvings depicting the Feathered Serpent and Tlaloc, the storm god, symbolizing the city's connection to water, fertility, and cosmic order.

The Ciudadela was likely the residence of the city's elite rulers, who controlled the political, economic, and religious life of Teotihuacan. The temple's underground tunnels and chambers suggest that it was also a site of secret rituals and burials, where the city's leaders sought to commune with the gods and ensure their divine mandate to rule. The Temple of the Feathered Serpent, with its elaborate iconography and strategic location, was a powerful symbol of the city's authority and its central role in Mesoamerican religious life.

The Residential Compounds: A Cosmopolitan Community

Teotihuacan was not just a city of temples and pyramids; it was also home to a diverse and cosmopolitan population, living in large, multi-family residential compounds that reflected the city's social organization and cultural diversity. These compounds, often elaborately decorated with murals, housed artisans, merchants, and farmers, as well as the city's elite.

The murals found in these residences, depicting gods, animals, and everyday scenes, provide a vivid glimpse into the lives of Teotihuacan's inhabitants. The presence of foreign artifacts and influences, from the Maya to the Zapotec, suggests that Teotihuacan was a melting pot of cultures, a city that welcomed and integrated people from across Mesoamerica. The residential compounds were not just places of habitation but centers of production and trade, where goods were crafted, exchanged, and sent across the region, fueling the city's economy and its influence far beyond its borders.

The Murals of Teotihuacan: A Kaleidoscope of Myths and Realities

Teotihuacan's murals are among the most remarkable artistic achievements of the ancient world, transforming the city's walls into vibrant canvases that told the stories of its gods, rulers, and people. These murals, with their bold colors and intricate designs, depicted a world where the divine and the mortal were intertwined, where myths were made manifest in the city's daily life.

Scenes of processions, rituals, and fantastical creatures filled the walls of temples, palaces, and homes, offering insights into the city's complex religious beliefs and social structures. The murals of Teotihuacan were not just decorative; they were didactic, conveying the city's cosmology and reinforcing the authority of its rulers. The vivid imagery of these murals continues to captivate and puzzle scholars, revealing the rich symbolic world of a civilization that, despite its influence, remains enigmatic and mysterious.

The Decline and Legacy

Teotihuacan's decline around 600 CE is one of the great mysteries of the ancient world. The city, once the most powerful and influential in Mesoamerica, was suddenly abandoned, its grand avenues and pyramids left to the ravages of time. The reasons for this decline—whether internal strife, environmental changes, or external invasions—remain a topic of debate among scholars.

Despite its fall, Teotihuacan's legacy endured, influencing the cultures and civilizations that followed. The Aztecs, who arrived centuries later, were so awed by the city's ruins that they named it Teotihuacan, meaning "the place where gods were created." They believed the city was the birthplace of the gods and the site where the universe was set in motion. The monumental architecture, urban planning, and religious symbolism of Teotihuacan left an indelible mark on Mesoamerican history, inspiring generations of builders, rulers, and priests.

Key Events

c. 100 BCE - Founding of Teotihuacan: Teotihuacan is established in the Valley of Mexico, quickly growing into one of the largest cities in Mesoamerica.

c. 200-600 CE - Peak Period: Teotihuacan reaches its height, with the construction of monumental structures such as the Pyramid of the Sun, the Pyramid of the Moon, and the Avenue of the Dead.

c. 450-650 CE - Cultural Influence: Teotihuacan exerts significant influence over much of Mesoamerica, with its art, architecture, and religious practices spreading widely.

Monte Albán: The Sky City of the Zapotecs

The Pinnacle of Power and Mystery

High atop a mountain in the Valley of Oaxaca, where the land stretches out like a patchwork quilt of ancient fields and verdant forests, lies Monte Albán—a city that once stood as the spiritual and political heart of the Zapotec civilization. More than just a city, Monte Albán was a marvel of engineering and vision, a place where the sky seemed to meet the earth, and where the Zapotecs carved their legacy into the very bones of the mountains. With its grand plazas, mysterious glyphs, and panoramic views of the valleys below, Monte Albán remains a symbol of the ambition, artistry, and spiritual depth of a people who sought to connect the heavens and the earth in a city above the clouds.

The Grand Plaza: A Stage for the Divine and the Elite

At the heart of Monte Albán is its expansive Grand Plaza, a massive open space flanked by temples, palaces, and pyramids that once thronged with the life of the city. The Grand Plaza was more than just a gathering place; it was a ceremonial stage where the Zapotec elite performed rituals, held public ceremonies, and demonstrated their power over both the people and the cosmos. The plaza's layout, aligned with the cardinal directions, reflected the Zapotecs' deep understanding of astronomy and their belief in the city as a microcosm of the universe.

Here, amid the towering structures and the wide-open sky, the rulers of Monte Albán would ascend the steep steps of their pyramids to commune with the gods, their prayers and offerings ensuring the continued prosperity of their realm. The Grand Plaza was the beating heart of the city, a place where the sacred and the secular were intertwined, and where the Zapotecs connected the rhythms of their daily lives with the eternal cycles of the heavens. It was a space designed to inspire awe and reverence, where every stone and every shadow played a role in the grand drama of life and death.

The Danzantes: Silent Guardians of Ancient Secrets

One of the most intriguing features of Monte Albán is the series of carved stone slabs known as the Danzantes, which depict figures in various contorted and dynamic poses. These carvings, some of the earliest known in Mesoamerica, have puzzled archaeologists and historians for centuries. The figures, with their twisted limbs and enigmatic expressions, are believed to represent captured enemies, perhaps sacrificial victims or dancers, their bodies immortalized in stone as a testament to the power and dominance of the Zapotec rulers.

The Danzantes are more than just artistic depictions; they are silent guardians of Monte Albán's ancient secrets, offering a glimpse into the rituals and beliefs that underpinned Zapotec society. Their stylized forms, carved with precision and purpose, speak of a culture that revered the mysteries of life and death, and that sought to control the forces of the universe through art, ritual, and sacrifice. The Danzantes stand as a testament to the complexity and depth of Zapotec culture, their presence a reminder that Monte Albán was a city where the visible and the invisible, the living and the dead, coexisted in a delicate balance.

The Observatory: A Window to the Heavens

Monte Albán's rulers were not only masters of the earth; they were also keen observers of the heavens. The city's observatory, known as Building J, is one of the most unique structures in Mesoamerica, with its unusual arrow-shaped design and alignment with the stars. This building, oriented at an angle distinct from the rest of the city's grid, is believed to have been used for astronomical observations, tracking the movements of the stars, planets, and the sun, which were integral to Zapotec religious and agricultural practices.

The observatory was a window to the heavens, where the Zapotec priests and astronomers could chart the courses of celestial bodies and align their rituals with the cosmic order. This connection to the sky was not just practical; it was deeply spiritual, reinforcing the idea that Monte Albán was a place where the earthly and the divine were in constant dialogue. The observatory is a testament to the Zapotecs' advanced knowledge of astronomy and their belief in the importance of understanding the cosmos to maintain harmony in the world below. It was here that the Zapotecs reached out to the heavens, seeking guidance and affirmation from the stars that watched over their city.

The Tombs of Monte Albán: Portals to the Afterlife

Beneath the surface of Monte Albán lies another world, one that speaks to the Zapotecs' profound beliefs about death and the afterlife. The tombs of Monte Albán, some of the most elaborate in Mesoamerica, were the final resting places of the city's elite, filled with treasures that would accompany them into the next world. These tombs, decorated with vivid murals and adorned with precious offerings, were not just places of burial; they were portals to the afterlife, where the dead could continue their journey in the company of the gods.

The most famous of these is Tomb 104, with its intricately painted walls depicting the underworld and the journey of the soul. The tombs were filled with jade, obsidian, and gold, along with ceremonial vessels and figurines, all intended to ensure that the deceased would be well-equipped in the afterlife. The presence of these tombs, hidden beneath the grand structures of the city above, reflects the Zapotecs' belief in the continuity of life beyond death and their desire to maintain their connection to the ancestors and the divine. The tombs of Monte Albán are more than just burial sites; they are sacred spaces that encapsulate the Zapotecs' vision of the universe as a cycle of life, death, and rebirth.

The Fall and Legacy of Monte Albán

Monte Albán's influence waned over the centuries, as regional powers shifted and the city eventually fell into decline. By the end of the 9th century CE, the city was largely abandoned, its grand plazas and temples left to the encroaching jungle. Yet, the legacy of Monte Albán endured, both in the physical remains of its structures and in the cultural and spiritual traditions that continued to influence the region.

In modern times, Monte Albán has been recognized as a UNESCO World Heritage site, drawing scholars, archaeologists, and visitors who seek to uncover the mysteries of this ancient city. The city's layout, architecture, and artifacts have provided invaluable insights into the lives of the Zapotecs and their contributions to Mesoamerican civilization. Monte Albán remains a symbol of the Zapotecs' ingenuity, spirituality, and connection to both the earth and the sky, a city that continues to inspire wonder and admiration.

Key Events

1. **c. 500 BCE** - Founding of Monte Albán: Monte Albán is established as the capital of the Zapotec civilization in the Oaxaca Valley of present-day Mexico.
2. **c. 200 BCE-200 CE** - Flourishing Period: Monte Albán becomes the political, cultural, and religious center of the Zapotecs, known for its monumental architecture, including pyramids, plazas, and tombs.
3. **c. 200-600 CE** - Zapotec Golden Age: The city reaches its peak, with extensive construction projects, including the famous Danzantes reliefs, and a thriving population that dominates the region.

Tikal: The Kingdom of the Sky and Jungle

The Sacred City of the Maya

Deep within the lush, dense jungles of northern Guatemala, where the canopy of green stretches endlessly and the sounds of wildlife fill the air, lies Tikal, a city that soared above the treetops and stood as one of the most powerful and enduring centers of the ancient Maya civilization around 300 BCE. More than just a city, Tikal was a kingdom in the sky, a place where towering temples reached toward the heavens, and the dense jungle whispered the secrets of an ancient people. With its monumental pyramids, sacred plazas, and vibrant history, Tikal remains a symbol of Maya ingenuity, spiritual depth, and the intricate dance between nature and civilization.

The Temples of Tikal: Pyramids Piercing the Sky

The skyline of Tikal was dominated by its towering pyramids, each crowned with a temple that reached above the jungle canopy, piercing the sky like stone mountains. These temples were not merely architectural marvels; they were sacred spaces where the Maya connected with their gods, ancestors, and the cosmos. The most iconic of these is Temple I, known as the Temple of the Great Jaguar, which rises over 150 feet into the sky. Its steep stairways and narrow summit were designed for the rituals of kings, where rulers would stand to perform ceremonies that ensured the prosperity of their people and the favor of the gods.

Facing Temple I is the equally majestic Temple II, or the Temple of the Masks, creating a grand stage for rituals and public gatherings in the Great Plaza. The alignment of these temples with celestial bodies and the surrounding landscape reflected the Maya's deep understanding of astronomy and their belief in the cyclical nature of time. Each temple, with its steep ascent and panoramic views, was a place where the earthly and the divine met, offering a glimpse into the spiritual life of the Maya and their quest to harmonize with the universe.

The Great Plaza: The Heartbeat of a Civilization

At the center of Tikal lies the Great Plaza, a vast open space surrounded by towering pyramids, royal palaces, and stone stelae. This plaza was the heart of Tikal's social, political, and religious life, where the city's rulers, priests, and citizens came together to celebrate, worship, and govern. The Great Plaza was more than just a meeting place; it was a symbolic center of the Maya cosmos, representing the four cardinal directions and the axis mundi, the world tree that connected the heavens, earth, and underworld.

The stelae that line the plaza are carved with the images of kings and hieroglyphic texts, chronicling the deeds of rulers, their conquests, and their divine right to rule. These monuments were not only records of history but also tools of propaganda, reinforcing the power and legitimacy of Tikal's dynasties. The plaza's open space was filled with the sounds of music, the chants of priests, and the footsteps of dancers, creating a vibrant scene that brought the city's population together in shared rituals and celebrations.

The Royal Acropolis: The Seat of Power

Adjacent to the Great Plaza is the Central Acropolis, a sprawling complex of palaces, courtyards, and administrative buildings that served as the residence of Tikal's elite and the seat of its political power. This acropolis was the home of the city's kings and their court, where decisions were made, alliances forged, and strategies devised to maintain Tikal's dominance in the region.

The acropolis was not only a place of governance but also a center of cultural and intellectual life. Its courtyards were adorned with sculptures and murals, reflecting the city's artistic achievements and its connection to the divine. The royal palace was a labyrinth of rooms and passageways, where the king and his family lived in relative seclusion, surrounded by the symbols of their authority. The acropolis was the nerve center of Tikal, where the city's fate was decided, and its future shaped.

The Reservoirs and Causeways: Lifelines of the City

Tikal's survival and prosperity in the heart of the dense jungle were made possible by its advanced engineering and understanding of the natural environment. The city's reservoirs, large artificial lakes, were essential for collecting and storing water during the dry season, ensuring a reliable water supply for its inhabitants. These reservoirs, carefully constructed with clay linings and connected by channels, were a testament to the Maya's ingenuity and their ability to thrive in a challenging environment.

The causeways, known as sacbeob, were elevated roads that connected different parts of the city and extended into the surrounding jungle, linking Tikal with other Maya centers. These causeways facilitated trade, communication, and military movement, making Tikal a hub of activity in the region. The reservoirs and causeways were the lifelines of Tikal, sustaining its population and enabling its growth into one of the most powerful cities in the Maya world.

The Ritual Ballgame: A Dance with the Gods

In the shadow of Tikal's towering temples, the Maya played their sacred ballgame, a ritual sport that was both entertainment and a deeply spiritual act. The ballgame, played on a large court near the Great Plaza, was a symbolic reenactment of the mythological battles between the gods of life and death. Players, adorned in elaborate costumes, used their hips to keep a rubber ball in motion, striving to pass it through stone hoops set high on the court walls.

The outcome of the game was believed to influence cosmic forces, determining the fate of the city and its people. The ballgame was also a political tool, used to settle disputes between rival city-states and demonstrate the power of the ruling elite. The ritual ballgame of Tikal was a dance with the gods, a dramatic and public expression of the Maya's beliefs in the cyclical nature of life, death, and rebirth.

The Decline and Rediscovery

Tikal's rise to power was followed by centuries of dominance, but like many ancient cities, it eventually faced decline. By the 10th century CE, Tikal had been largely abandoned, its great temples overtaken by the encroaching jungle. The reasons for Tikal's decline remain a topic of scholarly debate, with theories ranging from environmental degradation and overpopulation to warfare and shifting trade routes.

Despite its fall, Tikal's legacy endured, its towering temples and plazas lying in wait for rediscovery. In the 19th century, explorers and archaeologists uncovered the ruins of Tikal, revealing a city that once stood at the pinnacle of Maya civilization. Today, Tikal is a UNESCO World Heritage site, drawing visitors from around the world who come to marvel at its architectural grandeur and explore the mysteries of its past.

Key Events

1. **c. 1000 BCE** - Early Settlement: Tikal is established in the Petén Basin of modern-day Guatemala, becoming one of the earliest and largest Maya cities.
2. **c. 200-900 CE** - Classic Period: Tikal reaches its peak during the Classic Maya period, becoming a major political, cultural, and military center, with monumental architecture such as the Great Plaza and towering pyramids.

Printed in Great Britain
by Amazon